RETURN OF THE SINAI 1979

Clete Hinton

EAGLE EDITIONS
2007

EAGLE EDITIONS
AN IMPRINT OF HERITAGE BOOKS, INC.

Books, CDs, and more—Worldwide

For our listing of thousands of titles see our website
at
www.HeritageBooks.com

Published 2007 by
HERITAGE BOOKS, INC.
Publishing Division
65 East Main Street
Westminster, Maryland 21157-5026

Copyright © 2006 Clete Hinton

Other books by the author:
Arc of Crisis 1979
Camp David Accords

All rights reserved. No part of this book may be reproduced or transmitted in any form or by any means, electronic or mechanical, including photocopying, recording or by any information storage and retrieval system without written permission from the author, except for the inclusion of brief quotations in a review.

International Standard Book Number: 978-0-7884-4134-9

The Return of the Sinai - Index from 1979

1. Preface

2. The Signing of the Peace Treaty Between Egypt and Israel

3. The Egyptian Peace Treaty Sealed in the Sinai Desert   4-26-79

4. First Withdrawal - El Arish 5-28-79

5. Second Withdrawal - Western Sinai   7-25-79

6. Third Withdrawal - Southern Sinai 9-26-79

7. Fourth Withdrawal - Mount Sinai 11-16-79

8. Fifth Withdrawal - Rifidim - Mitla and Giddi Passes 1-12-80

9. Final Withdrawal - April 25, 1982 5-25-82

10. Treaty Proposal with the Palenstinians-Arafat and Pictures 9-14-93

11. Declaration of Peace Proposition - Jordan   7-6-94

Index

1.	Preface	1
2.	The Signing of the Peace Treaty Between Egypt and Israel	5
3.	Follow-up of the Camp David Accords	7
4.	Steps to Comprehensive Peace: Egyptian-Israeli Peace Treaty Sealed in Sinai Dessert	20
5.	First Withdrawal - Egyptian President, Sadat in El Arish	40
6.	Second Withdrawal - From Western Sinai	87
7.	Third Withdrawal - From Southern Sinai	124
8.	Fourth Withdrawal - From Mount Sinai	144
9.	Fifth Withdrawal - From Refidim (Mitla and Giddi Passes	149
10.	Treaty Proposal with the Palestinians - Arafat and Pictures	164
11.	Declaration of Peace Proposal - Jordan	170
12.	Passing of Hebron Accord - with Palestinians	181

Bibliography

A. Books - King James version of the Holy Bible - Isaiah Chapter 19:23-25.

B. Articles - U.S. Department of State Bulletin. Egypt and Israel signing of the Peace Treaty: The Camp David Accords: Government Printing Office - 1979.

C. Newspapers:
    Long Beach Press Telegram - 1979-1980
    Los Angeles Times - 1979 through 1997
    Orange County Register - Santa Ana, California - 1979 - 1980
    Daily Press - Victorville, California - 1981- 1997.

Preface

3-26-78

The signing of the Peace Treaty with Egypt and Israel is only the beginning of steps for a comprehensive peace in the Middle East. There are many radical movements that would disrupt the ongoing negotiations. The Palestinian Liberation Organization under the command of Yasser Arafat, has vowed to destroy the Accords and to harass all who agree with the President of Egypt, Anwar Sadat, and the Prime Minister of Israel, Menachem Begin, that peace and prosperity can be attained by patient and long suffering of the people involved.

Plans and preparation must be carefully weighed in the troublesome areas. Steps to a full autonomy for Palestinian refugees should be taken on step at a time, for the peace process to work effectively.

The United States can be a cohesive force in moderating the hatred and distrust that has existed for centuries between the Arabs and the Jews. Israel makes up most of the region once called Palestine, the Holy Land of the Bible. In ancient times, the Jews built a nation there, but Palestine fell to a series of conquerors. It became an Arab Territory, and then a Turkish land, although the Jews continued to live in Palestine in bondage.

To many Jews throughout the world, this land appeared to be the best to escape religious persecution they often faced in other countries. During the late 1800s, in the hope of establishing a free nation, Jewish immigrants began arriving in Palestine. They drained swamps, irrigated the desert, sank wells for water, planted forests, and farm settlements appeared amid what was uncultivated land. With extensive care and patience, the Jewish farmers grew with abundance.

In 1948, the Jews declared their independence, and called their land Israel. The towns sprung up, with factories, schools, and agriculture, and it has become the most advanced country in the Middle East. Independence and prosperity have not brought peace and security, however today she is on the threshold.

Preface - Egypt A Nation

Egypt has more than 33 million people. Almost all of it is covered by dry, windswept deserts. They are part of the Sahara region, the largest desert in the world. This country received hardly any rain, and its people could not exist without the life-giving Nile River.

Most Egyptians are farmers, and they depend on the precious water to irrigate their fields of cotton and agriculture products. Ninety-nine percent of the people live along the Nile or near the Suez Canal, which links the Mediterranean Sea with the Red Sea.

The Egyptians are a family oriented society. In early times, the husband ruled the family, but today women have more freedom, some receiving equal status. Women have the right to own property, can buy and sell goods, and about 30% can read and write. The government is slowly raising their standards. Education and health services are springing up as more people are living in rural areas.

Of the group dependent, most are poor peasants called, "Fellahin." A number of desert herdsmen are Nomadic, moving from place to place with their sheep and goats, called, "Bedouins." Pastureland is sometimes difficult to find, and the herdsmen gather together and share their goats milk, meat from the animals, and others sell their animals to buy or trade for grain and other necessities.

The life of the peasant or "Fellahin" is one of endless toil, and many rent fields from landlords, and are rarely out of debt. Arabic is their language, and they are chiefly of the Islamic faith, faithful to Allah. Their Holy Book is called the "Koran" and they pray five times a day.

With the signing of the Peace Accords, a cornerstone has been established to bring together a framework for a comprehensive peace in the Middle East, but other nations and people in the area must put aside their differences to improve the quality of life for all.

A substantial portion of the population of the Arab States are hopeful for peace, and an end to hatred and terrorism, destruction, and death, if they are allowed to rule themselves without reprisal. In the foreseeable future, Syria, Jordan, and the Palestinians, encouraged by Saudi Arabia, will join the peace negotiations. It is possible, a transition period must occur, preventing posturing and threats and attempts to weaken the ties of Israel and Egypt.

Prime Minister Menachem Begin of Israel, and Anwar Sadat of Egypt, moderated by President Jimmie Carter and the American State Department, have opened the door for a lasting peace. U.S. Resolution #242 and #238, was a foundation for the signing of "The Camp David Accords" peace treaty.

The UAR, United Arab Republic refused to participate, although they were asked. Each party must be able to achieve its purpose, to endure, and the issues must be addressed seriously, and reciprocal advantages should be derived from the negotiations. With Israel, the U.S. is committed in its foreign policy, both morally and strategically, and will support her as a sovereign state within a family of nations.

Beyond this, the people of Israel shall live in peace and security.

At the heart of Arab concerns is the West Bank and the Gaza Strip for the Palestinians. A political process is planned to reach their objectives. The 5 year transition period of the U.S. resolutions will develop a self-governing authority. It is expected the Israelis will withdraw and allow them free elections. The remaining military should be deployed to specific locations.

The legitimate rights of the Palestinians can be recognized.

The Middle East

Middle East is a term given to a region where the continents of Asia, Africa, and Europe meet. The United States Department of State defines the Middle East as consisting of the following countries:

The Republic of Cyprus, Egypt, UAR, Israel, Lebanon, Southern Yemen, The Sudan, Syria, Turkey, Yemen, and Iran.
The Kingdoms of Jordan and Saudi Arabia.
The Sheikdoms of Bahrain, Qutar, and the Trucial States.
The Sultanate of Muscat and Oman.
The Emirate of Kuwait.

    The Middle East is about the same size as the United States. It has been a central area of great culture, of economic and political importance since the beginning of recorded history. The City of Jerusalem has major shrines of the three religions: Christianity, Judaism, and Islamic.
    Oil is its greatest resource. The fields stretch from Iran around the Persian Gulf to Turkey and Egypt, and hold an estimated 2/3 of the world's known oil reserves. About 4 out of the 5 people make their living from agriculture. Wheat is their main crop, with farmers growing rice, millet, corn, fruit, and olives. Meat is mostly from sheep and goats, with a few cow ranches.
    The area has been a battleground of many would-be conquerors, because of its location. Possession of the Middle East has been the ambition of ancient pharaohs to the recent Napoleon Bonaparte of France.
    The Middle East can be divided into two natural regions; the Northern Mountains, and the Southern Plateaus. There are two large river systems; the Nile and the Tigris-Euphrates Rivers. The Nile has two sources; Lake Victoria and Lake Albert, Lake Edward from Uganda; and Lake Tana from Ethiopia that empties into the Mediterranean Sea.
    The Tigris River rises in Turkey, winding south through Iraq. The Euphrates River rises in the mountains of Turkey, but empties into the Persian Gulf. The rivers join in Southern Iraq at Shatt El Arab.
    Temperature varies from 115 degrees fahrenheit to zero in winter. The climate is very hot in summer, with mild winters. About 150 million people live and work in the Middle East. The language includes Turkish, Persian, Kurdish, Armenian, Greek, Hebrew and English.
    The Suez Canal was cut by France, to make Sea Lane, a route in 1869, from the North Atlantic and the Mediterranean Sea to the Indian Ocean.
    In 1947, the United Nations partitioned Palestine, separating the Arabs from the Jews. Through a series of wars, the Jews assembled to form a separate state. Jordan commanded a part of Palestine, and thousands of Palestinians fled to the land of Saudi Arabia.
    The Jewish nation called their land Israel. As it is today. Israel has found it can live with an Arab nation, Egypt, in peace.

"The Peace Treaty" - U.S. Dept. Of State Bulletin - May 1949

The signing of the peace treaty between Egypt and Israel Inspirations from President Carter, Prime Minister Begin, and President Anwar Sadat.

President Carter of the United States:

During the past thirty years, Israel and Egypt have waged war, but for the last sixteen months, these two great nations have waged peace. President Anwar Sadat of Egypt and Prime Minister Menachem Begin - have conducted a campaign with courage, tenacity, brilliance, and endurance of any general who led men and machines onto a field of battle.

The soil of the two nations is not drenched with young blood. The countrysides are free from litter and carnage of a wasteful war. The dedication and determination of these leaders and world statesmen have become a reality, and peace has come.

We must not minimize the obstacles which lie ahead. "We must rededicate ourselves to the goal of a broader peace, with justice for all who have lived in a state of conflict.

In the Koran we read: "But if the enemy incline toward peace, do thou also incline toward peace, and trust in God; for He is the one that heareth and knows all things."

President Anwar Sadat of Egypt:

The signing of a peace treaty with Israel is a turning point of monumental significance for all peace-loving nations. Those among us who are endowed with vision cannot fail to comprehend the dimensions of our sacred mission. The Egyptian people, with their heritage and awareness of history, have realized from the very beginning the value of this endeavor.

Today a new dawn is emerging out of the darkness of the past. A new chapter is being opened in the history of co-existence among nations, one that is worthy of our spiritual values and civilization.

President Carter of the United States has performed a miracle, devoting his skill, hard work, and above all, his firm belief in the ultimate triumph of good against evil to insure success of our mission. Happily, he was armed with the blessing of God, and the support of his people, and for that we are grateful to each and every American who contributed in his own way to the success of our enterprise.

We are heartened by the understanding of hundreds of thousands of Israelis who remained unwavering in their commitment to peace. The continuation of this spirit is vital to the coronation of our effort.

President Carter once said, "the United States is committed without reservation to seeing the peace process through until all parties to the Arab-Israeli conflict are at peace." We value such a pledge from a leader who raise the banners of morality and ethics as a substitute for power politics.

Prime Minister Menachem Begin of Israel:

I have come from the land of Israel, the land of Zion and Jerusalem, and here I am in humility and with pride as a son of the Jewish people, as one of the generation of the Holocaust and redemption.

The ancient Jewish people gave the world a vision of eternal peace, of universal disarmament, of abolishing the teaching and learning of war.

"And they shall beat their spears into pruning hooks: nation shall not lift up sword against nation, neither shall they learn war anymore."

Despite the tragedies of the past, we must never forsake that vision, that human dream, that unshakable faith.

"Peace is the beauty of life; it is the sunshine; it is the smile of a child, the love of a mother, the joy of a father, the togetherness of a family. It is the advancement of man, the victory of a just cause, the triumph of truth. Peace is all these and more."

The President of the United States, Jimmy Carter is a (mirabile dictu) an intransigent righter for peace.

It is a great day in your life, Mr. President of the Arab Republic of Egypt. In the face of adversity and hostility, you have demonstrated the human value that can change history - civil courage.

When our forefathers returned from their first exile to Jerusalem and Zion they said, "De Profundis," Save us, Save us. This is our prayer of thanksgiving.

FOLLOW-UP OF THE CAMP DAVID ACCORDS

4-2-79
Cairo, Egypt
Begin honors Egyptian war dead

Prime Minister Menachem Begin arrived in Cairo today to a cool welcome, and then began his historic visit of reconciliation by touring the Pyramids and to honor Egypt's war dead.

Despite a lackluster welcome from Egyptian authorities worried by outrage over the peace treaty with Israel, Begin was in high spirits and clearly moved by the drama of being the first Israeli leader to visit an Arab capital.

"This is a great day for Israel," he replied, as he alit from a Egyptian Air Force helicopter which flew him to the Pyramids in Southern Cairo.

He began a 24 hour visit by laying a wreath on the tomb of the unknown soldier, honoring tens of thousands of Egyptians who died in wars against Israel over the last 30 years.

Calling it an emotional moment, Begin told reporters: "I laid a wreath in the name of the Israeli people and the Israel defense forces, in honor of the unknown soldier who died for his country."

There were no cheering crowds at the airport, no signs praising Begin in November 1977 to begin his dramatic peace crusade.

4-2-79
Cairo, Egypt
Arab ambassadors protest Israeli-Egyptian Treaty

Arab ambassadors began an exodus from Cairo today in protest of Egypt's treaty with Israel, but the government of Sadat said it would not be deterred from peace by the Arab outrage.

An Arab summit conference in Baghdad, Iraq, ended with the announcement that 18 nations would punish Sadat by cutting all diplomatic and economic ties with Egypt. The ambassadors of Saudi Arabia, Tunisia, Kuwait, Jordan, and Bahrain left Cairo before the arrival of Prime Minister Menachem Begin of Israel, leaving their embassy staffs behind.

Egyptian officials said they would wait to see what extent the sanctions are carried out before deciding how to react.

The ambassadors of Qatar and the United Arab Emirates were the last to leave the Arab capital.

The ambassadors of Somalia and Morocco were out of the country and it was not known if they would participate in the sanctions against Egypt.

4-2-79
Baghdad, Iraq
Danger of subversion - By the Soviets

Being the tough talk against the Egyptian-Israeli peace treaty, in this militant, oil rich country, is a danger rarely mentioned in the controlled press; the danger of Soviet takeover. The danger is regarded as acute by a handful of top officials, who are pushing Iraq to lead the Third World, and who exert domination.

Indeed, in irony, the anti-Soviet warning being sounded throughout the Middle East by President Carter, Menachem Begin, and Anwar Sadat of Egypt, is to seek Arab acceptance of the new treaty. Iraq is the only Arab state that has a friendship treaty with Moscow.

In addition to justifiable fear over the Soviets to use a small virulent Community party as a lever to heighten their influence, they expect eventual control of the ruling, nationalist, Baath party. The 2 million Kurds, one sixth of the population, and the sectarian difficulties between the Moslem sects, could be infected by both the Kurdish revolt and Shiite Moslems, real people who would help with the revolution in Iran.

Although the secretive government says almost nothing about a takeover publicly, one respects their authority, described as a matter of life and death, in predictions. It is also concerned of Soviet pressure for more oil from their country, whose reserves may prove larger than Saudi Arabia. Moscow, in the past, has brought oil from Iraq, sold it to the satellites for huge profits, and charged outrageous prices for Soviet hardware to defend their borders from invaders.

4-5-79

Prime Minister Menachem Begin - Meeting with Sadat in Sinai Cairo, Egypt:
President Anwar Sadat of Egypt and Prime Minister Menachem Begin of Israel agreed today to meet in Israel's Negev Desert, and to keep their peace effort in defiance of the vehemence and opposition of other Arab leaders.

Begin then returned to Israel, where he told reporters at Tel Aviv airport, named after the late Ben Gurion, that he had received friendly hospitality, and he said Sadat and I are real friends.

The Prime Minister stated the two had reached agreement on important issues. Before leaving Cairo, he announced they both will meet in El Arish, the capital of the Sinai, on May 27, 1979. That is the day after Israel gives up that city on the Mediterranean coast, as the first step in its 3 year withdrawal from the Sinai Peninsula.

While the Prime Minister was in Egypt, he was royally treated by his host, President Sadat, and raised a toast, for saying, "Hallelujah." In God's good time other Arabs will join us in search for a peaceful settlement, after 30 years of war and hostility."

For the Israelis who would later watch television, it was an intense, emotional drama, to see their Prime Minister at the Pyramids of Egypt. When there is peace, we will go to the Pyramids, the parents of the Jews tell their children. We will pray constantly that war will cease, we can join hands in fellowship, and bring to our families a hope, perhaps a reality, we can live together, without watching over our shoulder that we will be struck down.

4-4-79

Arab terrorist Qaddafi lives to destroy Israel
Tripoli, Libya

An irreconcilable Libyan dictator, Maummar Qaddafi, may have nuclear weapons, and may soon test an atomic bomb in the Libyan desert. It is true that Qaddafi sent an emissary to Peking in 1970 to ask the late Chou En-Lai to sell Libya an atomic bomb. Intelligence reports claim that he has attempted to purchase nuclear weapons or the ingredients to produce them ever since.

Late last year, the Soviet Union agreed to construct a nuclear reactor in Libya. An Arab source pointed out that India was able to build an atomic bomb from the byproducts of peaceful nuclear energy. Was the world surprised when India did it? Should the world be surprised if Libya were able to do it?

Qaddafi is concerned about a reported build-up on his eastern border. It has been speculated that the Israeli-Egyptian peace treaty might free Sadat to attack Libya, which has been a thorn in his side. He predicts that "as the Sah of Iran vanishes from power, so will President Anwar Sadat." U.S. weapons, now pouring into Egypt, will be turned against Israel. "All the Arab nations will fight together and support the Palestinian peoples," and all the arms from the Americans and other countries will be used in this struggle."

Muammar Qaddafi's heart perhaps is true. He has not lavished his nation's oil wealth upon himself. He has spent billions to improve the lot of the poor in Libya, but he also has spent billions to arm himself and his adherents for the final struggle against Israel.

4-5-79
Hot line between Israel and Egypt
Jerusalem -

Israel began putting together the steps toward normalization of relations with Egypt, including a hot line linking President Anwar Sadat and Prime Minster Menachem Begin.
Begin's cabinet and the Knesset (parliament) gave prompt approval of Begin's report on his visit to Cairo, clearing the way for decisions on actual peacemaking.
A direct telephone line was established so that the two leaders can call at any time for consultation.
The Prime Minister of Israel asked government ministers to draft proposals for normalization in the fields of education, culture, and science. An eleven member cabinet in Israel was requested to state its position on the proposed autonomy for the West Bank and Gaza, and to select five ministers to meet with Egyptian counterparts next month when negotiations on the autonomy itself begin.
The exchange of peace documents as ratified by the two nations will be made in the Sinai Desert. They will be coordinated at the Sinai field mission, a listening post operated in western Sinai by the U.S. State Department.
The Minister of Defense, Ezer Weizman, will be going there April 15, 1979. He plans to discuss the Israeli withdrawal with Egyptian War Minister, Kamel Hassan Ali.
Israel officials said that although the border will be officially opened May 27, it would probably be weeks before there is free access for ordinary tourists to cross the line.

4-8-79
Diplomatic touch wins for Sadat
Cairo, Egypt

The Egyptian-Israeli peace treaty moved forward last week. The moderate acceptance of Prime Minister Menachem Begin's visit turned to joy and gladness, with President Sadat hosting his friend at the royal palace with renewed vigor.

Two days after Begin's departure, Sadat, in a marathon speech to the People's Assembly of Egypt, began selling the treaty to the home folks and to the Arab world. Sadat's appeal, mixed with wit and rancor, deciphered every group - the Palestinians, other Arab states, local Egyptian critics - opposed to the treaty.

Local opposition, signed by some 20 independent members of the assembly, ranging from communists on the extreme left, to fundamental Moslems on the extreme right, have no coherence.

One complaint was the Palestinians have no assurance the treaty would bring an independent state. The Egyptian President made an impassioned appeal over the heads of the leaders, to participate in a treaty program for autonomy. What is better, he asked, "autonomy or words." Demonstrations or withdrawal? Slogans or the liberation of prisoners?

To be sure, the struggle to make the treaty operational depends on how the Israelis handle the Palestinian question.

With Sadat's political artistry, he once again shows that he is a winner.

4-8-79
Egypt recalls seven ambassadors.
Cairo, Egypt

From seven Arab countries, Egypt is recalling her ambassadors, retaliating for the political and economic sanctions imposed for its peace treaty with Israel.

The move, coupled with the withdrawal from Cairo of Envoys from many Arab League nations, further isolates Egypt, the most populace Arab country that shares the Muslim language.

The rich supporter, Saudi Arabia, Qutar, The Arab Emirates, Bahrain, Tunisia, Kuwait, and Morroco, have been instrumental in maintaining a solid united front, and the hardliners refuse to budge with Israel.

Premier Mustapha Khalil, repeated that Egypt would not withdraw from the Arab League, as the militants have demanded. Calling it a slap on the hand, the Arab League said the peace treaty is insufficient, because it does not provide for a Palestinian State, and the return of East Jeralem, the Holy site of Islam for the Arabs.

Egypt insists that the treaty is only a step toward a solution of the Mideast conflict, and the Palestinians should begin with an autonomous state, and eventually seek independence.

As for Jerusalem, Egypt says the city is part of the West Bank that will be returned with further negotiations.

P.L.O. declares an all out war with Egypt
Damascus, Syria

The Palestine Liberation Organization declares an all out offensive against the Israeli-Egyptian peace treaty, particularly inside the Israeli-occupied territories.

The P.L.O.'s central council endorsed measures to intensify guerilla and political action aimed at undermining Israeli plans for the autonomy of the West Bank and the Gaza Strip. The 55 member central council refrained from making any decision on the demands by the more radical leaders for violent actions against Egyptian and American targets, in addition to the offensive against Israel.

The president of the council, Khaled Fahoum, stated that the decision has been taken "to step up military activities against the Israelis in the occupied territories" and to "strengthen the resistance of the Arabs in Jordan, the West Bank, and the Gaza Strip."

Syria's minister of information, Ahmed Iskandar Ahmed, said the Egyptian-Israeli treaty would bring war - not peace - to the Middle East. Ahmed called the treaty, "a military alliance between Sadat and Begin against the Arab nations." We will spare no effort to destroy Sadat," the minister of information stated; He is a threat to the Egyptian people, and his treachery makes him expendable.

Will Libyan leader assassinate Sadat?
In the shadow of Israeli peace negotiations, a team of assassins have been watching for an opportunity to upset the peace process, and turn triumph into tragedy.

These grim plotters have actually cemented a friendship with the Prime Minister and President of Egypt, but they haven't abandoned their chance for murder. The story goes back to the summer of 1977, when a group of terrorists allegedly carried Libyan documents into Cairo, Egypt. The plot is shadowy, but high on their hit list was the name of Anwar Sadat. The american, Ambassador Herman Eilts, was also marked for assassination. The man behind the plan was Mauamar Khadafi. Early in his political career, he was under the spell of the charismatic dictator, Gamal Nassar, who raised the banner of Pan-Arabian nationalism.

Nassar's death, and Sadat's succession, only strengthened Khadafi's determination, to unite Libya and Egypt, as one step to create one great nation. His dream has not come to fruition, and he feels Sadat has become a traitor. Sadat calls him "Magnoun," meaning crazy.

In a quiet manner, the United States has handled the situation, and the President of Egypt has been given high honors for his courage. In the meantime, Sadat has dealt well with his foes, providing a different result. Now Israel and Egypt are at peace, freeing the combat divisions to move from the border of the Jewish state to the Libyan border.

The politics of the reprisal can cut two ways; intelligence reports claim there have been assassination plots directed at Khadafi.

Israelis use restraint in business with Egyptians
Tel Aviv, Israel

Israeli leaders have decided upon a policy of restraint in pursuing business opportunities in Egypt following the signing of the historic peace treaty between the two nations. They are now taking a sober look at the prospects of unilateral trade.

With the exception of oil - which Israel badly needs and which was one of the last stumbling blocks to agreement on the treaty - Israelis see a limited market for their products and technology in their big neighbor.

Despite the stated policy of Prime Minister Menachem Begin's government of a freer and economic business climate, Israeli commercial relations with Egypt are likely to get started under a tight rein. Officials want to keep a watchful eye on Israeli entrepreneurs eager to explore Egyptian enterprises.

Business leaders stressed the importance of getting commercial ties between the two countries off and the right foot. "It is imperative that we create a spirit of partnership. We should look for Egyptian areas of strength. We should not appear as teachers."

Joint ventures undoubtedly will be the method adopted to begin Egyptian - Israeli business relationships. Joint cooperation will be the best way of creating understanding, and help collapse the walls of distrust. Egypt has the manpower and raw materials, and we have the high concentration of technology and skilled labor, stated Minister of Finance, dan Halperin.

American companies could be a valuable third partner in such projects. It might be easier to proceed in business relationships if a third party is involved.

Israelis bomb P.L.O. bases in Lebanon
Tel Aviv, Israel

Israeli warplanes streaked deep into Lebanon and bombed two Palestinian guerilla bases just hours after a terrorist bomb blast killed one person and wounded 33 others in an open-air market in Tel Aviv, officials reported.

One of the bases attacked was just six miles south of Beirut. The air raid was Israel's first since the signing of the Egyptian-Israeli peace treaty March 26, 1979.

The planes hit bases at Damour and Ras el-ain and all returned safely, a military spokesman stated.

The P.L.O. said the jets attacked the city of Tyre, but an Israeli official stated the targets were camps of Al Fatah, major military arm of the Palestine Liberation Organization.

The Israelis often launch air strikes into southern Lebanon in their eye-for-an-eye war with Palestinian guerillas who infiltrate across their borders to plant bombs in populated areas.

Arabs boycott of Egypt analyzed by U.S.
Washington, D.C.

Secretary of State Cyrus Vance stated that the United States expects Saudi Arabia and other Arab states to keep their previous commitments to Egypt, but delay any new assistance because of Egypt's signing of the peace treaty with Israel.

Testifying on the peace treaty and the administrations special request for 4.8 billion dollars in additional military and economic aid for Israel and Egypt, Vance told the Foreign Relations Committee that Saudi Arabia will carry out its pledge made last year to pay for Egypt's purchase from the United States of 50 F-5E fighter planes at a cost of $525 million.

"In respect to the future, economic assistance may not be forthcoming to Egypt."

In the meantime, the United States and other Western states will have to fill the gap, and help Egypt meet its pressing needs. So far, no other state has offered aid.

"It is fair to ask why there should be such a price for peace." Vance said. The answer is the "Middle East is volatile, and carries its own risks." In order for both governments to lead their people through these unchartered waters, they must be confident they can deal effectively with threats to their continued security.

Meanwhile, in Cairo, Egypt, President Anwar Sadat established April 19, 1979, as a date for an Egyptian referendum on the peace treaty with Israel. He said he will ask Egypt's 9.5 million voters to give him authority to call new elections "in order to establish guidelines of democracy for a new era."

Criticizing Arab moderates who joined hardliners in imposing sanctions against Egypt for signing the treaty, Sadat said, "the lowest, humblest Egyptian will snub the Cadillac-riding Arabs because he knows that it was his blood and that of his brothers which quadrupled the price of oil." Peace for Egypt is "love," sweat, and tears."

Under the constitution in Egypt, President Sadat must receive the approval of the voters to hold new elections. Elections must be held 60 days after parliament is dissolved.

Aid to Egypt will bring quick, visible gains
Cairo Egypt

The United States will supply economic aid to Egypt as part of the peace process with Israel. The key is to provide planned small projects with a fast and visible payoff.

Egypt's need for help is beyond question. President Anwar Sadat has grounded the peace treaty with Israel on a pledge that peace will bring prosperity. If the treaty is to win enduring support, it must yield benefits.

Constant war with Israel has left practically nothing for expanding and maintaining urban services, housing, transport, power and communications - necessary to support the burgeoning population of the cities.

The countryside is not much better off. The high birth rate means that illiteracy is outrunning education and disease is outpacing health programs. Food production cannot keep up with consumption.

In the long run the cycle can be broken by a strategy of rural development. This will involve family planning, reclamation, provisions of more services to the countryside, the building of new towns, and the development of industry in rural areas.

Food is probably the most immediate priority. There are shortages of vegetable oil and lentils, two basic items of Egyptian diet. The United States can provide wheat, which it now supplies and other vital products for a healthy diet.

Housing is a disaster area. Thousands of Egyptians are living in a cemetery known as the "City of the Dead." Years will be required before the shortage of shelter can be met.

There is a golden opportunity for exchange visits between Israelis and Egyptians. The friendliness of the Egyptians, their genuine assurance melts the hardest of Israeli hearts. These kind of experiences offer the best hope for peace progress.

The private foundations could make a great contribution by promoting exchange visits of writers, businessmen, doctors, and other citizens.

Gloom in Lebanon over peace treaty
Beirut, Lebanon

The Egyptian-Israeli peace treaty that set off a wave of euphoria in America, Egypt, and Israel has generated a sense of failure, deep anger, and frustration at the United States and gloom among Palestinians and other Arabs in Lebanon.

An indication of distress was an explosion that wiped out the first and second floors of the American John F. Kennedy Library and cultural center.

The members in the P.L.O. have united in escalating operations in the occupied territories in Israel and the West Bank of the Jordan River. In addition there will be mass political protests and military operations against them.

The Sadat-Begin treaty has brought together Habash and his (Popular Front) with the Palestinian Liberation Organization in defeating the peace treaty of Egypt and Israel. Bassam Abu Sharif, P.L.O. leader states, "there will be an explosion soon in an Arab country, maybe Egypt, the Sudan, or somewhere that the regime works with the American-Israeli alliance."

"The treaty that Sadat has made is an arms agreement with America, not a peace," said a Lebanese politician who in the past has opposed P.L.O. activities. The other Arab countries, and especially the Palestinians, will not buy it, no matter how you present it.

Israelis polish manners for visits to Egypt
Tel Aviv, Israel

Don't kiss or hug in public. Don't refuse an invitation to coffee or tea. If you are a woman, do not wear shorts or a short skirt, no matter how hot it is.

This is part of the advice Israelis are hearing about how to behave in Egypt when the border gates are lifted to allow tourism between the two former enemies.

The government hopes the personal contact of tourists will put a friendly seal on the Israel-Egypt peace treaty, but there are tentative plans to limit the number of permits to go to Cairo, just as Jerusalem does not want Egypt flooding Israel with their people.

Israel is preoccupied with going to see the land of the Pharaohs. The newspapers feature travel articles on the wonders of Egypt.

Hanna Bavly, Minister on manners for diplomats, wrote in the newspaper Maariv, "Egyptians are used to dressing with care and elegance, the men as well as the women." "It is important that the first impression be positive."

Mrs. Bavly advised Israelis to learn some Arabic greetings, to drink mineral water instead of tap water, to listen politely instead of interrupting, and not to agree too heartily when an Egyptian makes self depreciating jokes.

An organization, "A Beautiful People in a Beautiful Land," is preparing a brochure advising Israelis on how to behave abroad, and with the signing of the peace pact, Egypt is being added explaining, courtesies and deportment.

About a half-million Israelis, 15 percent of the population, are expected to travel this year.

Reprisals threatened by Arafat against U.S.
Beirut, Lebanon

The leader of the Palestinian Liberation Organization, Yasser Arafat, assailed the Carter Administration for "pushing us into a corner" and warned that "many events" such as the recent spate of attacks against Israel "are coming on the horizon."

Arafat promised Palestinian blows against American interests in the Middle East, as well as attacks against Israel and Egypt, and "a holy war" to recapture Israel-occupied East Jerusalem by force.

The Palestinian chief, after two unsuccessful raids on Israel, a foiled airport attack in Brussels Belgium, heavy exchanges of artillery fire between his forces and those of Israeli-backed Christian militias in Southern Lebanon, and the bombing of the American cultural center in Beirut, took no credit for other guerila activities.

Asked under what conditions would Arafat agree to start direct talks with the United States, he said that any negotiations must be under the auspices of the United States, and on the condition that the United States abide by "all the U.N. resolutions which deal with the Palestinian problem and which the Palestinian people have accepted."

Arafat repeated the P.L.O. position that the group would settle for an independent state, "in any part of the Palestine from which Israel will withdraw, or is liberated."

Arafat stated that he saw little hope of gaining Palestinian objectives peacefully. "After carrying on our armed struggle, we have achieved many victories, liberated our people, and come from refugees to freedom fighters," he declared.

Sadat relaxes, thinks through big issues
Cairo, Egypt

Anwar Sadat rises every morning between 8 and 9 a.m. For half an hour he reads the papers and breakfasts on papaya and a bit of honey. Then he goes for a walk in the garden.

For 2 ½ years when he was a prisoner of the British during World War II, he lived in a tiny cell. Now he moves around.

Sadat lives in no one place. In summer he is in Alexandria, winter in Aswan, spring and fall in Ismalia and Cairo.

The President of Egypt settles down to work about 11 in the morning. For the next four or five hours he sees his ministers or other visitors.

After his meetings, Sadat regularly takes a walk - roughly 2 ½ miles. The most striking feature of his routine is the large amount of time he spends by himself.

Far more than any other leader in the Middle East, Sadat has figured out the historic needs of his country, and has taken the steps required to achieve them. He has identified peace with Israel as the prime objective.

On many domestic issues, nobody is prepared to make decisions without the approval of the Egyptian President. Sadat's main philosophy is that he has an extraordinary rapport with the Egyptian people, and the faithful protect him from the radical Arabs, who would overthrow his government.

Israel retaliates for raid
Jerusalem, Israel

Israel naval vessels shelled Palestinian targets in northern Lebanon in responses to a predawn raid by four Palestinian guerillas on a costal town of Nahariya.

Beirut radio quoted Palestianian sources as saying that at least 10 civilians had been wounded in the attack.

Two girls, ages 2 and 4, were among the four Israelis killed in the raid. Prime Minister Menachem Begin canceled his appointments to be able to attend memorial services for the girls and their father in Haifa.

Ezer Weizman, Israel's defense minister, postponed a state visit to Egypt in order to go to Nahariya with his chief of staff, General Rafael Eitan, to view the scene of the Palestinian attack.

Israeli investigators, who described the attack, said that four Palestinians, members of the Lebanese Palestine Liberation Front came ashore in a rubber power boat. They had come from Tyre, a port in southern Lebanon.

Begin phoned President Anwar Sadat of Egypt to tell him of the decision to postpone Weizman's visit. The Prime Minister's office said that Sadat is sharing the sorrow of the Israeli people, and for those who died in Nahariya.

4-23-79
Military advancement of Saudi Arabia
Dhahran, Saudi Arabia

Prince Bandar bin Sultan of Saudi Arabia escorted a group of Americans around Dhahran Air Force Base, the showpiece of the military, pointing with pride to sleek F-5 fighter planes and modern single family houses for the pilots and ground crews.

When the American official addressed the 30 year old nephew of King Khales as "Your Highness," the prince stated, "I prefer to be called major." "I worked hard to become a major in our air force. I was born a prince."

Bandar's preference for military instead of royal titles is strikingly unusual in a country that is governed in feudal fashion by the royal family, and where Western-style military rank, command structure, and weapons were virtually unknown a generation ago.

The ability of the Saudi military is an issue of vital concern to the United States, not only because the country is a pivotal one in the Middle East, but also our country is more dependent on Saudi's vast reserves of oil

Saudi and U.S. officials agree that the most serious potential military threats are posed by South Yemen and Ethiopia, two Soviet backed Marxist states.

Before 1950, Saudi Arabia's armed forces were primarily equipped with vintage rifles, curved swords, spears, camels, and swift Arabian horses. King Ibn Saud, in 1950, nearing the end of his 20 year reign, sought U.S. aid in modernizing its armed forces. The military started slowly, but today Saudi Arabia is the leading foreign nation for U.S. arms assistance, building its military around American made planes, tanks, armored personnel carriers, artillery, and rockets.

On the United States-built air base in Dhahran, the Saudi air force is training pilots to fly the 100 F-5 jets that the country began to obtain in 1973. Training of the more sophisticated F-15's will begin in the early 1980's.

The Saudi defense forces are divided into two parts, each commanded by a senior member of the royal family. The national guard, with 15,000 to 30,000 men, is paterned by the British palace guard units. It is commanded by Prince Abdullah. The Army, Navy, and Air Force together make up the second unit, with 40,000 to 50,000 men. It is patterned after U.S. military units and is commanded by Prince Sultan.

Before 1950, the national guard was known as the "white army," because its members wore traditional white desert robes. All the members of the white army were recruited from Bedouin tribes of central Arabia. Today most members of the guard are Bedouins who sometimes wear robes and sometimes Western-style uniforms.

The Army, Navy, and Air Force are more western in appearance. The role of these services is defense of the country against attack from outside.

A pentagon official said that the United States has been carefully cultivating its military ties to Saudi Arabia for more than 30 years. "We should not forget that we are dealing with the absolute center core of another culture." The Saudi's do not want to be an extension of any great power."

4-23-79
Israeli immigrant from South Africa saves neighbors
Nahariya, Israel

Shmuel El-Ad looked at Charlie Shapira's bullet-shattered door and told his neighbors: "I owe my life to you."

Shapira shot one of the four Palestinian terrorists who stormed the apartment building. The three other terrorists grabbed two hostages and fled the area.

"If you didn't have a gun they would have gone through the whole complex and killed all of us," El-Ad told the 36 year old immigrant from South Africa.

Shapira, who grabbed a .38 caliber revolver when the terrorists fired through his door, waited until a Palestinian entered the apartment and killed him.

Across the hall was the apartment of Dani Heran, and his wife Smadar and two small daughters. Heran and his daughters died in the attack. Heran managed a textile factory in nearby Maalot, the scene of two terrorist attacks in recent years.

The floor of the Heran apartment was littered with spent cartridges, and the stairwell was pitted by shrapnel from grenades. Outside, a pickup trucks headlights were shot out, and bullet holes had shattered the windshield.

The wife of El-Ad, Gayle, stated, "I never wanted my husband to have a gun," I felt it was too dangerous; but after this I've changed my mind. We were totally at the mercy of the terrorists.

4-25-79
Strauss named as Chief Mideast Mediator
Washington, D.C.

President Carter appointed Texan Robert S. Strauss, his special trade negotiator, as Chief U.S. mediator in the next phase of Mideast peace talks on Palestinian autonomy.

"By accepting this difficult but very important challange, Bob Strauss will be relieving Secretary of State Cyrus Vance and me of our time consuming and heavy personal role in the peace talks," Carter stated.

Strauss served as Carter's adviser on anti-inflation programs and was Democratic national chairman at the time Carter won the 1976 presidential election.

Strauss, a jew, said he did not believe his ethnic background would hamper him in any way in his new post.

The Egyptians and Israelis agreed as part of their peace settlement to begin negotiations on establishing autonomous Palestinian governments in Israeli-occupied Gaza Strip and West Bank of the Jordan River.

The goal is to hold elections within a year after those negotiations begin. The autonomous governments in turn would run those regions for a five year interim period, during which Israel and the Arabs would negotiate the ultimate fate of the two territories.

The President of the United States has cleared his selection by telephone with both Egyptian President Anwar Sadat and Israel's Prime Minister Menachem Begin.

Their response was positive and enthusiastic.

4-25-79
Israel's third day of reprisals against Palestinians
Jerusalem, Israel

Israeli planes and ships bombed and shelled Palestinian targets in southern Lebanon in the third day of reprisals for the guerilla attack in the city of Nahariya.

In Cairo, Egypt, a government official said the Israeli attack on southern Lebanon would have "negative effects" on the implementation of the Egyptian-Israeli peace treaty. The spokesman also condemned announced Israeli plans for additional West Bank settlements as "illegal and contrary to the peace treaty."

In Jerusalem, Prime Minister Menachem Begin appeared before the Knesset foreign affairs and defense committee and, according to Israel radio, said the settlements would be only on public lands, not those owned by the local Arab population.

Begin stated he would recommend to his cabinet that the death penalty be imposed on terrorists found guilty of acts of "inhuman cruelty" during attacks on Israel. There is no civil death penalty here except for war crimes, tried in the military courts.

Despite the Nahariya raid, Israel's reprisals and Egypt's angry response, plans were going ahead for the exchange of the articles of ratification of the peace treaty at the Sinai Field Mission, an American listening post east of the Suez Canal. The exchange will make the peace treaty operative.

STEPS TO COMPREHENSIVE PEACE
Egyptian-Israeli peace treaty sealed in Sinai Desert

4-26-79
Um Khasiba, U.N. Sinai buffer zone

Israel and Egypt sealed their historic peace treaty at a remote American surveillance station in the Sinai Desert.

Israeli and Egyptian delegates exchanged ratification documents after they consulted with Jerusalem and Cairo to clear up a problem over the texts that delayed the signing two hours.

Fighting continued, meanwhile, on the Israel-Lebanon border. Three Israelis were hurt by rockets fired from southern Lebanon into northern Israel by Palestinians. Israeli jets, gunboats and artillery pounded Palestinian camps in retaliation.

The formal exchange of treaty documents ends the 31-year state of war between Egypt and Israel and sets in motion timetables for Israeli troop withdrawals in the Sinai and negotiations on Palestinian autonomy. It also permits Israeli ships to use the Suez Canal.

The ceremony in the Sinai buffer area lasted only 30 minutes. Flags of Egypt, Israel, the United Nations, and the United States were raised and the national anthems of the three countries were played.

Israel radio said the text problem concerned a word missing from the Egyptian version of a side letter on Palestinian autonomy negotiations. The official Middle East News Agency in Cairo said the delay was caused when Egypt insisted that all documents dealing with self-rule be exchanged along with the treaty. Israel agreed to the demand.

At the banquet in Cairo, Israeli Defense Minister Ezer Weizman and his counterpart Kamal Hassan Ali, toasted the formal end of a state of war between their countries. Weizman was in Cairo to discuss details of Israel's withdrawal from the Sinai.

4-27-79
Middle East cost .S. billions
Washington, D.C.

War and instability in the Middle East have cost the United States an estimated $55 to $70 billion, according to State Department figures made available to congress.

The cost of the 1973-1974 Arab embargo and rising oil prices since that time have cost the Americans an estimated $315 billion, the department said.

The Senate Foreign Relations Committee voted 9-1 on April 26, 1979 to recommend the Senate approve the Middle East package for peace.

This includes 4.8 billion in loans and grants for Egypt and Israel, only 1.47 billion of which involves out-of-pocket costs to the United States.

The cumulative cost of higher prices since 1973 of oil has cost the U.S. over $300 billion. The price for peace will cost the Americans far less.

Senator Frank Church of the Foreign Relations Committee says, "When people write me and say don't squander 1.47 billion for peace over the next three years and then ignore the enormous amounts we have spent for war, we have a duty to put it in perspective."

"If war comes again and the oil is cut off, our factories would close, our autos would stand idle, and we soon would be turning off our lights," Church said.

The bill for the loans to Egypt and Israel calls for full repayment at 9 percent interest.

The new aid package, intended to help implement the Israeli-Egyptian peace treaty, involves military credit sales of 2.2 billion for Israel and 1.5 billion for Egypt.

Israel would get $800 million in direct grants to pay the costs of moving two air bases from the Sinai Desert to the Negev Desert in Israel. Egypt would get $300 million in specific economic aid.

4-29-79
Possible nuclear confrontation in Middle East
Jerusalem, Israel

The Middle East, despite a first tentative step toward peace, is moving closer each day to a possible confrontation.

Israel possesses atomic potential: If it has no bombs, it is only because the wires have not been connected.

Its enemies are offering, and spending tens of millions of dollars in a clear attempt to get nuclear weapons of their own.

Israeli officials have warned that the French sale of nuclear research reactors and uranium to Iraq could give Iraq the bomb.

The French reactors were ready for delivery when seven charges of skillfully placed plastic explosives severely damaged them in a factory near Toulon, France, early this month, setting back Iraq's reactor program and its need for uranium, two years.

Piracy, theft, collusion and spurious documentation are rife in the fringes of international nuclear dealings.

Despite efforts of world leaders to forestall the entry of nuclear weapons in the Middle East, the threat is obviously growing as Israel's enemies amass the financing and know-how to match Israeli atomic potential.

The Iraqi, the United States fears, is attempting to develop nuclear reprocessing capability. Many nations, including the West Europeans, advocate the reprocessing of spent nuclear fuel as an economical means of producing nuclear energy through breeder reactors. A byproduct of reprocessing is plutonium, which can be used to make a bomb. Iraq may have intended to divert highly enriched uranium fuel from the two research reactors France was building for it.

In the Islamic world Pakistan is diverting huge sums into technology for making an atomic bomb. Pakistan is being aided by Libya, Saudi Arabia, and Kuwait for the purpose of adding nuclear weapons to an Islamic armory. You can write your own scenario of what might happen in this pan-Islamic theatre.

4-29-79

In Israel, pirated uranium and a 26-megawatt research reactor provided by France in the late 1950s without provision for international safeguards have given Israel a plutonium capacity sufficient for one bomb a year since the middle 1960s, intelligence sources stated. Israel is also developing laser enrichment techniques for upgrading uranium for use in weapons.

The major powers have stepped in to try to halt moves which could lead to proliferation. The United States cut off foreign aid to Pakistan when the military regime there secretly began building a centrifuge to enrich uranium to a degree that could be used for weapons. The Soviet Union reportedly has dropped plans to build three reactors in Libya.

"The only way to prevent a holocaust will be for the states to establish safeguards agreed to by all the major powers. The greatest threat will be from smaller nations newly in possession of a bomb - and the danger among them will be from those who place hatred above consequences.

4-30-79
Arab terrorists injure three Israeli children
Tel Aviv, Israel

A bomb blast injured three children waiting for a school bus. The three children were not seriously injured. One was treated for shock and the other two for minor shrapnel wounds.

In Beirut, Lebanon, the Palestinian Liberation Organization said its guerillas were responsible for the attack, and claimed several Israeli soldiers were killed in the explosion.

The bombing in Kfar Sava, eight miles northeast of Tel Aviv, was the latest in a wave of terror attacks against Israel aimed at disrupting the Israeli-Egyptian peace.

Police are telling Israelis to be especially alert for attacks with the approach of Israel's 31st Independence Day celebration.

In the Sinai Desert, meanwhile, Israeli and Egyptian generals met at Tassa, a United Nations post, for their first detailed discussion of the return of Sinai territory to Egyptian rule. Good will and understanding will be used to solve future problems.

The Israeli Cabinet voted by a vote of 7-5 with one abstention and four members absent to reinstate the death penalty for crimes of Extreme Cruelty by terrorists. Cabinet Secretary, Arieh Naor, stated that this action cancels "the insurance policy" for captured terrorists.

Death penalty approved by Israel
Jerusalem, Israel

The Israeli cabinet, after a lengthy debate, supported Prime Minister Menachem Begin's recommendation that the death penalty be applied to terrorists.

Israeli law provides for the death penalty in civil cases - including "crimes against the Jewish people" - as well as in military cases. Terrorism - indiscriminate attacks against civilians - is classified as a military offense. Beginning in 1967, the government ordered prosecutors not to ask for the death penalty.

The leaders of Israel have traditionally opposed capital punishment because of the Jews experience at the hands of the German Nazis. An official stated that "we of all people should hold human life sacred."

But the Palestinian guerilla raid into Nahariya on April 22, 1979, in which four Israelis died crystalized public opinion in favor of the death penalty.

"There are some incidents so terrifying that it would be an injustice not to ask for the death penalty," said Justice Minister Shmuel Tamir after the cabinet session.

The Prime Minister recommended that any death sentence be carried out by a firing squad rather than hanging, apparently since the world - and the terrorists - would consider the firing squad less cruel.

4-30-79
Israel shielded by Jordan from terrorists
Al Qurn Fortress, Jordan

Jordan - King Hussein's alert, professional soldiers at this outpost, along with their equally alert Israeli enemies just yards away from a bend in the Jordan River, have a common foe.

The enemy armies are both on the lookout for what each considers its greatest threat - Palestinian terrorists attempting to slip into Israel from the Jordan side of the river.

To the Israelis, the Palestinians are a direct threat. Four armed commandos crossed on Easter Sunday the Jordan River, but they were spotted and killed just short of their objective. It was a small Israeli settlement, where they apparently intended to kill as many people as they could before being caught or killed.

To the Jordanians, the possibility that the four crossed from their side was so chilling that the local battalion commander, Major Yahya Yussef, lead a painstaking three day investigation to determine if they really passed through his lines from Jordan into Israel.

Although the incident and its aftermath may seem trivial in the broad spectrum of the Middle East conflict, it shows how delicately balanced the Hashemite Kingdom of Jordan is as it seeks to reject the Israeli-Egyptian peace treaty while constantly reassuring Israel that it has no hostile intentions along the border.

Memories of the late 1960s and early 1970s when this lush river bank farmland was a battleground, are still fresh, and Jordan does not want to relive them.

The wounds of that clash, which drove the Palestinian guerilas into Syria and Lebanon, have not healed, despite numerous attampts by Arab mediators to strike an accord between P.L.O. leader Yasser Arafat and King Hussein.

The orders of Major Yussef are to see that there are no incidents that might offend the Israelis. In a written contract, each farmer pledges, under threat of criminal penalties, "to arrest suspicious persons on sight and bring them to the nearest army post."

4-30-79
Israel welcomes dissidents as heros
Tel Aviv, Israel

Edward Kuznetsov and Mark Dymshits arrived in Israel to a heroes' welcome today. They were the last of seven Soviet Jews freed by the Kremlin after nine years in prison for plotting to escape from the Soviet Union by hijacked airliner.
"Blessed be he who has sustained us and brought us to this day," said Prime Minister Menachem Begin, quoting a Jewish prayer celebrating joyous occasions.
Kuznetsov, 52, and Dymshits, 40, both pale and gaunt from their prison years but smiling broadly, arrived at Ben Gurion Airport on a flight from New York. They and three other Russian dissidents were swapped in New York in the United States for two convicted Soviet spies.
The men were welcomed by an emotional crowd of relatives, friends, and government officials led by Begin, himself a former prisoner in a Soviet labor camp.
"Thanks to your efforts we have arrived to be with you," said Dymshits. I am happy that after nine years I can join my country and my family in my homeland. There is many more thousands of Jews who want to leave the Soviet Union. A struggle is still before us.
The two Jewish dissidents were met with tears and hugs from relatives, flowers presented by school children, and the ceremonious awarding of Israeli citizenship cards to the new immigrants.
Prime Minister Begin thanked President Carter for negotiating the release of Kuznetsov and Dymshits. "Words cannot express what we feel towards our comrades this day."

Suez Canal open to Israeli ships
Suez City, Egypt

To the shouts of Salaam and Shalom, an Israeli freighter sailed through the Suez Canal, flag waving, horn glaring proof that peace has indeed come between Egypt and Israel.
The 4,500 ton Ashdod was the first vessel flying the Israeli flag allowed to pass through the 101-mile waterway, Israeli officials said.
April 30, 1979, will long be remembered as a red letter day for Israel and Egypt. It is a milestone in the normalization fo relations under the Israeli-Egyptian treaty of peace, which guarantees Israeli ships unhindered passage through the canal.
The Ashdod, following the custom of the Suez, flew both Israeli and Egyptian colors as it began its northbound passage at Suez City, southern entrance to the canal. It had come from the Israeli port of Eilat on the Gulf of Aquaba and was on its way, empty, to the port of Haifa, on the Mediterranean Sea.

About a 100 jubilant Egyptians, including soldiers and civilians waiting to cross the canal to the Sinai Desert, waved and cheered in Arabic, Salaam, Shalom, the Hebrew word for peace, as the freighter steamed past. Sirens wailed and ship foghorns sounded welcome.

The last Israeli ship to enter the Suez Canal, the "Bat Galim, tried to pass through in 1954, but was seized by the Egyptians, and the crew was held for three months as prisoners of war.

5-2-79
Mideast treaty signals new age for Israel
Jerusalem, Israel

Israel celebrates its 31st birthday today, treasuring its freshly signed peace treaty with Egypt and hoping it signals the start of a new age.

"This agreement means our infancy is over," said one government official. "Maybe now we can begin to see the day when we can concentrate on building our economy and solving our social problems. All we ever wanted was to be a state with the power over our own destiny."

The treaty which ended the state of war with Egypt was signed in Washington on March 26, 1979, by Israeli Prime Minister Menachem Begin and Egyptian President Anwar Sadat. It took effect on week ago, following a ceremony at an outpost in the Sinai Desert.

Israel declared its independence on May 15, 1948. The day is commemorated by its Hebrew calendar anniversary, which falls this year on May 2.

The euphoric sense that the accord would usher in an era of tranquility and prosperity has been shattered by the hostility of the Arab states. Sixteen Arab nations have severed relations with Egypt. Israel has bombed Palestinian bases in Lebanon to retaliate for persistent terrorist attacks.

But the face of the Mideast already has been transformed. Some of the dreams after Sadat's visit to Jerusalem in 1977 have come true.

Begin made a state visit to Cairo this year and fulfilled his wish to see the pyramids built by his ancestors. Israeli and Egyptian generals have begun meeting regularly to work out details of Israel's withdrawal from Sinai.

Israel expects austerity and higher inflation as the price for redeploying its Sinai forces on a new defense line in the Negev Desert inside Israel. If the vision enshrined in its complex clauses and compromises become reality, Israel will have won the long struggle for acceptance in the Middle East.

5-3-79
Land rights contested by Arabs, Israelis
Hebron, Israeli Occupied West Bank

The growing confrontation between Jews and Arabs in Hebron is apparent in the field of vines across the road from Kiryat, Arba, an Israeli settlement adjoining the Arab city of Hebron.

The barbed wire that the Israelis put up around the Arab-farmed land had been cut and pulled aside.

In the field, 5 year old vines lay shriveling in the spring sun, neatly severed with a power saw. Hundreds have been cut in the last two weeks.

Across the road, on a commanding rise, stand the closely spaced apartment towers of Kiryat Arba, where 2000 Jews live in the midst of the Arab highlands of Judea. Guards with sub-machine guns carefully inspect the cars of Arabs entering the compound.

The vines were cut on land the Jewish settlement had coveted - and been denied by Israel's Supreme Court - as a site for expansion.

The land dispute is tied in with a more serious issue: the rights of Israelis to settle in Hebron, which with 50,000 residents, is the second largest city in the Occupied West Bank.

Hebron, where the Patriarch Abraham and his family are said to be buried, is a holy site to religious Jews, second only to Jerusalem.

5-4-79
Control of West Bank retained by Israel
Jerusalem, Israel

Prime Minister Menachem Begin, outlining his plan for autonomy on the West Bank and the Gaza Strip, said that Israel's military government should retain sovereignty there.

"The agreement reached last September at Camp David, Maryland, by Begin, President Anwar Sadat, and President Carter states that the Israeli military government and its civilian administration will withdraw."

The Prime Minister of Israel proposes that its military government be withdrawn to Tel Aviv - but continue to function as the ultimate authority for the occupied areas, a majority of Arab residents.

Begin emphasizes that a Palestinian "self governing" council should have no legislative role under a system of autonomy, but only administrative authority.

"It is a legal point, and almost theoretical, " an Israeli official responded. "We cannot allow a vacuum of control. If the Palestinians' self-governing council, at some stage declares Palestinian independence there has to be a military government to keep harmony."

In Cairo, a Foreign Minister official said: "Statements issued for local consumption, if they include pre-conditions conflicting with what has been agreed upon, may obstruct efforts for a just, lasting, and comprehensive peace."

5-6-79
Egypt calls for Islamic Summit Conference
Cairo, Egypt

in a diplomatic counter attack against its Arab critics, Egypt has called for an Islamic summit conference to discuss the "liberation of the Arab section of Jerusalem, which was annexed by Israel nearly 12 years ago.

The call, made in a foreign ministry statement, was given wide circulation in the Cairo press. The statement proposes that the Islamic meeting be held in Fez, Morocco.

If the conference is sanctioned, Egypt is prepared to attend, although Morocco is one of the countries breaking relations with Egypt since the signing of the peace accords. This has left the Egyptians with diplomatic ties to only Sudan, Oman, and Somalia in the Arab world.

A frequent complaint by Sadat's adversaries is that Camp David agreements and the subsequent Israeli-Egyptian peace treaty have ignored the future of Arab-Jerusalem. They have alleged that President Sadat sold out on the question of Arab autonomy as part of a separate commitment with Israel.

Israelis encourage Palestinians to settle in Jordan
Amman, Jordan

Government officials say they believe that Israel has embarked on a campaign to drive Jordanians out of their own country in order to make Jordan a homeland for the Palestinians.

Some of the leading Jordanians expressed this belief in recent interviews, citing what they perceive as an intense Israeli propaganda campaign to undermine King Hussein's rule and incite hostility among the Palestinians, who constitute a majority of this nation's 3 million people.

"We know that the Israelis have hoped Jordan would become a Palestinian homeland, conveniently leaving the West Bank under permanent Israeli occupation," a senior officer stated.

The officials pointed to a spate of reports from Jerusalem and from Beirut, Lebanon, alleging that a series of recent events in Jordan added up to government instability, a split in King Hussein's royal family and the possibility of an uprising among the Palestinian population.

The deaths of two Jordanian leaders close to the royal household fueled speculation that a critical confrontation between the King and crown prince Hassan was imminent.

The director of Jordan public security, General Ghazi Arabiyat, was killed in an automobile crash early this month as he was being driven into Amman from the airport following a meeting of Arab world police chiefs in Doha, Qatar.

A few days later an uncle of King Hussein, Sherif Nasser Ibn Jemil, former commander in chief of the Jordanian army, died at the wheel of his car while driving to Amman from his country estate.

The rumors of crisis were enhanced by Hussein's absence from his country, which magnified the split with the crown prince.

The mysterious deaths of the Police chief and the King's uncle were coincidental and unrelated. The Kings absence was strictly non-political according to palace sources. The king was sorrowful of his uncle's death and sought solace away from his empire, vacationing in Britian, Austria, and Morocco.

5-8-79
El Arish returned to Egyptian control
El Arish, Israeli occupied Sinai

Israeli and Egyptian officials met to work out plans for restoring this major community to Egyptian control and also to Egypt's economy.

After having been linked to the economy of Israel for almost 12 years, El Arish is being joined to that of Egypt, where the per capita income is one-tenth of Israel's and the minimum wage one-fifth.

The joint commission formed by the two nations for the transfer was guarded in its announcements, but it appears that Egypt:

Would probably allow 5,000 workers from El Arish to continue to cross into Israel to hold jobs there.

Would not let Israelis continue to operate five factories in the city, including the major processing plant for the city's biggest industry, fishing.

"Two-thirds of the work force here works in Israel, and Israeli official said." "We have information from Cairo that Egypt will let the workers continue to cross."

When the Israeli occupation ends on May 25, 1979, the doors of the Kitan factory will be closed, but an official of the plant said the firm will leave its equipment intact when it withdraws in the hope that Egypt will get the shop running again and resume exports to Israel.

El Arish was a city of around 65,000, provincial capital of the Sinai, when Israel captured it after a tough battle in the six-day war. Twenty five thousand residents fled, according to mayor Ahmed Abdullah Eldangir, who states many want to return. The mayor was appointed by the Israeli military government in 1970.

El Arish is a natural oasis, with its own water wells. Many of the houses in the dusty city are abandoned, and many pocked with bullet holes from the 1967 war, but Egyptian flags are flying in El Arish and the city is prepared for a festival.

5-8-79
Lebanon rejects peace overtures by Begin
Jerusalem, Israel

The Prime Minister of Israel has invited the President of Lebanon, Elias Sarkis, to a series of peace talks, although Israeli planes are continuing to bomb Palestinian targets inside Lebanon.

Begin's offer was promptly rejected, both by the Lebanese, who labeled it "amazing" in light of the renewed attacks, and within Israel by the leader of the opposing Labor Party, Shimon Peres, who suggested that Syria would have to be involved in such discussions.

Begin issued his invitation to Elias Sarkis in the form of a report to the Israeli parliament at the state of its summer session.

"I invite the President of Lebanon to come to Jerusalem to confer with me," the Israeli leader said. "For my part, I am prepared to leave on a civilian plane for Beirut."

Peres, Israel's opposition leader, stated that Begin, by inviting the Lebanese leader to talk about peace has taken "a very brave step," but Lebanon is under Syrian occupation, and must have their permission.

The 30,000 man Arab League security force in Lebanon, brought in to keep the peace at the close of the 1976 civil war, is largely Syrian.

The Prime Minister of Israel replied that Israel and Lebanon could make peace in a matter of days "because there are no territorial disputes." The main problem is the presence in Lebanon of Palestinian refugees, who number about 195,000 people. Saudi Arabia and Libya have plenty of land, water, and oil, and could relocate the refugees in their countries.

In another development, Egypt announced that it would not agree to the establishment of an air link with Israel until 15 months after the two countries exchange documents ratifying their peace treaty.

"The basic position . . . Egypt is that the normalization of relations with Israel will begin nine months after the exchange of documents ratifying the peace accords," a government spokesman said.

5-9-79
Doubt expressed on Saudi aid to Egypt

Officials of the Carter cabinet expressed doubt that Saudi Arabia would meet its said to Egypt.

Both Defense Secretary Harold Brown and Secretary of State Cyrus Vance, testifying before the House Foreign Affairs Committee, underscored the downturn in U.S.-Saudi relations.

Vance, who had expressed earlier confidence that the Saudi aid commitments to Egypt would go through as promised, testified that 50 F-5E jet fighters sold to Egypt for 525 million dollars, questioned as who is to pay was "still under investigation."

Last month, after the Egyptian-Israeli peace treaty was formally ratified, Saudi Arabia disproved of the policies of the United States, and abruptly broke diplomatic relations with Egypt.

Egyptian President Anwar Sadat, in a May Day speech, bitterly denounced the Saudi leadership. The uncertainty of Saudi intentions is counted from this time.

Unilateral support and concord is needed to make the peace accords operable. Patience and understanding of each of the nations involved will bring peace to the Middle East.

5-9-79
Egypt boycotts Islamic meeting
Fez, Morocco

Facing certain censure from fellow Moslem nations, Egypt boycotted the Islamic meeting, even though a place had been set aside for the Egyptian representative at the residence of Morocco's King Hassan.

A majority of foreign ministers of 43 nations that constitute the Islamic world had decided to temporarily suspend Egypt from membership in the Islamic Conference, as punishment for signing a peace treaty with Israel.

The censure from the worldwide Islamic organization was softened by the last-minute diplomatic maneuvering in which Egypt chose to boycott the conference rather than attend and face the certainty of being voted out. Morocco's Hassan was instrumental in arranging the plan.

The Islamic conference was formed in 1969, out of Arab and Islamic anger over the burning of Islam's third-holy shrine, the Al Aqsa mosque in Jerusalem. Saudi Arabian Foreign Minister Saud al Faisal stated that the liberation of Jerusalem remains the concern of the conference.

This organization has expanded, and now operates Islamic newspapers, broadcasting stations, and development banks funded from oil-rich states of the Persian Gulf.

5-9-79
United States improves security in the Mideast
Washington, D.C.

Yasser Arafat, chairman of the Palestine Liberation Organization and leader of the Fatah, the main Palestinian guerilla group, has warned several times since the Middle East summit at Camp David last September that American interests will be under attack because of the U.S. role in arranging the Egyptian-Israeli peace treaty.

Analysts in Washington disagree as to whether Arafat's threat should be taken as a signal for physical violence against Americans or a general warning of economic and political reprisals.

A recent upsurge in terrorist attacks against civilian targets in Israel has been traced to a series of meetings in December of last year between Arafat and some of his more militant colleagues. As a result, there is some apprehension that "Black September," Fatah's international terrorist wing, may be revived from a dormant state after the assassination by Israeli intelligence agents of most of its field operators in 1975.

Egyptian authorities late last month arrested a team of Palestinians carrying plastic explosives in toothpaste tubes. The captured men identified themselves as "Eagles of the Palestinian Revolution."

The United States has organized anti-terrorist forces from the elite military exclusively dedicated to hostage rescue and similar anti-terrorist reprisals. We will be prepared against violence from all adversaries.

5-10-79
Israeli force turned back by U.N. troops in Lebanon
Jerusalem, Israel

A large Israeli force pursued a band of fleeing Palestinian guerillas into Lebanon and was halted and turned back by United Nations troops after a five hour confrontation.

The U.N. forces refused to let the Israelis search for Palestinians in a village four miles inside Lebanon. The Israelis finally withdrew empty handed.

"No shots were fired and there was no violence," a U.N. spokesman said of the incursion.

The incident was the first showdown between the 6000 man United Nations forces and the Israeli army. Israel was clearly violating the U.N. mandate to halt passage of armed personnel through the border area. Israel stated that the peace keeping forces had interfered in its pursuit of the terrorists.

The Israeli military issued a statement accusing the U.N. forces of "shielding terrorists" and said, "It is unthinkable that terrorists who attempt to carry out an attack against Israeli civilians and fail should be allowed to find shelter across the border."

Major Haddad of the Christian Militia of Lebanon regularly report capturing Palestinian infiltrators attempting to cross through the Christian-controlled enclave into Israel, but there are no Christian villages in the area adjacent to Manara, and it would not be difficult for Palestinians to pass through the border undetected.

A guerilla, captured by Major Haddad, stated that he and his comrades had come from Tyre, a Lebanese seaport dominated by the Palestine Liberation Organization, and had passed through Shakra, a border town, on their way to Israel.

5-10-79
Egyptian aid from Arab states frozen
Jidda, Saudi Arabia

A fund established by four oil-rich Arab states to shore up Egypt's economy has "frozen all its operations in Egypt," a Saudi newspaper reported.

In Cairo, Egyptian officials were not immediately available to comment on the report. Premier Mustapha Khalil stated recently that Arab assistance was not calculated in Egypt's 1979 budget.

Many Egyptian officials have said they expected the Arab oil states to cut off aid in line with a decision by 16 Arab nations and Iran to punish them for signing a peace treaty with Israel.

The fund, known as the Gulf Organization for the Development of Egypt, involves Saudi Arabia, Kuwait, Qatar, and the United Arab Emirates.

It was set up in 1977 after street riots over increased food prices in Egypt.

5-13-79
Sadat by public subscription to ask U.S. to pay for fighters
Mit Abul Kom, Egypt

President sadat said he no longer expected Saudi Arabia to finance the purchase of 50 American jet fighters for Egypt, and would ask the American people to raise the money for them by public subscription.

The F-5E jets, which the Saudis had agreed to pay for, cost 525 million dollars. Sadat stated, "I do not want to finance this project from the Carter administration, or the U.S. Congress. I want wider participation. It is the significance of it that I need."

Sadat said the thought of appealing directly to the American people on the F-5's occurred to him only two days ago and he had not worked out the details.

The President of Egypt said he would make his request over American television "whenever I hear officially that the Saudis will be going back on their word."

Saudi Arabia has made a down payment on the planes. The balance of the financing has been left in doubt by Saudis in opposition to the peace accords signed by Israel and Egypt.

Sadat added a contention that the present Saudi leadership under King Khalid was not up to the standard of the late King Faisal.

Speaking of the possibilities that the sale of the F-15's from the United States to Saudi Arabia was in doubt, the President of Egypt stated, "They are thinking of shifting their position from the F-15 to the Mirage 2000 from France."

The Egyptian leader conceded that his position with the Arabs had been deteriorated by recent Israeli raids against Palestinian guerillas in Lebanon.

5-14-79
Economic plan to fight Israel's inflation
Jerusalem, Israel

Warning that the Israeli inflation will reach 60 percent this year because of the cause of peace, Finance Minister Simcha Ehrlich proposed a five year austerity plan.

He told the Israeli cabinet that relocating military bases from the Sinai Peninsula to Israel's Negev Desert would bring about a record high inflation rate exceeding 40 percent.

Ehrlich proposed diverting $150 million from this year's $12 billion budget to help pay for the Negev relocation, a move required by the peace agreement with Egypt.

"No price is too high to pay for peace," the finance minister stated.

"We must put an end to the dangerous feeling in the public at large that we will be able to increase public spending and develop welfare and social services and cut taxes as a result of peace," Ehrlich told the cabinet.

"Peace involves tremendous government spending and any addition to that will take a heavy drain from the economy."

"Our cabinet is not like President Carter's," an Israeli official stated. These people are not appointed, but are elected representatives, each represents his own party in the Begin coalition.

The United States has promised a $2.8 billion loan to help replace two air fields Israel is giving up when the Sinai returns to Egypt. Other costs in the Negev relocation must be born by Israel.

Ehrlich's five step program include:

Freezing virtually all construction projects except for apartments, which are in short supply.

Continuing mini-devaluations of the Israeli pound to encourage exports.

Repayment of government loans and mortgages at a rate tied to the cost of living index.

5-15-79
Saudi Arabia closes arms company in Egypt
Cairo, Egypt

In a fresh reprisal against Egypt for signing the peace treaty with Israel, Saudi Arabia's defense minister announced the dissolution of the 1 billion dollar Egyptian based Arab arms manufacturing company.

This is the heaviest blow struck at Egypt's country. Egypt stands to lose up to 15,000 jobs, a major source of imported technology and a source of weapons the President of Egypt has been counting on to supply needed equipment for his armed forces.

A committee representing the four participating states in the armed company - Saudi Arabia, Qatar, The United Emirates, and Egypt - has been formed to liquidate the company, the Saudi defense minister, Prince Sultan Ibn Abdul Aziz, added in a statement published by the official Saudi News Agency.

The Arms Organization for industrialization was formed by the four states in 1975 and has since produced rockets, bombs, armored vehicles, and automatic weapons for Arab armies.

The organization was set up to end Arab dependence on imported weapons, acquired Western military technology, and aid the Egyptian economy.

In January of this year, the Arab groups and an American Motors Co. opened a jeep plant. The jointly owned operation was to produce about 10,000 jeeps a year, all of which could be fitted with the British Swingfire antitank missle, which had been scheduled later this year under another contract. Operations are to cease July 1, 1979.

5-15-79
Terrorist bomb strikes resort town of Tiberias
Tel Aviv, Israel

A terrorist bomb ripped apart a sidewalk marketplace in the northern Israeli resort town of Triberias, killing two young boys and wounding 32 other persons. The latest attack threatened to spark a new round of Israeli reprisal raids which have left 80 Lebanese and Palestinians dead since April 22.

Yasser Arafat's P.L.O. claimed responsibility for the bombing and shattered the festive atmosphere in the popular vacation town on the Sea of Galilee.

The deaths brought the number of Israelis killed in terrorist attacks to 15.

In Qatar, a top side to Arafat repeated the P.L.O. vow to attack American targets. The bombing in Tiberias coincides with a warning by Arafat that Israel will start a war with Lebanon.

5-17-79
Sadat and Begin to discuss self-determination of Palestinians
Cairo, Egypt

Anwar Sadat ruled out including Palestinian representatives in the upcoming Egyptian-Israeli conference on Palestinian self-rule in the occupied West Bank of the Jordan River, scheduled to start May 25, 1979. – "We shall not determine the fate of the Palestinians in these meetings," Sadat replied: "I am not negotiating for them and I do not encourage anyone to negotiate for them. I am negotiating with the Israelis to alleviate the suffering and put the Palestinians on the right channel to self-determination through full autonomy.

Meanwhile, the Egyptian leaders renewed its call to Israel to ratify the nuclear test ban treaty as proof of its sincerity for peace in the Middle East.

Deputy Foreign Minister Butros Ghali, asked Israel to "take this step for the sake of establishing real peace. It would also confirm to the Arab world Israel's desire for peace."

5-18-79
Begin will request sovereignty over the West Bank and the Gaza Strip five years from now, Prime Minster Menachem Begin told a high level committee of Israel's position on autonomy plans for Israeli-occupied areas.

The committee, except for Defense Minister Ezer Weizman, approved Begin's proposals.

The 22 part proposal was presented by Begin as Israel's bargaining position when this country begins negotiating with Egypt over the proposed autonomy for Arabs in the West Bank and Gaza.

Among the key points in these pronouncements are:

Israel will demand ultimate Sovereignty over the occupied areas.

The Ultimate authority for control of the areas will remain in the hands of the Israeli military government.

Israel will continue to be responsible for security and public order.

Israel sovereignty over public lands and water resources will continue.

Settlements by Israeli civilians will continue.

Begin's plan, in effect, would continue the present status of the West Bank and the Gaza Strip, except for allowing the largely Palestinian inhabitants self-rule over local administration measures such as health, schools and welfare.

Under the basic autonomy plan agreed to at Camp David summit, and approved by Egypt and Israel, the powers involved decide by negotiations within a five year period the ultimate sovereignty over the West Bank and Gaza.

The Prime Minister is convinced that Israel has a claim to the West Bank of the Jordan River on the basis of Biblical Jewish heritage.

5-18-79
United States may police the Midest
Washington, D.C.

Carter officials are studying the possibility of sending a force of several thousand U.S. soldiers to police the Middle East if the Soviets carry out its threat to veto U.N. troops in matters of security, administration sources stated.

The American officials still hope to persuade the Soviet Union not to oppose a U.N. unit at the Security Council meeting in July which will decide the issue.

The strong dissent has triggered contingency planning within the Administration for alternatives to the United Nations force to police Israel's withdrawal from the Sinai Peninsula over the next three years.

The State Department, uncertain of domestic and Arab political reaction to a U.S. military force for the Sinai, is hoping to lessen criticism by organizing a multinational force outside U.N. auspices, probably with U.S. leadership and financing.

Another option under study is the policing of the agreement by Egyptian and Israeli armies.

5-20-79
Robert Strauss, new peace negotiator
Washington, D.C.

President Carter's new Mideast peace negotiator, Robert Strauss, has promised a fresh beginning in the Mideast talks that will make them "new and different."

In his first beginning with reporters since he was appointed to the job in April, Strauss stated, "I am in a strong negotiator, an advocate of position. I do not know any other way."

Strauss, former chairman of the Democratic National Committee, and most recent top foreign trade negotiator, as asked by the President to represent the United States in talks beginning this week over the crucial Palestinian question - the future of the West Bank of the Jordan River and the Gaza Strip.

Secretary of State Cyrus Vance will open the meeting Friday in Israel, but Strauss will assume command in June.

The purpose with Egypt, Israel, and the United States is to develop plans for autonomy, or self-rule for Palestinian Arabs in keeping with last year's Camp David Accords.

After both Egypt and Israel have expressed their initial positions, the United States will emerge with strong positions of its own in an effort to find compromises.

Strauss said, "We are going to be a full partner, in the negotiations, in every respect."

5-21-79
Palestinian refugee over thirty years
Nablus, Israel

Israeli-occupied West Bank - It will be thirty years next month since Abu Abdullah Ez Eldin became an official refugee - and the United Nations became his keeper.

It was supposed to have been only a temporary arrangement. The United Nations would care for the people for a while - until other Palestinians who fled their homes in the Arab-Israeli war of 1948 found new places to live.

The agency that was created to deal with their problems, the United Nations Relief and Works Agency for Palestinian Refugees in the Near East is still administering aid - including those of more than 5,000 people at the Balata camp, on the southern end of the West Bank city of Nabulus. Ez Eldin is one of them.

"This is fit for animals, not humans," stated the 70 year old refugee. He lives in a 9 by 12 concrete block cubicle. Ez Eldin is one of 875,000 Palestinians who became homeless in 1948. He left Jaffa, the Arab section of Tel Aviv, during the fighting that summer. The history of the Middle East war and politics has kept him a refugee ever since.

In the occupied territories, the crowded conditions under which the refugees live, make the camps perfect spawning grounds for anti-Israeli underground activities. Israel responds with heavy retribution, which in turn convinces the people interned of the righteousness of the P.L.O. cause.

Ez Eldin is proud of his accomplishments under severe conditions. He has installed running water, a grape arbor, and he has a tiny grocery store in front of his two cubicles. Two of his seven children died when the family lived in tents before homes were built in 1956. He says, "I will go back to Jaffa. If not me, my son, or my grandson. We want to be free, and to control our own lives."

5-22-79
Egypt and Israel to negotiate self-rule of Palestinians

Jerusalem, Israel
Israel will take a tough and detailed proposal for the open negotiations with the United States and Egypt on Palestinian self-rule in the West Bank of the Jordan River and the Gaza Strip.

The sources, asking not to be named, said the cabinet adopted proposals that were even more specific than those drafted by Prime Minister Menachem Begin.

Meanwhile, in Beirut, Lebanon, a communique from Yasser Arafat's Palestinian Liberation Organization said Israeli gunners and Christian militiamen fired on Rashidiyeh refugee camp and the town of Ras el Ein, both of which are below the Lebanese port city of Tyre, 12 miles north of the Israeli border.

The Israeli Cabinet Secretary Arieh Naor announced that Israel's plan for self-rule applied only to the Palestinian inhabitants, with Israel continuing to control the land and resources. The document, in accordance with the demands of the Secretary of defense, is a set of guidelines for negotiations, implying room for compromise.

The pronouncement states that the source for authority of the autonomous regime will be the Israeli military government - meaning, Israel could dismiss a self-governing Arab council if the body oversteps its mandate.

On May 25, 1979, Prime Minster Begin and President Anwar Sadat will meet in the Sinai Desert town of El Arish in a ceremony marking the return to Egyptian control of the first section of the Sinai to be evacuated.

5-24-79
Difficulties arise in border exchange at El Arish, Sinai

Egypt has refused an Israeli request that the Sinai border at El Arish between the two countries be opened eight months before the peace treaty normalization. Also Butros Ghali, Egypt's foreign Minister, rejected a request by Israel to permit Jewish settlers at Neot Sinai to keep 500 acres of vegetable farmland at El Arish after Israel returns the town to Egyptian control on May 25, 1979. A strong attempt will be made by 150 settlers camped on the farm to resist evacuation.

In another area in Lebanon Israeli war planes attacked three Palestinian villages in retaliation for guerilla bombing several hours earlier that killed two Israeli women and a baby at a bus stop in Tel Aviv. A Palestinian Liberation Organization communique in Beirut said that 14 Palestinians and Lebanese, including civilians, were killed and 50 wounded in the Israeli attacks. Western newsmen, visiting one of the villages saw the bodies of three guerillas, and stated they were killed by a bomb dropped on an anti-aircraft position.

5-25-79
Strauss - Vance differ on Mideast peace process
Washington, D.C.

The first stage of the peace process will come to a conclusion this weekend with the reversion to Egypt of a major slice of the Sinai Desert occupied by the Israelis. The next step is the discussion of autonomy for two parts of Israeli-occupied territory predominantly populated by Palestinian Arabs - the Gaza Strip and the West Bank of the Jordan River.

The Israelis, who oppose Palestinian independence, and the Egyptians, who lean toward it, have prepared opening positions that are far apart.

The new peace negotiator, Robert Strauss, feels that the nations involved should work out their differences methodically, as Egypt's President Anwar Sadat stated recently; allow a pause to "Let the dust settle."

The Secretary of State, Cyrus Vance is of the opinion that the key to peace in the Middle East is a settlement that satisfies the Palestinians. He has debated that, unless the Palestinians were satisfied, Egypt would become isolated in the Arab world, and their would be a deterioration of American relations with Saudi Arabia, Iran, and other oil-producing states of the Persian Gulf.

At present, it is too early to tell whether Vance or Strauss will prevail in strategy, but it seems unlikely that the Secretary of State can convince the Israelis and the Egyptians to proceed with dispatch and reckless abandon. Both Prime Minister Menachem Begin and President Anwar Sadat prefer to approach the peace negotiations cautiously.

5-25-79
Palestinian bases inside Lebanon attacked
Tel Aviv, Israel

Israeli warplanes strafed and bombed mountain and coastal Palestinian bases deep inside Lebanon for the second straight day, hours after Arab terrorists shelled a northern Israeli border area. Lebanese authorities said the raids killed 35 persons and wounded 50.

Syrian Mig-21 Jets crossed the border on "protective patrol missions" over Lebanon's eastern Bekaa Valley after the Israelis attack.

A voice of the Christian Phalange Party said the Syrian overflights were designed to shield a string of Soviet-made ground to air missle bases in the valley against foreseeable raids.

Farther to the south, near El Arish, capital of the occupied Sinai, defiant settlers who had resisted eviction by throwing stones and vegetables at Israeli soldiers, finally relented and gave up their farms so the area could be turned over to Egypt today.

Meanwhile in Alexandria, Egypt, Secretary of State Cyrus Vance and President Anwar Sadat reviewed together the Mideast situation in preparation for the next round of Egyptian-Israeli peace talks concerning the future of Palestinians.

"There are obstacles and it will be a difficult negotiation," Vance stated after their one hour meeting at Sadat's villa on the Mediterranean.

"All of us know the importance of these consultations, and I believe that in the long run we shall achieve our objectives."

Israel and Egypt begin talks today in the southern Negev Desert city of Beersheba. The future of the West Bank and Gaza Strip and their one million inhabitants will be decided in these negotiations. The United States can act as a moderator in the hope of bringing a lasting peace.

The final contingent of Israeli troops, which had occupied the Sinai town since the 1967 war, pulled out and Egyptian forces took over the 425 square-mile El Arish sector on the Mediterranean coast in the first stage of the Israeli withdrawal from occupied territory.

There was an explosion of joy by the 45,000 residents who mingled with hundreds of Egyptians, shaking hands, shouting congratulations, and embracing with thanksgiving and praise.

The ceremony coincides with the opening of talks between the two nations in Beersheba, 60 miles to the northeast of El Arish.

THe autonomy talks, which are to be completed in a year, and Israel's withdrawal from Sinai over three years, are the dual outcome of the Israeli Egyptian peace treaty.

"The negotiations that open today are of great importance to the destinies of the Arab and Israeli peoples," Secretary of State Cyrus Vance said upon his arrival in Tel Aviv from Cairo.

Egyptians prepared for the arrival of President Anwar Sadat, who will be joined by Vance and Israeli Prime Minister Menachem Begin, before all three leave for Beersheba. Sadat stated, "This occasion sends a message to those who oppose peace. It will be a turning point in history - peace and brotherhood instead of violence."

Major General Dan Shomron, chief of Israel's Southern Command, represented the official to surrender the section of Sinai and Abdul Hamed Hamdi of Egypt, Egypt's representative to accept the occupied land.

5-27-79
El Arish returned to Egyptian control
El Arish, Egypt

Israel returned El Arish, the largest town in the Sinai, to Egypt on May 25, 1979, ending 12 years of occupation in its first surrender of conquered Arab land in more than three years. In Beersheba, the two nations opened negotiations on the future of the Palestinians.

"Long live Egypt," thousands of El Arish residents roared as the red, white and black flag was raised in a brief military ceremony. The return of El Arish is the first concrete implementation of the Israeli-Egyptian peace accords signed March 26, 1979, in Washington, D.C. in the United States.

Interior Minister Yosef Burg headed the Israeli delegation and U.S. Secretary of State Cyrus Vance represented the Americans. Neither the Palestinians nor Jordan were represented at the talks, though they have been invited to attend.

Major General Dan Shomron, who led the 1976 raid into Uganda's Entebbe airport, handed over El Arish to Egyptian General Abdel Hamdil Hamdi, a former chief of intelligence, who will be governor of Northern Sinai.

"We did not conquer this area out of a desire for expansion, but because of the state of war that threatened our very existence," Shamron said. "The evacuation of El Arish, and the continuing evacuation of the Sinai, is the clearest and sharpest expression of our desire for peace."

"Amdi, Egypt's assistant defense minister, called it a "great honor for me to be the first Egyptian soldier to raise our flag on the land of El Arish after 12 years of struggle."

Red, white, and black flags imprinted with a gold eagle festooned the Sinai town, and Sadat's portrait gazed down from posters and billboards. This is truly a momentous occasion for the republic of Egypt and its people.

FIRST WITHDRAWAL -
EGYPTIAN-ISRAELI PEACE TREATY SEALED
IN SINAI DESERT

5-28-79
Sadat welcomed in El Arish
El Arish, Egypt

President Anwar el-Sadat was accorded a tumultuous welcome when he arrived in El Arish for ceremonies and prayers celebrating the return of the northern Sinai town to Egyptian rule.

The jostling crowds of cheerful, waving townspeople were swelled by other Sinai inhabitants and by officials and parliamentarians brought in from Cairo. Portraits of the Egyptian leader and banners supporting his peace policy dominated the area.

Meanwhile in Cairo, U.S. Secretary of State Cyrus Vance informed Egypt and Israel that the United States intends to make a major effort in coming months to convince the Palestinians and their supporters that Washington is sympathetic to their problems and is working on their behalf in the latest negotiations.

Officials traveling with Vance said the Carter administration is deeply puzzled about the opposition to the Egyptian-Israeli accords in the Arab world, and is determined to make a good faith gesture to turn around the unanimous condemnation that has greeted Sadat in this region.

As soon as the Israelis pulled out, the Egyptians tore down or painted over nearly all the Hebrew signs and substituted Arabic-language ones. Israeli license plates disappeared overnight from most local cars. A single-story building identified as belonging to the Israeli Sinai military area was changed to the Ministry of Education of El Arish and Sinai.

U.S. State Department Bulletin
SECURITY OF ISRAEL BY TRANSFER OF SINAI TO EGYPT

Israel needs to be certain of its security during and after withdrawal from the Sinai. This matter of security is an important element in the negotiations. The United States agrees that a continuing strong Israeli defense capability is essential.

The Jewish state presently maintains a large portion of its active military force structure in the Sinai Desert. In accordance with the peace treaty of Egypt, within three years "Israel will withdraw all its armed forces . . . behind the international boundary . . . and Egypt will resume the exercise of full sovereignty over the Sinai. Relocation of Israel forces has implications for her security in three specific areas; airbase requirements, ground forces, and early-warning demands.
Airbases:
Israel now has four airbases in the Sinai, two of which are forward operating bases at Refidim and Ophir, and two which are main operating bases at Etam and Etzion. Within 9 months Israel must abandon Refidim, and within three years Israel must give up the three remaining bases. The bases at Etam and Etzion are of prime concern

because they normally house the Israeli squadrons deployed in the Sinai. Two new operating bases are required to replace these active squadrons to maintain the Israeli security from radical rejectionists.

Construction of these facilities without U.S. assistance would be an extraordinary burden on the Jewish state. It would strain her economy already experiencing severe inflation, and it would overtax her construction industry. The President of the United States has agreed to assist in the construction of the two airbases by providing funds and management assistance.

The two proposed bases will be located at Ovda and Matred in Negev Desert. These sites are the most suitable in terms of terrain, location, availability, and construction cost. The U.S. Air Force will be the project manager for this undertaking; the Corp of Engineers will be the construction agent. The American government will work in partnership with Israel; both parties will share responsibility to assure the completion of construction for initial operational capability prior to the date agreed for final relocation of Israeli forces in the Negev.

Ground force relocation

In addition to the airbase construction, there are other costs which will be imposed on Israel as a result of the withdrawal. One such cost involves the ground forces. Israel presently maintains two active armored divisions in the Sinai. These units, with their supporting infrastructure, will have to be displaced from their present Sinai locations. Supporting liaisons will also be required - road networks, water and power lines, and land lines communication - for Army and air force redeployments.

Naval force relocation

Israel will move its Sharm-el-Sheikh and El Tur naval facilities to Elat and its Mediterranean Naval Facility at Defna to Ashdod.

Early warning systems

The loss of the Sinai reduces early warning capability of the Jewish state. New construction and procurement is vital for this nation to continue with security that will prevent radical elements from piercing their defenses.

Israel is confident that it can defend itself against external attack. To insure this confidence, modernization of Israel's forces must continue.

This policy of helping Israel help itself does not absolve the United States from maintaining a watchful attitude toward the security of Israel. We must continually be concerned with the protection of all friendly regional states, because vital American interests are at stake, in the Middle East.

5-29-79
Palestinians from El Arish deported to Gaza
El Arish, Egypt

With deportations, evictions and investigations of collaborators, Egypt has resumed its administration of El Arish, provincial capital of the Sinai Peninsula.

Even before Israel formally ended its occupation, the Egyptians ordered the deportation of 150 families - perhaps 1000 people - who had come to El Arish from the Israeli-held Gaza Strip.

The Palestinians were sent back to the Gaza Strip, where the Israeli military government is helping them build new homes.

A bedouin leader said that many of his people were being evicted from homes they occupied after 1967, when the Israelis captured the city during the six-day war. The bedouins are seeking other homes here or returning to the desert.

Egypt believes, as do other Arab nations, that the Palestinians should remain a refugee problem and a political issue to be used against Israel until they are restored to their original homes in what is now Israel. Israel believes that the Palestinian problem should be solved by settling the refugees where they now are, rather than returning them to their homes.

Egypt, by deporting the Palestinians, is proving its loyalty to the Arab policy, and Israel, by settling them in homes in Gaza, hope to show how the refugees can settle down.

Israel officials stated that the Palestinians are happy with the prospect of life in suburban Gaza, which is more fertile and developed, a stretch of the Mediterranean coast, than in the sandy oasis of El Arish. For most of the refugees, this is at least their third move since 1948.

5-29-79
Prisoners in administrative detention released by Israel
Jerusalem, Israel

Israel released 16 Arab prisoners as a goodwill gesture to Egyptian President Anwar Sadat, and three Israeli ships prepared to pass through the Suez Canal in another symbolic step toward normalized relations between the former enemies.

Sadat said Egyptian and Israeli ministers will start working immediately on procedures for opening the borders between the two countries. He replied that this consideration will give "momentum to the peace process."

The Israelis did not identify the released prisoners, but said 10 had been held in administrative detention without specific charges. The six remaining prisoners were listed as minor offenders, meaning they had been convicted by military courts of security offenses not involving loss of life.

Nine of the detainees were released into the West Bank of the Jordan River, the Gaza Strip or northern Sinai, an Israeli military spokesman said. The other seven were sent to Egypt.

Israeli sources indicated other Arab prisoners may be released soon.

5-29-79
Israeli ships steam into Suez Canal

Three Israeli navy ships steamed into the Suez Canal today to cheers of "Shalom" from Egyptian workers on the canal banks. They were the first Israeli military vessels to use the 101 mile waterway.

"I would have never believed it if I wasn't seeing it," Yitzhak Davidi, commander of the Israeli landing ship Ashdod, told reporters on the ship after he welcomed an Egyptian pilot aboard.

The landing ships Achziv and the Ashkelon, also loaded trucks from the Israeli occupation force in the Southern Sinai, followed the Ashdod through the entrance at 8:30 a.m. for the northward passage.

Egyptians rushed to the banks of the canal to see the Israeli vessels and shouted "Shalom" - the Hebrew word for "peace."

The Egyptian-Israeli peace treaty guarantees passage for Israeli shipping through the Suez. The first Israeli flagship through the canal, the freighter Ashdod, made its initial passage April 28, 1979, with a crew of 22, but no cargo.

The three 1,000 ton landing craft, which had departed from the Israeli navy base at Sharm el Sheikh in the Sinai, were scheduled to complete their 15 hour voyage through the canal by midnight and continue on to Haifa on the Mediterranean coast.

In another step of the unfolding peace between the two countries, Egyptian President Anwar Sadat said that foreign airlines can begin service between Tel Aviv and Cairo . . . "There is no restriction, no boycott, let them come," he replied to the news reporters.

5-31-79
Support package for the Mideast approved by the House of Representatives
Washington, D.C.

After being amended at the request of Rep. William Dannemeyer of Fullerton, California, President Carter's support package of $4.8 billion was ratified by the House of Representatives, 347-28; and approved by the Senate.

Final action by both houses on the measure, which involves $1.47 billion in direct taxpayer expenditures, is expected early next week.

Under the complete package of overseas expenses in the Middle East, Israel will receive an estimated $3 billion in various forms of military aid, and Egypt will get about $1.5 billion with economic assistance of $300 million.

Dannemeyer's amendment requires President Carter to submit to congress, within 90 days, a detailed and comprehensive report on direct and indirect costs to the united States, stemming from implementation of the Mideast Accords. Dannemeyer stated, "While we all hope for peace in the Middle East, passage of this amendment is a step in finding how much this peace process will cost us."

The majority of the House and Senate support the President, and refuse to negotiate with the P.L.O., unless the Arab community recognize Israel's right to exist.

6-1-79
Israel eases bombardment of South Lebanon
Tel Aviv, Israel

The Israeli bombardment of southern Lebanon let up just hours before a United Nations session was held to discuss the fighting. Nevertheless, warplanes swept over the Lebanese coast as a reminder of Israeli strength.

Israeli Defense Minister Ezer Weizman served notice to Arab states not to expect the occupied West Bank of the Jordan River, Gaza Strip and Golan Heights to be handed back the way Israel returned the Sinai Peninsula to Egypt. Egyptian Premier Mustapha Khalil said Israeli settlements in those territories "created a serious situation" and blocked the chance for overall Middle East peace.

In another Mideast development, Saudi Arabia, which had expressed annoyance at American participation in the Egyptian-Israeli accord, gave permission for its commercial flights to cross Saudi airspace. Moscow has weekly flights to Yemen via Kuwait.
The Palestine news agency WAFA said the "situation is almost quiet at the frontier after six days of constant shelling."
Lebanon has galled for a Security Council meeting in New York City to consider "rapidly deteriorating defense in South Lebanon." Provincial authorities stated that rebel Lebanese army Major Saad Haddad, his rightist Christian militiamen and Israeli border gunners had been shelling Palestinian strongholds almost daily.
Defense Minister Weizman told the newspaper Maariv in Tel Aviv that the handing over of part of the Sinai to Egypt was an isolated agreement.
"Judea, Samaria, (biblical names for the West Bank,) and the Gaza Strip are part of the land of Israel from the spiritual, historical, and without a doubt, secular point of view," Weizman said in an interview marking the Jewish holiday of Shavout. (Pentecost)

6-3-79
Bomb blast at Kennedy Center in Beirut, Lebanon
Beirut, Lebanon

Half an hour after midnight on April 16, 1979, a blast shattered the quiet of Abdel Aziz St. In the mainly Moslem western sector of Beirut.
No one was hurt, but the bomb caused $20,000 damage to the entrance of the John F. Kennedy Center, operated by the U.S. Embassy in Lebanon.
"Running an American cultural center in Beirut these days requires steady nerves and a sense of humor," replied Boulos Malik, the embassy counselor for press and culture affairs.
The bombing of the center and the embassy rocket attack - which caused less extensive damage - provides graphic examples of the difficulties confronting American missions abroad in the wake of the Egyptian-Israeli peace treaty. Aware of the widespread and determined Arab opposition to the U.S. sponsored pact, Secretary of State Cyrus Vance ordered extra security precautions at American embassies throughout the Middle East.

Malik stated that American cultural centers also were in the Arab capitals of Amman, Cairo, Damascus, Casablanca, Khartoum, and Tunis.
The problems of projecting American culture are unique in Beirut. The uncertain political climate in Lebanon has made use of local talent of trained Lebanese and embassy personnel.

The purpose of the John F. Kennedy Center is to support reconstruction and the role of the central government. The center has an 11,000 volume library used extensively by students, professors, and business people for improving the Lebanese way of life.

6-3-79
Egyptian-Israelis developing tourism

Last fall, before Israel and Egypt signed their peace treaty, American Society of travel Agents convened in Acapulco, Mexico.

Israeli and Egyptian travel agents, hoteliers, and government tourism officials got together at each others hospitality suites.

"What happened was remarkable," said Israel Zuriel, Israel's commissioner of tourism for North America. "An Egyptian belly dancer performed for us and we danced the "hora." Very informally, we discussed the possibility of normalizing tourist links.

Now that a peace treaty has been signed, that unofficial gathering looks like a prophetic prelude to what may become official meetings between representatives of both countries.

This will mean that the borders of the two nations will be open, and relations begin to normalize. This will signal some interesting changes for unilateral travel in the Middle East. The people will be able to fly directly between Tel Aviv and Cairo rather than having to travel to a neutral third country first, as it is today. New routes may open. Wouldn't it be interesting to drive or take a tour bus from Israel to Egypt on the Mediterranean coast?

"Some questions have to be resolved," said Nabil Heikal, director of the Egyptian Tourist Office in New York City, New York. Talks cannot begin until after the withdrawal of the armies. Then negotiations will be needed on how currency will be handled and exchanged, whether visas will be required, how much money tourists will be required to have, and other matters."

It will be important to know if the airlines, Egyptair and ElAl (who are armed in all major world airports with soldiers) - will be allowed to carry firearms in Cairo.

Land travel - whether by car or by rail - faces the additional problem of security. While Israel and Egypt may be at peace, the possibility of terrorist attacks are very real.

Perhaps the most important benefit which may derive from the Begin-Sadat accord is that some of the money used for armaments might find its way in development of tourist attractions. One way would be the restoration of historical monuments and sites.

Egypt, particularly needs money to preserve its archaeological treasures. In the Valley of the Kings, only a few of the decorated tombs have been excavated. Israel, too, has many important historical sites which could be restored, and made more accessible to the tourist.

Peace also can spur development of hotels and a new Red Sea resort. Only time will tell if these projected ideas can be accomplished. With cooperation and united effort by both countries, they can build a framework together for a lasting peace.

6-4-79
Settlement on West Bank approved by Israeli Cabinet
Jerusalem, Israel

The Israeli cabinet rejected an attempt to halt construction of a new Jewish settlement in the West Bank of the Jordan River, and ordered the army to expropriate Arab-held land needed for the site.

Deputy Prime Minister Yigael Yadin had sought unsuccessfully to block the start of the ElonMoreh settlement near Nablus, about 30 miles north of Jerusalem. The cabinet overruled his appeal in an 8-5 vote.

Yadin and members of his Democratic Movement for Change oppose Israeli settlement in areas where there are large Arab populations, as at Nablus, the largest city in the West Bank. Defense Minister Ezer Weizman and Foreign Minister Moshe Dayan joined Yadin's group in opposing the move.

Prime Minister Menachem Begin was not at the meeting, but government sources said he gave Yadin a proxy to cast his vote in favor of going ahead with the construction of the settlement.

Workers will start fencing off the new site this week. It is on a bare hill near the village of Rujeib, and part of the site belongs to local Arabs. The military government was ordered to proceed with requisitioning the land. The Arab owners will be paid, as under the right of eminent domain in the United States.

Elon Moreh is a project of the nationalist religious group Gush Emunim, (faith bloc), which has originally settled without permission not far from the new location.

The Prime Minister of Israel stated, "We ask our friends in Egypt not to get themselves entangled with declarations." Begin was referring to recent Egyptian statements that Jewish settlements in occupied territories are illegal, that East Jerusalem should be returned to Arab sovereignty and that autonomy in the occupied territories is the first step to a Palestinian state.

At a cabinet meeting, Defense Minister Weizman told the government that the assassination of the Arab religious leader of Gaza, Shiek Hassem Huzandair, "will impede cooperation between Israelis and Arabs of the occupied territories." The sheik was stabbed to death, and a Palestinian guerilla contingent said he had been killed for collaborating with Israel.

The religious leader was one of the few officials in the Gaza area - the formerly Egyptian-administered strip on the Mediterranean at the Sinai Peninsula border - to support Israel's proposed autonomy plan for Arabs in that area. Violence still prevails and radical insurgents will do anything to disrupt the peace keeping process.

6-5-79
Homes of terror suspects seized on West Bank
Ramallah, Israel-occupied West Bank

Israeli forces sealed off or destroyed four homes in which Palestinians accused of terrorism had lived. The Israelis also prevented two West Bank mayors from talking publicly about the armies actions.

In the early morning, troops went to four homes in and around Ramallah, ordered the residents out, with their belongings, blew up one building and sealed off parts of three others with concrete blocks and cement.

The military government said that members of a guerilla unit had killed four Israelis and wounded dozens of others in time-bomb attacks, and were living in the four houses.

A law empowering the government to destroy the homes of subversives has been in effect since the Ottoman Turks ruled Palestine before the British came in 1917. The British used it against the Jewish underground before Israeli independence.

An arrest was made of a twenty-one year old school teacher in the village of Beit Sira, as a terrorist, caught planting a bomb. She had been trained in Syria, and was in charge off one of the Arab cells in the West Bank.

Meanwhile in Cairo, Egypt Israeli Foreign Minister Moshe Dayan flew to the Arab state to explain Israel's new Jewish settlements in occupied areas of the West Bank.

"There are some basic points in our policy which we do not intend to change," Dayan stated at a Cairo press conference. "We have the full right to establish settlements and maintain the unity of Jerusalem. My view is that the solution is for us to live together."

Egypt's Defense Minister Butros Ghali said, "In spite of our basic differences, I believe that through more negotiations we can overcome our difficulties."

6-6-79
China agrees to supply weapons to Egypt
Cairo, Egypt

President Anwar Sadat has agreed to supplies of weapons from China, a development that gives him an important political boost and brings China into the Middle East Arms participation.

Sadat gave no details of the deal, which came as a surprise to most observers, but Western sources here said it involves the sale by China of several squadrons of Mig-19 jet fighters, possibly as many as 60 planes.

The Mig-19 is a relatively old, Soviet-designed airplane which the Chinese have been building since the early 1960s. Its acquisition would have meant little to an Egypt at war with Israel, but it could be a useful asset to an Egypt now at peace with Prime Minister Begin's people. Sadat's government can restructure its armed forces for a different kind of mission in the Red Sea region and in Africa.

In his annual speech to troops stationed in the Suez Canal, the President of Egypt said he was planning to ask the United States for permission to manufacture sophisticated American weapons under licenses. The United States has emerged as an important arms supplier in Egypt, but it is not clear whether Sadat discussed this proposal with a Pentagon survey team to assess Egypt's military needs.

If licenses to make American weapons are granted, the work would be done in factories set up over the past three years by the Arab Organization for Industrialization, a weapons-manufacturing consortium of Egypt, Saudi Arabia, Qatar, and the United Arab Emirates. That organization broke up last month when the three oil states pulled out in protest over the Israeli-Egyptian peace treaty.

The organization will continue to run in a new form as the Egyptian Organization for Military Industrialization. Even if the Persian Gulf Arabs withdraw what remains to be spent of the 1.4 billion dollars in capital they have supplied, the reconditioned factories still exist, the Egyptian workers have been trained, and the manufacture of jeeps under an agreement with American Motors continues.

China is itself short of modern, sophisticated weapons and has not participated in a rush to supply arms to Middle East countries. But Peking developed a military supply relationship with Egypt in 1967 when China sent some spare parts for Egypt's Soviet-supplied weapons after Sadat severed relations with the Soviet Union.

Little has been heard from China since then, and there was no advance indication of the sale of airplanes to Egypt.

When the Soviet Union cut off shipments of weapons and spare parts to Egypt after the 1973 Middle East war, the President of Egypt proclaimed a policy of diversifying the country's sources of weapons.

6-6-79
Cairo Egypt

For a nation that sowed the seeds of Mideast peace, Egypt today appears to be reaping a case of security jitters. They are told they have the third largest standing army, upwards of a million people, but from the comfort of an alliance with 20 other arab nations, Egypt now faces an economic boycott from 16 of them.

Unfortunately the peace with Israel is turning less than a panacea. Instead of having one major enemy, Egypt is now confronted with 16 former allies. The real enemy lies within Egypt. The psychological damage left by the strongman, Gamal Nassar, dates back to the revolution of 1952. That experience led to adoption of policies that have become the life-style that is difficult to change. One out of every three employable Egyptians draws his or her salary from the government. University education is free, and every graduate is assured a lifetime job. There are few positions available in private industry, with a good standard of living, consequently they wind up working for the government.

The average per capita wage is $286 a year. Only the protein chick-pea, the basis of the peasant's diet, prevents widespread malnutrition. Egypt's population is over 40 million and continues to rise.

A massive government housing program gives an appearance from the air of prosperity, but at ground level, the slums are overwhelming.

Cairo draws most of its water from the Nile river, yet only five percent of the soil is arable.

6-7-79
Close cooperation exists between United States and Saudi Arabia
Washington, D.C.

Although relations between the United States and Saudi Arabia have been chilled by the U.S.-backed Israeli-Egyptian peace treaty, military cooperation of Washington and Riyadh, Saudi Arabia has never been closer, a senior Pentagon official stated today.

"What we have been engaged in with the Saudis is discussion (on defense) in the area," the government official said. They have substantial concerns about outside intervention and we have been able to offer them assurances that they will not be invaded and overrun. This confidence has produced the best possible attitude on military relations.

The Saudis are in an uncomfortable position. They have problems with security threats from outside the area. They have problems with security threats from outside the area. They also have potential outbreak from the more radical Arab states who view the United States as an enemy, and supporter of the State of Israel.

The United States is engaged in a similar diplomatic balancing act, attempting to maintain close relations with both Egypt and Saudi Arabia, despite the bitter differences between the two Arab states over Egypt's peace treaty with Israel.

6-7-79
Egypt, Israel agree to travel by air and sea
Cairo, Egypt

"Egypt and Israel have decided to allow ordinary citizens of the two countries to travel back and forth," Egyptian Premier Mustapha Khalil announced to reporters.

"They can travel only by air or by sea, not over land through the Sinai Peninsula, and will require clearance in advance," Khalil said, but the only other restrictions are those applied by the two countries to any other foreign traveler.

Khalil had concluded a three day visit from Moshe Dayan of Israel in how to implement the open border policy presented by President Sadat and Prime Minister Menachem Begin last month.

The outcome of Israel's Foreign Minister was different from what the press in both countries had predicted. Egyptian and Israeli reports had said the two nations would probably allow Israeli fishermen and Egyptian workers in the Sinai to cross the border to work, but limit other travel to journalists, scholars, and professionals on specific missions.

Israel's requests for fishermen to use Lake Barawil and for the workers to go back to their jobs was turned down by Egypt in Dayan's first round of talks, but restrictions on other travelers apparently was approved instead as a compromise.

6-7-79
Lebanon pullback announced by P.L.O.
Beirut, Lebanon

In an effort to avert further Israeli raids on southern Lebanon, Yasser Arafat's Palestine Liberation Organization and its Moslem allies said they would pull back from southern cities and villages.

The P.L.O. news agency announced that offices in the city of Tyre would be closed and guerillas would "keep clear of southern villages so the enemy may have no excuse to take action against these villages."

In the last two months, Israel has flown air raids against guerilla targets in the south and launched land and sea artillery barrage that reportedly killed more than 120 Palestinians and Lebanese.

The raids were made in retaliation for guerilla attacks in Israel that have killed 18 Israelis and wounded more than 200 this year. The attacks and the Israeli raids have escalated since the March 26th signing of the Egyptian-Israeli peace accords, which has been condemned by most of the Arab world.

Tyre, 50 miles south of Beirut and 12 miles north of the Israeli frontier has Palestinian refugee camps on its southern, eastern, and northern outskirts.

In Washington D.C., a State Department spokesman said the P.L.O. reported withdrawal plans could not be confirmed.

6-8-79
Israel attempts to justify new settlement

The Israeli cabinet approved a plan by Gush Emunim, the Jewish Zealots, who act as if they have the right to build anywhere in the Biblical land of Israel. They want to settle near Nablus, on the West Bank.

Nablus is an active town where Arab feelings run high, and is the center of Palestinian nationalism. The land for the settlements was confiscated by Israeli authority from private Arab owners.

How does Israel justify the settlement location? It argues that those people in the Jordan Valley, should remain as guards for the outposts under the peace arrangement. The land seizure may not apply in this case. It can exist only as long as the Jews protect the region.

At Camp David, Maryland, in the U.S., Resolution 242, which calls on Israel to withdraw from occupied territory, no border adjustment would allow Israeli forces to continue their operation in a populous Arab center, such as Nablus.
The real challenge is not to Sadat of Egypt, or to President Carter of the United States, but to the character of Israel. Its government wants to exercise sovereignty on the West Bank, and control the inhabitants, without giving them a voice of protest. Autonomy must not have the threat of coercion. The Palestinians should be able to exercise their rights and govern themselves.

6-10-79
Secretary of State, Cyrus Vance, calls for consolidation in the Mideast

The Secretary of State is a strong defender of the Carter administration. With the Egyptian-Israeli peace treaty in reality, and with a strategic arms limitation treaty,

(SALT) with the Soviet Union set for a signing ceremony in Vienna, Austria, Vance has accomplished much for his foreign policy, and for the United States.

Senate ratification of the arms treaty with the Egyptians and the Israelis is Vance has accomplished much for his foreign policy, and for the United States.
Senate ratification of the arms treaty with the Egyptians and the Israelis is Vance's main target. Defense Secretary, Harold Brown, and a host of arms specialists will follow-up with the Mideast talks.

Vance, normally not demonstrative, was excited attending the ceremony of the withdrawal of Israel from El Arish in the Sinai Desert. The Secretary of State's lawyer approach to foreign policy has appeared vindicated.

The era of good feeling is a reminder of the administration's summit meeting at Camp David last summer. The accords, developed there are a framework of Vance's clear emergence as a dominant figure managing U.S. interests abroad. The SALT consolidates his position.

6-10-79
Israeli settlement of Elon Moreh protested
Tel Aviv, Israel

Several thousand Israelis demonstrated against the new Jewish settlement of Elon Moreh, urging removal of the 2-day old outpost in the occupied West Bank of the Jordan River.

The protest near the settlement site was organized by "the Peace Now" movement, which vows to oppose a campaign by the zealots of "Gush Emunim," who are grouped together to increase settlements in the West Bank.

No incidents were reported. The estimated 4000 demonstrators were kept about a hundred yards from the hilltop outpost by the military.

Meanwhile, Egyptian Vice President Hosni Mubarak arrived in Washington D.C. for a five-day visit to the United States during which he was to deliver a personal message to President Carter from Egyptian President Anwar Sadat.

Mubarak will discuss developments in Egyptian-Israeli relations and plans in establishing Palestinian autonomy in the Gaza Strip and the West Bank.

In Alexandria, Egypt, tomorrow, Israel and Egypt will resume their talks, with a United States team participating as a "full partner," official sources reported.

Elon Moreh, two miles from the Arab city of Nablus, was established with government approval, five years after the Gush Emunim attempted to build a settlement there.

A Peace Now member told a reporter, "We came here to encourage the government to reconsider withdrawing from this settlement."

The planned enclave has been criticized by Egypt and the United States as harmful to negotiations in steps for a comprehensive peace.

Only tents and a few prefabricated buildings now stand on the site, but Elon Moreh pioneers envision a town with hundreds of families.

6-11-79
Begin criticized at Palestinian peace talks
Alexandra, Egypt

Israel and Egypt opened the second round of negotiations on Palestinian autonomy in Alexandria in an atmosphere clouded by the chief Israeli negotiator's anger criticizing Prime Minister Menachem Begin.

Israeli Interior Minister Yosef Burg said he objected to an editorial in the newspaper Al Akhbar from Cairo which accused Begin of trying "to set fire to the negotiations on autonomy."

In Tel Aviv, Israel, Begin responded to growing criticism of the Israeli policy of establishing Jewish settlements in occupied Arab land, denied that the controversial outposts are obstacles to the peace process. The presence of Jews in Judea and Samaria is not a provocation. Judea and Samaria are biblical names for the West Bank and the Jordan River.

The Interior Minister called the editorial a "personal attack on Prime Minister Menachem Begin. "These are contrary devices to the advancement of peace."

The United States negotiating team, headed by James Leonard, stated it was time that public discussions cease, and serious talks "begin behind closed doors" to come to grips with the issues.

6-13-79
Autonomy for Egypt, Israel, tentative in West Bank
Alexandria, Egypt

Egypt and Israel ended two days of procedural talks on Palestinian autonomy with every indication President Anwar Sadat and Prime Minister Menachem Begin will have to solve major problems together. The two nations began their meetings with public argument over Israeli settlements in occupied territories, and ended with a meeting in Israel to set an agenda for the next negotiating phase.

Authoritative conference sources stated that several issues will have to be clarified before progress can be made in joint decisions.

A ministerial meeting is scheduled for June 25-26, and Egyptian Foreign Minister Butros Ghali said the ministers will take over if the officials are unable to draw up an agenda.

The United States is the third party in the negotiations, but U.S. sources say the United States delegation does not want to intervene prematurely with suggestions that might cause division between Egypt and Israel.

Robert Strauss, appointed by President Carter as chief negotiator, is not supposed to arrive in the Middle East vicinity until the beginning of next month. The steps to a comprehensive peace should be surveyed carefully, and time be given for the collaborating countries to find answers that both nations can live with.

6-14-79
Negotiating team for Israel on autonomy headed by a moderate
Jerusalem, Israel

Josef Burg, who heads the Israeli negotiating team in the delicate talks on Palestinian autonomy in the West Bank and Gaza Strip is a politician who hates decisions and loves committees.

He is 70 years old, has been an Israeli cabinet member for 28 years, and - a rare event in the rough-and-tumble politics of Israel - has few enemies. He is not a power among dynamic leaders of the young nation, and is sometimes dismissed as "an unimportant man." His loyalty to Prime Minister Menachem Begin has been rewarded with one of the most important jobs in the Middle East - and ultimately, in the international arena.

Among the six delegates on the Israeli side are cabinet members such as Ezer Weizman, Defense Minister, Moshe Dayan, the hard minded Foreign Minister, and Ariel Sharon, the hawkish Minister of Agriculture. "Any one of them might speak for themselves," one Israeli official said, "But Burg will speak for Begin only."

Burg thinks of himself as a "bridger and a compromiser." He is neither a dove nor a hawk. He is a crisis avoider.

After one of the initial negotiating sessions in Alexandria this week, Yosef Burg returned to Jerusalem, shrugging off what some might have considered a slight.

Egyptian Premier Mustapha Khalil, head of the Egyptian negotiating team, who by protocol ranks with Begin - had suggested that Israel upgrade its top negotiator to match his own rank.

At an airport press conference, Burg stated that he was not rebuffed by the Premier. "I can only say that I will be pleased to be his host when he arrives in Israel."

The Israeli press has reported that an in-depth study prepared by the U.S. Embassy in Tel Aviv suggested that Burg may turn out to be an important "moderate" at the peace talks.

There have been indications from both sides that neither is eager to leap into full negotiations in an effort to solve the problems of a comprehensive peace overnight. They are expected to show caution, and Yosef Burg is a cautious man.

The chief negotiator of Israel told the Tel Aviv newspaper Maariv, "Historical developments are not to be measured with a stopwatch, but with a calendar."

"If we are to consolidate an atmosphere of calm and peace between ourselves and Egypt," Burg stated before the first session, "this will also attract the moderates among the leaders in Judea and Samaria (the West Bank) to join the negotiations. If we can succeed in the war against the Palestinian Liberation Organization and terrorists, more moderates will join the peace accords."

Yosef Burg became a member of the Cabinet of David Ben-Gurion in 1951 as Minister of Health. He was born in Dresden, Germany, and he came to Israel in 1939 after working underground to help Jews flee to the free state. "Negotiations cannot change positions of principle, he said recently. They can provide a basis for existence, and for co-existence."

6-15-79
Peace-keeping force to remain in Lebanon
United Nations

The U.N. Security Council voted to keep its 6,000-man peacekeeping force in southern Lebanon for another six months, and demanded that Israel immediately halt its attacks in the region and its aid to Christian militiamen.

The decision came amid new warnings - including one from U.N. Secretary General Kurt Waldheim - that the United Nations soon may be forced to pull troops out of Lebanon if Israel continues its actions.

The council voted 12-0 to renew the U.N. force's mandate until Dec. 19, 1979. The Soviet Union and Czechoslovakia abstained, and China did not participate in the voting.

Lebanon contends that Israel's actions have complicated a major aim of the U.N. peacekeeping mission - to return control of southern Lebanon to the Beirut government.

Israel U.N. ambassador Yehuda Blum defended his countries actions as necessary to its own security.

Radical Libyan and Palestinian leaders met in Tripoli to counter attacks by Israel in southern Lebanon. Abdul Salam Jalloud, a senior member of Libya's General People's Congress, stressed the need for Arab unity in an opening address to the committee members.

In Tunisian, the Arab Inter-parliamentary Union decided to suspend Egypt membership. The suspension follows moves to expel the Arab Republic Union representative for signing a peace treaty with Israel.

6-17-79
Divided Jerusalem not negotiable in the future
Jerusalem, Israel

Arabs and Israelis agree on one thing - that Jerusalem is not negotiable.

The Egyptian-Israeli peace talks on the question of autonomy in the occupied territories is not a problem with the Palestinians of the West Bank or the Gaza Strip. It is Jerusalem, and neither side desires to give in to the other.

The Saudis and the Arab Emirates believe that Anwar Sadat, President of Egypt, compromised when he signed the peace accords with Israel. The State of Israel, on the other hand, have made it clear to the world that Jerusalem is holy ground, and Israel's eternal capital, not to be divided.

Jerusalem is an emotive city, and the people hold it precious above reasons of territorial demands. As former Israeli ambassador Simcha Dinitz stated, "Jerusalem is the cradle of our faith, the magnet of our longings, the center of all our spiritual and national being, the place returned to in agony and joy.

The difference between the Egyptian reasoning and the Israeli thoughts is the matter of sovereignty and autonomy. The mayor of Jerusalem, Ted Kollek, proposes a borough system, legalizing Arab administration of holy places and their right to govern themselves, and elect their own supervisors, but sovereignty would remain with Israel. The Palestinians and other Arab nations find this unacceptable.

At the present time there appears to be an impasse, neither Arab or Jew wishes to relinquish the holy city. Everything else is negotiable, but not this city.

6-17-79
Jerusalem, a city of three faiths

In Jerusalem, you will see the lights on the Mount of Olives where Christ was taken by the soldiers to be crucified. A patina (film or incrustation) usually green, covers the very stones that built Jerusalem. The cobblestones worn by the feet of, among others, Egyptians, Babylonians, Romans, Crusaders, Turks, British, Israelis, and a multitude of Christians and pilgrims, are in evidence today after thousands of years.

Jerusalem sits on the edge of a desert that stretches beyond Israel's borders through Jordan and Saudi Arabia. It has no sea, is not on any major trade routes, and has no mineral wealth, yet it has existed for more than 4000 years.

The name Jerusalem, as it appears in Hebrew, (Yerushalayim) is derived from the word "yara and salem" meaning, "founded by God." The city is holy to followers of three great religions, Moslems, who believe that Mohammed, the founder of Islam, rose to heaven from Jerusalem; Jews, because it was their political and religious center in Biblical times; and Christians, events of Jesus' life took place here, and it was in Jerusalem that he was crucified and ascended to heaven.

One always goes "up" to Jerusalem. The usage has a mystical intent, Israelis will tell you, but it also describes the city's geography. It is perched on a high hill amid the hills of Judea.

With a population of over 400,000 people, this is Israel's largest city, and unofficially its capital - Army headquarters are in Tel Aviv, but many government offices are here, including the Knesset, or assembly building.

The Knesset is in "new" Jerusalem, a modern city. There are sites of interest, among them, the Israel museum with the Shrine of the Book (built to house the Dead Sea Scrolls, the "Yad Vashem," memorial to the six million Jews murdered in Nazi death camps, but what draws more people than any other area is one square mile in "Old Jerusalem."

The Old City is divided into four neighborhoods - quarters, residents call them - the Armenian, Christian, Moslem, and Jewish.

Most of what is the Jewish Quarter, had been annexed by Jordan in 1948. It was reclaimed by the Israelis in the 1967 war.

Jordan has not allowed Jews to live in the Old City of Jerusalem, or even visit there during Jordan's reign. The color of this city is the color of old lace. Over time, it has been built and rebuilt with limestone, quarried nearby, and shaped by stonecutters, who in any given century, use the same tools as their ancestors.

In the Bible, or the Torah, or the Koran, there is a keen interest in Jerusalem.

Jews, when they arrive, rush to the Western Wailing Wall, along with the southwestern wall, which is all that remains of the Second Temple Enclosure, that was destroyed by the Emperor, Titus, in the year 70 A.D. The wall is a symbol of lost glory, and it often brings tears to the people who worship there. Another fact is; dew forms on the stones in the early morning, and the wall seems to weep, with the people.

Jerusalem is the third holiest city, after Mecca and Medina in Saudi Arabia; and the Dome of the Rock, built in 691 A.D. This is also the site where Mohammad ascended to heaven aboard his legendary steed, "El Burak."

Christians can take their choice of the many places where Jesus spent lifetime on earth. Gethsemane, The garden on the slope of the Mount of Olives, is where Jesus Christ ate his last supper with his disciples. It is also the place where he laid for three days in a tomb, before ascending into heaven. Some historians say that the Church of the Holy Sepulcher is built over the burial place of Jesus. A garden tomb, on the Nablus Road is another location.

Jerusalem seems to wear different faiths. You can stand in the forecourt of the Greek Orthodox church, and the Roman Catholic church of the Holy Sepulchre at noon and listen to a muezzin on the next door minaret, call Moslems to prayer.

6-18-79
Weizman resigns from the Israeli Panel
Tel Aviv, Israel

Ezer Weizman announced his resignation from the six-man ministerial team, negotiating with Egypt and the United States for Autonomy on the Israeli occupied West Bank of the Jordan River. Weizman has expressed public reservations about the guidelines drawn up by the cabinet for the negotiations and is said to oppose establishment of the "Elon Moreh," a Jewish settlement near Nablus. Israel radio quoted Weizman as saying he would not take in any further meetings but would continue to express his views to the cabinet.

Near Nablus, a demonstration by thousands of Palestinian Nationalists dissolved into a rock-throwing melee, into the streets before the Israeli troops could quell the disturbance with tear gas. A handful of injuries were reported on each side.

In Tel Aviv, about 12,000 people demonstrated against the government's decision to proceed to the Elon Moreh. In the meantime, the mayor of Nablus, Bassam Shakaa, led his Arabian followers through the city with chants of "Allah Hu Akhbar," God is great; and "Palestine for Arabs;" and "No to Zionists," And No to the Autonomy."

Shakaa, with other Arab leaders spoke to the Israeli Military Chief, and were refused permission to continue the march. The Mayor was hoisted onto the shoulders of two men to tell the crowd to turn back to the city hall. The band of marchers retreated away from their projected goal three miles away.

6-18-79
Israel's good faith eminent in peace talks.

No progress had been anticipated in the initial rounds of the Egyptian-Israeli consultation on the future of the Palestinians in occupied territories, and that expectation has been right so far. The distance between the two sides has not diminished. More talks will be held later this month, and certainly more after that to deal with the deadlock.

The immediate question is, how to work with the election of local Palestinians in forming some type of civic authority. The larger issue is what will happen after five years, to the Israeli occupation. Egypt projects that the autonomous Palestinian homeland should emerge. The Israeli position is not to permit this to happen because full autonomy is a danger to the security of the Jewish State.

There is near-unanimity of opposition in Israel to the creation of any Palestinian Entity that would be under the control of the PLO, Palestinian Liberation Organization. There is need for on-the ground measures to safeguard Israel's frontier. The concurrence ends here, as divergence of views on settlements in Judea and Sameria appear openly. What is required is to meet the Jewish nation security, and at the same time, satisfy the Palestinian hopes and aspirations.

Israel Supreme Court temporarily halts Elon Moreh
Jerusalem, Israel

The Israeli Supreme Court issued an injunction to halt work on Elon Moreh, the controversial settlement launched June 7, 1979 on Arab-owned land in the West Bank.

The three-judge court gave the government 30 days to show cause why it should not leave the site, and criticized it for the manner in which it seized the land.

"I understand the bitterness and anger of the Arab landowners," said court President Moshe Landau. He stated that the owners had not received written notice that their land was being taken until four days after the site was occupied.

The Supreme Court action came as Israeli Foreign Minister Moshe Dayan was explaining to the nine nations of the European Common Market that Israel's settlement policy was not illegal.

Dayan summoned the ambassadors of the nine nations to the Foreign Ministry in Jerusalem, reading to them a sharply worded message declaring that the market statement had caused "irreparable damage to the hopes of peace in the Middle East."

Dayan said the Israeli settlements were "strictly in accord with international law."

The government submitted the opinion of Army Chief of Staff Raphael Eitan that Elon Moreh, which is on a hilltop near the West Bank Arab city of Nablus, overlooks the area's main north-south and is of strategic importance.

An attorney for the Arab owners presented a letter from former Chief of Staff Chaim Bar-Lev denying that the site had any strategic importance.

The high court did not rule on the military aspects but took issue with the legality in which the land for the Elon Moreh was seized.

There are 16 prefabricated structures and 10 tents at the location. The court has ordered that no more settlers be moved to Elon Moreh, and no new improvements be made, until the case is decided. Security work to protect existing facilities may continue.

Libyan leader, Khadafy organizes a people's policy

Tripoli, Libya

"We consider government is an instrument of dictatorship, Government must disappear."

The speaker is the Libyan leader, Mohammar Khadafy. He says, "I accept the title of leader of the revolution, but I do not lead with authority." My job is to enable the masses to govern themselves."

To clarify this announcement, Khadafy has given up all his official posts, has disbanded the military command council which led the revolution and has proclaimed Libya the world's first (Jamahiriyah) a term of his own, meaning republic of the masses.

He remains the revolutionary guardian and spiritual caretaker. His theory rejects classes, parties, parliaments, plebiscites, and every other form of administration in the search for a system of real democracy. He proposes that people should make decisions to benefit others and every adult entitled to join a popular congress, a local forum for discussions and acceptances.

A General People's Congress is elected which states the countries policy for a year, but does not decide it. The policy is decided in the people's committees. At the Congress it is put in final form.

His country is flexible Socialism, proclaiming common ownership of land and the means of production, but equally guaranteeing private rights over food, housing, clothing, and personal transportation.

"Partners, not wage workers," is a slogan spoken by the people. The rise of modern nationalism coincides with the discovery of oil for the 2.8 million Libyans, and has made them rich and masters of their own fate.

Literacy, freedom of poverty, decent housing, enough to eat, have decreased the desire for political power of the populace.

6-21-79
Constitutional union proclaimed between Syria, Iraq
Baghdad, Iraq

The two militant Arab foes of the Egyptian-Israeli peace treaty announced in a joint communique that they have placed their combined Soviet-supplied armies under a unified command pending the proclamation of the two nation constitutional union."

The Baath Socialist governments began to patch up a 13 year old feud last October 26, 1979, when they signed a "unity charter" in Damascus, the Syrian capital.

The unification will end a split that began when an Iraqi-backed Marxist faction of the Baath Party - which rules both nations - staged a military coup in Damascus in February 1966, and ousted a Baath faction.

The Nationalists regained control with another military coup in November 1970, and Lieutenant General Hafez Assad became president. The bad feeling between Marxist Baathists in Iraq and the Nationalists in Syria was heightened in 1975 by a dispute over division of the waters of the Euphrates River and in 1976 by Syria's intervention in the Lebanese civil war to prevent victory for the leftest Lebanese Moslems and Palestinians supported by Iraq.

The reunion is a result of the two nation's opposition to Egyptian President Anwar Sadat's peacekeeping with Israel. Syria and Iraq have led the fight to isolate Egypt from the rest of the Arab world and sabotage the treaty.

The agreement to go ahead with unity plans was reached between Assad and Iraqui President Ahmed Hassan Al-Bakr in Baghdad. In principle, 21 million people and the two nations will be joined together with one central government, on army, one flag, one national anthem, and one federal Parliament.

6-22-79
Clandestine activities on Birzeit university

The Israeli military government closed Birzeit University on the West Bank of the Jordan River in the city of Ramallah - Israeli-occupied West Bank on May 3, 1979, charging the Palestinian Arab students with involvement of illegal activities.

University officials are working to graduate 100 seniors who might otherwise lose a year of school, but they are doing it secretly out of fear that the military government might consider clandestine classes illegal.

In the psychodrama of the West Bank, they know a lot about the student-role - the role of the militant, adopted by many, and the role of the victim, applied now to all. Arrest is not a negligible danger for Birzeit's 1200 students. Hundreds of them have been arrested if only for questioning, in the last few years. Most of the students openly support the Palestine Liberation Organization, but few take part in demonstrations.

"The Israelis say that it is the foreign faculty members who are inciting the students," a professor stated in the university that it is the government itself."

According to military sources, the institutions was closed after a long series of disturbances and incitement encouraged by the college's teachers and administrators.

In recent years Birzeit has become a center for hostile political activity and has departed, both in scope, from accepted academic framework. These activities have found expression in the initiation and organization of radical subversion in Judea and Samaria. (West Bank)

0-23-79
Sadat asks Premier Khalil to form new government
Cairo, Egypt

President Anwar Sadat, in a formal move after the recent landslide election of his party, accepted the resignation of Premier Mustapha Khalil's 35-member coalition. The Eqyptian President immediately requested his Premier to form a new government to usher Egypt into a new era of peaceful relations with Israel, official sources revealed.

Khalil, a United States educated engineer, became Premier last October and has been Egypt's chief negotiator at peace talks with Israel since his appointment.

Meanwhile in Israel, Defense Minister Ezer Weizman may reconsider his leaving the Herut (Israel's cabinet officers council), in which he has been in opposition to Prime Minister Menachem Begin over the new Israeli settlement of "Elon Moreh" on the West Bank of the Jordan River. Most of the official delegates believe that Begin will be able to persuade Weizman to remain.

Land of promises seen in Sands of Sinai

Rogers Cannell does not take the Bible literally, but he believes there is a basic fact in the Exodus account of how Moses struck the rock at Massah to draw water from the Sinai desert.

Cannell is an Oakland, California engineer who worked on a project in Yemen four years ago. He began reading the Bible, and was impressed by the references to water in the Sinai.

As an engineer and senior officer of the Oakland firm of Woodward-Clyde Consultants, he foresaw the importance of the Sinai in an eventual Mideast settlement. He anticipated the establishment of United States and Egypt rejected that idea in favor of total Egyptian control. A consortium of Arab Consulting Engineers along with the U.S. have a planned contract to develop the Sinai Desert.

Geological studies and satellite photographs have pointed toward the existence of groundwater in the desert that the children of Israel wandered through on their way from Egypt to the promise land.

Even more encouraging was an encounter with General Abdel Halim Abu-Ghazala, military attache at the Egyptian Embassy. Abu-Ghazala was one of 13 Colonels who overthrew King Farouk and installed the military government that preceded Gamal Abdel Nasser, at the time a tank commander in 1950. He found that even in fairly shallow surface, wells produced water in the almost rainless territory.

Groundwater appears to be present in the narrow plain along the Gulf of Suez and the Gulf of Aquaba. The large central plain of the Sinai is underlain by sedimentary rocks that offer good water potential.

Water is of paramount importance. A pipeline under the Suez, which formerly brought water from the Nile River area for the city of Ismalia is being repaired and two lines added, but this is not enough for expansion of Egyptian culture and peoples.

Since the estrangement of most of the Arab world by Egypt's signing of the peace treaty with Israel, the United States has become the sole foreign backer.

No nation can afford to repeat mistakes like those made in Iran, where zeal for progress resulted in the completion of irrigation systems before farmers were trained to use them, and before transportation and marketing plans were prepared for new crops.

A gigantic grid system has been proposed, dividing the region into squares. The altitude, terrain, average temperature, water and soil conditions of each square are then matched with potential crops and land use.

If the water resources are there the Sinai can become a miraculous problem solver for Egypt.

Sadat, new Nasser to the Fellaheen
Cairo, Egypt

President Anwar Sadat has a vitally important and overlooked fact going for him during the current boycott of his country by most of the Arab world, which continues to oppose the Israeli-Egyptian peace accords; an entirely new loyalty and fervent support from Egyptians 25 million peasants, or (Fellaheen).

In villages up and down the Nile Valley, the traditional Islamic greeting of "light of the morning" has been replaced by "Sabah el Salaam" or "peace of the morning." When you receive this kind of cultural adjustment to peace, the man who made it happen is glorified.

Among the Fellaheen, Sadat radiates the kind of charisma once exuded by Nasser, and he is viewed as a devout Moslem.

The culture of medieval Islam pervades almost every aspect of daily life. Cairo is the seat of Islam's premier Al Azhar University, and Egypt's recent exclusion from the Islamic conference has caused a great deal of pain to the people.

The impression is that now Egypt's fellow Arabs have done their worst - barring a force exodus of Egyptian workers from the Persian Gulf - the longer Sadat survives as President, the more likely he and the Egyptian-Israeli peace themselves will survive.

It depends, as it has from the start, on the Americans. The United States needs to provide confidence, both to the Israelis and the Egyptians, and to encourage Israel to make concessions to the Palestinians for a true and comprehensive peace.

Revival of Islam for West Bank Arabs
Nablus, Israel occupied West Bank

The Islamic revolution is surfacing on the West Bank.

When 1500 Nablus residents marched against Israeli troops a week ago they were led by young men chanting "Allahu akbar" - God is great - and waving copies of the Koran, the sacred book of the Moslems.

When a student body election was held at Najah University in Nablus May 9, 1979, the Islamic slate defeated the Palestine nationalist ticket and the Communist slate.

The Moslem Brotherhood, a fundamentalist religious group long active on the West Bank, is gaining strength and making insistent demands. The group insists, for example, that separate classes be provided for men and women in their universities.

"The reaction to the Israeli occupation creates a religious revival," said Mousa Jayyousi, a Nablus attorney and a member of the university's board of directors.

A Nablus educator relates, "Religious people tell our young: "So long as we are so far from the rule of God, God will not be with us. What has politics accomplished for us? We are still occupied. Let us find strength in God."

Nablus, the largest city (population 80,000) in the Arab populated West Bank area, has a historic resistance to occupation - resistance to the British before the Israelis and to generations of Ottoman Turks. Although conservative, it is not a Moslem stronghold, and the Islamic trend there seems to be a spontaneous new approach to fighting the Israeli presence.

Political asylum offered to Shah in Egypt
Cairo, Egypt

President Anwar Sadat extended a public invitation to the deposed Shah of Iran and his family to accept political asylum in Egypt.

In Tehran, Iran's revolutionary government revoked Shah Mohammed Reza Pahlavi's passport in an effort to block his travel in search of sanctuary and eventually force his return to Iran.

Sadat, addressing the opening session of his newly elected Parliament, said, "It hurts me much," that many countries have refused to shelter the Shah because they fear reprisals from Iranian terrorists.

Sadat welcomed the Shah in Aswan last January when the monarch went into exile. Since then, the Shah has found temporary homes in Morocco, the Bahamas, and now in Mexico. The United States and European countries have not appeared eager for the Shah to establish permanent residence.

Sadat told the 390 members of his Parliament that he was submitting a draft decree that would give the Shah and others refuge "in the name of the principles of Islam, Christianity, and Egypt's civilization."

Members of Parliament applauded the President of Egypt's humane consideration. Sadat also rebuffed other Arab leaders in opposing the Israeli-Egyptian peace treaty.

Iranian Foreign Minister Ibrahim Yazdi, speaking in a state radio interview in Tehran, said he hoped the revocation of the Shah's passport would force him home.

"If he doesn't have a passport, he cannot travel, or else he will have to use another country's passport," Yazdi stated.

The Shah of Iran at the present time is in Cuernavaca, Mexico, and there is no official word of his extradition.

6-25-79
Weizman to remain in Israel's Cabinet, will leave panel
Jerusalem, Israel

Defense Minister Ezer Weizman, who threatened last week to resign his cabinet position in opposition to the government's West Bank policy, stayed on in that post but quit as a member of the Israeli delegation to the Palestinian autonomy negotiations with Egypt.

Weizman split with Prime Minister Menachem Begin over Israel's new Elon Moreh settlement.

Begin and Weizman met privately before the regular cabinet session to "Clear the air." At Begin's suggestion, the cabinet agreed to allow Weizman to leave the committee, which opens its third negotiating meeting at Herzliya, on the coast north of Tel Aviv today.

The talks are aimed at planning elections in the Arab areas occupied by Israel in the 1967 war and shaping self-governing administrations there. Meanwhile in Tel Aviv, Israel, jets attacked five Palestinian strongholds in southern Lebanon, the military command said, hours after a terrorist bomb exploded in the Tel Aviv central bus station.

The bus station blast killed two Arabs who evidently had planned to plant the device when it was detonated.

In Beirut, Lebanon, the Palestine Liberation Organization said the 35 minute air raid killed one man and wounded eight others, mostly women and children.

A brief Israeli announcement stated that Israeli planes hit terrorist concentrations.

A spokesman for the governor's office in Sidon, a provincial capital 15 miles south of Beirut, said the towns of Aaqbiyeh and Adloun took the brunt of the Israel raid.

Negotiations in Herzliya begin
Herzliya, Israel

Egyptian and Israeli negotiators met at this Israeli beach resort in an attempt to coincide negotiations on Palestinian autonomy.

At the end of the first day's meetings it appeared the two sides were cordially disagreeing on the basic approach to the talks. Israel wanted to talk about specifics and Egypt about philosophy.

The United States took part in the talks but submitted no proposals. It was the third meeting of the two panels since May. The Herzliya consultations end June 26, 1979.

Officials stated the meetings were "productive and constructive," and were free from dispute.

Israeli spokesman Dan Pattir said, "The Egyptian delegation presented its ideas relating to the basic framework of the autonomy talks. The Israeli panel believed in speaking in concrete terms of what should be in the autonomy."

Egyptian spokesman Izzat Abdelatif reported, "Who will hold authority over the autonomy once it was established? Elections can lead to setting up a self-governing system for the West Bank and the Gaza Strip."

It was reported that Interior Minister Josef Burg said, "The two day session is helpful, constructive and will be fruitful."

Mustafa Khalil, head of the Egyptian delegation, said he was looking to the future for more substantive commitments, and he was hoping to include Palestinians in the agendas to follow. The next session is to be in Alexandria, Egypt, on July 5 and 6, 1979.

Khalil stated that the United States can be a catalyst and as one of the components of a chemical reaction.

6-27-79
United States signs 15 year oil pact with Israel
Washington, D.C.

The United States and Israel have signed a 15 year agreement providing for U.S. sales of oil to Israel in the event that Israel is a target of an oil embargo.

The text of the agreement worked out over the past three months by Israeli and American officials, was signed last week and made public by the State Department.

It provides that:

The United States will sell oil to Israel only to the extent that the State of Israel is unable to make its own independent arrangements for oil supplies. If an oil embargo also is imposed against the United States, the agreement will not be activated.

The U.S. oil sale commitment will be in effect from November 1979 until 1984.

The price paid by Israel for the oil would be comparable to the world market prices. Israel will reimburse the United States for all the costs incurred.

Meanwhile over Lebanon, Israeli and Syrian warplanes battled in the sky for the first time in five years. The Israelis used U.S. made F-15 fighters in combat.

A military communique issued in Damascus, the Syrian capital indicated four Syrian planes were downed.

In Tel Aviv, a United States Embassy official stated the Phantom Jets were sold to the Israelis on the condition they be used for legitimate self-defense.

In Cairo, Egypt, their government condemned the Israeli attacks on Palestinian targets, which pre-empted the air reprisal, saying they pose grave danger to the Mideast process.

6-28-79
U.S. to enlarge military force in Middle East.
Washington, D.C.

The Carter administration's top foreign policy and defense aides have recommended that the United States strengthen its military presence in the Indian Ocean and the Persian Gulf.

The recommendation, which has been forwarded to President Carter, constitutes a turning point in American policy in this region. The high level proposal is likely to result in gradual but significant augmentation of naval and air forces for the coming year.

Officials stated that the American expansion resulted from a study in which several agencies examined changes in regional security, including the West's growing dependence on oil from the Persian Gulf, political and military gains by the Soviet Union, and turbulence in Iran and elsewhere.

Two high level meetings were conducted at the White House last week, conducted jointly by Secretary of State Cyrus Vance and Secretary of Defense Harold Brown. A consensus emerged that there was a need of ensuring what a senior administration aide called, "our strategic position in the region."

The Pentagon has been asked to prepare a list of deployment possibilities," including the establishment of a permanent fleet for the Indian Ocean and the dispatch of land-based combat aircraft at regular intervals to countries around the Persian gulf.

Begin rejects protests of use of F-15's
Tel Aviv, Israel

Prime Minister Menachem Begin brushes off protests about Israel's use of American made F-15 Eagle jets in dogfights with Syrian warplanes over Lebanon.

Begin stated that the most modern planes in the Israeli arsenal - were carrying out a legitimate act of self defense when they shot down five Syrian Soviet made Mig-21 fighters.

In Damascus, the state controlled Syrian newspaper said the country's decision to challenge the escalating Israeli strikes against Palestinian targets was "neither temporary nor casual," and hinted more resistance could be expected.

Begin's report came with a meeting with U.S. Ambassador Samuel Lewis, who relayed the information to Washington. Lewis was told that the Israelis did not want any confrontation with the Syrian Air Force.

7-2-79
Middle East negotiator Robert Strauss special ambassador

Robert S. Strauss takes over President Carter's Middle East peace process on July 1, 1979. He expressed his determination to carve out a role for himself as the broker of political answers to difficult problems, and a broader Arab-Israeli peace settlement.

Shortly before arriving in Israel at the start of a seven day trip that will help shape an administration decision on how fast and how far to push the issue of self-rule, Strauss told reporters that he expects to generate "a bit of flap" in his first active days as Carter's special ambassador at-large to the Middle East.

Strauss intends to seek out and talk to local Palestinians when he visits the occupied West Bank. He expects the symbolism of both acts to stir political controversy that would convince both sides he is serious about "taking scars" and promoting settlement issues.

Strauss will sit in this week on the fourth round of talks between Israel and Egypt, which have stalled over an agenda for the year-long negotiations to establish a self-governing Palestinian authority on the Israeli-occupied West Bank and the Gaza Strip as promised in the Camp David peace accords.

Strauss made clear to reporters traveling with him that he would not invest much time or effort on detailed negotiating sessions, where Egypt has called on the United States to be a "full partner."

Comparing his new role to his highly successful efforts as Carter's special trade representative, he is anticipating a comprehensive and agreeable pact for all sides of the negotiations.

Mossad, Israel's intelligence bureau, with beautiful women and resourceful men
Tel Aviv, Israel

The four leading intelligence agencies in the world are America's CIA, Great Britain's MI-6, the Soviet Union's KGB, and Israel's Mossad.

Of these four, Mossad - an abbreviation for the Hebrew words meaning "Institution for Intelligence and Special Assignments" - is the smallest and the most romantic, probably because it employs some of the most beautiful women spies in the world, and very effective in maintaining its primary objective, the survival of Israel.

The Mossad's recent coup was in stimulating the peace movement between Israel and Egypt negotiated by President Carter of the United States. Some time ago,

Mossad agents learned of a Libyan-Soviet plot to assassinate President Sadat of Egypt. The word was passed on to Israel's Prime Minister Menachem Begin, who in turn passed it along to Sadat and eventually the CIA. When the information was checked out, it proved to be accurate. Grateful to Israel, Sadat decided, in spite of intense Arab opposition - to go to Jerusalem and maneuver for peace.

Under Isser Harel, a Russian who emigrated to Palestine in 1930 when he was 17 years old, and his successors - Meir Amit, Yitzhak Zamir, and Yitzhak Hosi - the Mossad has achieved other spectacular intelligence triumphs. A few months ago its "hit team" blew up the Palestinian leader's intelligence chief who was responsible for the 1972 murders of Israeli athletes at the Olympic Games in Munich, Germany.

In 1960, after three years of painstaking investigation, the Mossad tracked Adolf Eichmann, the Nazi concentration camp murderer, to Argentina, then brilliantly kidnaped and flew back to Israel, where he was tried and executed.

In 1966, a beautiful Mossad agent influenced an Iraqi Pilot Munir Redfa, into defecting to Israel with a Mig-21 Soviet made fighter airplane. Redfa, who had been trained by the U.S. Air Force, and sent later by Iraq for advanced training to the Soviet Union, was one of the few Iraqi pilots entrusted with then the most modern Soviet Plane.

In August 1966, Redfa flew his Mig-21 from Iraq to Israel, where he and his family, (spirited out of Iraq) now live as Israeli citizens under assumed names. As for the Mossad agent, she still works for the Israelis.

The aim of the Mossad now is to maintain Israel's nuclear superiority in the Middle East, and to prevent the development in Islamic countries of nuclear weaponry. At the present time the intelligence bureau of Israel is concerned with Pakistan, where a uranium-enrichment plant reportedly has received vital equipment from two Swiss firms.

The United States Assistant Secretary Thomas Pickering states, "The Pakistan program is not peaceful, but related to an effort to detonate a nuclear explosion."

If Pakistan develops an atomic bomb for itself, will it not then be duty bound to develop one for the radical Arab leader Muammar Qadaffi, who has threatened to destroy the Israeli State?

The Mossad wants to prevent this from happening, consequently constant alertness is necessary, and the intelligence agency has the human forces to parry any attack, and are prepared for any eventuality.

Israel invites, Shah accepts invitation to stay
Tel Aviv, Israel

Shah Mohammad Reza Pahlavi has accepted an invitation from an Israeli millionaire to stay in his maximum security vill a near Tel Aviv, official sources reported.

The exiled Iranian ruler will accept Samuel Flatto-Sharon's invitation after an abortive attempt was made on his life in Mexico. He is due to arrive in Israel in late July or early August of this year.

Flatto-Sharon is a member of the Israeli Parliament. He was born in Poland and became a resident of France after World War II. He came to Israel a few years ago and ran for the Knesset in 1977.

Meanwhile, President Carter's Mideast negotiator Robert Strauss is encouraging Prime Minister Menachem Begin to move faster on Palestinian autonomy negotiations. He will be present when Egypt, Israel and the United States negotiating teams meet in Alexandria, Egypt this week.

In Cairo, the State Minister of Foreign Affairs, Butros Ghali, called on Palestinians to join the talks because "without the Palestinians, there can be no autonomy."

7-4-79
Sensors of Sinai monitored by Americans
Umm Khashiba, Sinai Buffer Zone

For three years Carl Kachikis has been a supervisor of warning stations in the Sinai desert at two strategic mountain passes separating Israeli and Egyptian forces. He is one of 160 Americans assuming the role as peacemaker in the war torn area.

The tense days on the desolate plateau overlooking the Mitla and Gidi passes, 20 miles from the Suez Canal, now seem far away since Egypt and Israel have signed the peace accords.

Nevertheless, the American surveillance team continues to use sophisticated sensors to monitor everything in their 250-mile area of responsibility.

"If a rabbit moves, I know it," stated a technician Paul Penn, scanning an elaborate console at a station overlooking the Gidi Pass.

Egypt takes control next January, and the Americans will dismantle the surveillance stations.

"But until the lines are changed, this is very important," Kachikis said. "Whoever controls Mitla and Gidi controls Sinai."

Tanks and other heavy armored vehicles, unable to traverse the Northern Sinai sands or the Southern Sinai mountains, can cross the Peninsula only through the two passes.

The area became part of the United Nations buffer zone under the 1975 Sinai II disengagement Accord negotiated by Henry Kissinger, then the U.S. Secretary of State. The United States built three early-warning stations.

"We think we have made a contribution toward peace by our presence," said Ken Hartung, the Field Mission Director. We have good credibility and a reputation for impartiality.

So far most of our calls have been against Israel, though none was serious. The monitors have logged 62 intrusions by Israel, none by Egypt. All are reported within minutes to Washington, D.C., Cairo, Egypt, and Jerusalem, Israel.

7-4-79
Israel's urban renewal delayed by politics
Jerusalem, Israel

Moshe and Regine want a window in the tiny livingroom of their home in the Jerusalem slum of Musrara. The added light will help fight the mold on the whitewashed walls.

Contributors in Los Angeles, California have adopted Musrara as a special project, and $2 million in pledges are available to help people like Moshe, a young fireman, his wife, Ragine, and their five-month old daughter.

An Israeli political fight over control of urban renewal funds has delayed work on Musrara's rehabilitation. The Musrara's project, located in the heart of the Jewish capital, can turn out to be a prototype for the plan.

There are about 160 neighborhood distressed communities that Project Renewal, a one billion dollar nationwide program are designed to deal with.

Some plans were detailed to help the people buy houses and rehabilitate them. A mixture of middle and lower income residents could move into some of the boarded up Arab houses in Musrara, move families from nearby apartments into them, and refurbish the old units, adding private baths and kitchens, which most lack. In a year the residents could be back in their old homes.

Additionally, the plans of the local director would include consolidating social services in the area, to treat social ills - unemployment among young men, school dropouts, the need for a clinic, as housing is improved.

The difficulty lies with the National Housing Ministry, who has control and is not willing to delegate the responsibility or funding to the local government.

7-5-79
P.L.O. threats will not alter U.S. stance in Mideast
Cairo, Egypt

Robert Strauss, President Carter's Middle East troubleshooter, stated that the United States will not alter its stance on Palestinian autonomy by threats to block critical sea lanes that carry oil to the West.

Strauss was responding to hints by Palestinian Liberation Organization leader Yasser Arafat, who suggested the P.L.O. might resort to sinking an oil supertanker or two in the Strait of Hormuz to block oil routes.

The 65-mile wide sea passage separates the Persian Gulf from the Gulf of Oman and lies between the east coast of the Arabian peninsula and Iran.

The Persian Gulf suppliers provide the United States with about 36 percent of its total of OPEC supplied oil.

The Middle East peace negotiator says, "As long as I am involved, we will not be subjected to threats by anybody on any subject."

Meanwhile in Tel Aviv, Israel, the government has asked a Quaker group, a citizens affiliate of the United States, to stop providing legal aid to West Bank Arabs arrested on security charges, because the assistance goes beyond humanitarian activity. A spokesman for The American Friends Service Committee said in Jerusalem that the government's action will deprive many indigent Arabs of legal assistance, particularly students accused of taking part in demonstrations.

7-6-79
Progress made on Palestinian Issue
Alexandria, Egypt

Robert Strauss, President Carter's special negotiator in the Middle East, held his first direct talks on Palestinian autonomy, and announced "some progress" toward heading off a deadlock between Egypt and Israel. "It went very well," Strauss reported.

He, the Egyptians, and the Israelis are attempting to agree on an autonomy plan for the 1.1 million Palestinians living on Israeli-occupied West Bank of the Jordan River and in the Gaza Strip.

The two days of talks, which ends today, are the fourth session on the Palestinian question. The earlier talks, ended with participants unable to agree on an agenda for future negotiations that are to continue for the next 11 months.

An air of restrained expectation surrounded the latest consultations, held in the San Stefano Hotel by the Mediterranean Sea, a site protected by high walls and guards carrying automatic rifles.

The stage was set, Strauss stated in the opening 90-minute morning session on the fifth of July, for "a breakthrough, not a breakdown," but we are not going to solve gut issues or resolve any major obstacles. Instead, "Our role is to move the process to the next stage," after the discord of earlier sessions.

"We hope that by the end of this meeting we will have groups working on specific issues, with deadlines to report" to the full negotiating body, Strauss told reporters before the talks. Although the savvy negotiator did not say so, it seemed apparent the talks in subcommittees would concentrate on the mechanics of holding an election in the occupied territories and on dismantling Israel's military government.

Egypt, however, presumably will stick to its position that Jewish settlements on the land won by Israel in the 1967 Mideast War and the status of Jerusalem be discussed at some point.

Yosef Burg, Israel's Interior Minister and leader of its delegation, said after the session that it had been "good and objective" and added, "We have opened the door. Now we have to see what walks in."

Egyptian spokesman Ezzat Abdel Latif said the talks had been "business-like and cordial."

Some of the officials believe that real progress will have to wait until Egyptian President Anwar Sadat and Israeli Prime Minster Menachem Begin meet in Alexandria.

In other developments, the Israeli radio reported that Lebanese Christian militiamen had crossed lines set up by U.N. forces to attack Palestinian guerillas in southern Lebanon. Their enclave was reported as north of the Israeli border, and attackers blew up buildings in the guerilla camps.

7-6-79
Logjam in Mideast broken
Alexandria, Egypt

U.S. mediator Robert Strauss announced what he termed a "breakthrough" today in unsnarling the logjam that had been holding up the talks between Israel and Egypt on the issue of Palestinian autonomy.

"They arrived at a broad solution sooner than I thought they would," Strauss said at a news conference after the two former enemies accepted his working concept for group participation.

In a joint communique, the three sides agreed they would assign the working groups to discuss how to hold an election for the Palestinian Arabs living in the occupied territories, and what powers and responsibilities the elective council would have.

"We have a structure now for coming to grips with practical problems and it will let progress go forward," Strauss related to officials.

A communique read at the news conference said a working group would begin holding sessions within two weeks to plan for a Palestinian council to administer home rule in the Israeli occupied areas. The full delegation will meet again in Israel on August 5, 1979.

7-8-79
Begin's settlement policy - a challenge - and his reply
From the American Jewish community

Since the signing of the Israeli-Egyptian peace treaty on March 26, 1979, the Israeli government's policy of creating new Jewish settlements in the mostly-Palestinian West Bank has aroused heated international controversy. Recently, a number of prominent members of the Jewish community signed an open letter to Israel's Prime Minister Menachem Begin opposing this policy as an obstacle to peace. The Prime Minster replies with a letter of his own. The texts of both messages are as follows:

Dear Mr. Prime Minster:

We are ardent friends of Israel. We are pledged to a strong and prosperous Israel, and to an Israel at peace with all its neighbors. We have watched with admiration the conclusions of the treaty with Egypt, and we salute the courage and vision which you brought to that historic achievement.

We are profoundly distressed, however, by the decision of our government to create new settlements on the West Bank. Such a move seems imprudent as critical negotiations on the future of the territories are about to commence. The recent establishment of "Elon Moreh" impairs Israel's credibility in the eyes of the inhabitants of the area, with which Israel must find an honorable way to live, and in the eyes of the world. We understand that there are legal and historical arguments for the Jewish settlement, but a policy which requires the expropriation of Arab land unrelated to Israel's security needs, and which presumes to occupy permanently a region populated by over three-quarters of a million Palestinian Arabs, we find morally unacceptable and perilous for the democratic character of the Jewish State. We appeal to you to reconsider this policy, which makes the Palestinian problem more difficult, and delays a full and comprehensive peace in the Middle East.

Prime Minister Begin's answer:

Gentlemen:
I received your cabled letter after 24 hours publication in our media. May I say this is a questionable procedure.

As for the subject matter of your complaint, here is my reply:

Jews have a perfect right to live in any area in "Eretz Israel." This is the land of our forefathers to which we have returned as of right. Just as we are entitled to dwell in Tel Aviv, Jaffa, Haifa, Petah, Tikya, Rehovot, or for that matter in Jerusalem, so do we have the absolute right to live in all parts of Judea, Samaria, and the Gaza district. This right of our people is inseparably bound with the needs and demands of our vital national security. Please remember, gentlemen, that in our small country there is a genocidal rampage being conducted by the so-called Palestine Liberation Organization. If from Samaria came from these professional killers and destroyed the lives of mothers and children, should not the government of Israel attempt to stem such movements aimed at murder of our men in any conceivable way?

Of course, nobody can give an assurance that we shall always succeed in preventing these atrocities. Five justices of the Supreme Court of Israel unanimously answered this question on which the lives of our children do depend. I quote:

"One does not have to be a military and security expert to realize that terrorist elements operate more easily in an area inhabited by a population that is indifferent or is sympathetic towards the enemy than in an area where there is indifferent or is sympathetic towards the enemy than in an area where there are also persons likely to look out for them, and to report any suspicious movement to the authorities. Such persons will offer them no hide-out, assistance, or supplies. The matter is simple and needs no elaboration."

You write to me, "inter-alia." "We have watched and admired with concordance your treaty with Egypt, and we salute the courage and the vision which you brought to that historic moment."

Thank you gentlemen, I will continue to work for my people and country, hopefully, not without the qualities you describe.

Menachem Begin

7-8-79
Libya may break diplomatic relations with U.S.
Washington, DC

Libya, which already has threatened an oil cutoff, recently informed a high ranking Carter administration envoy that it may be forced to break diplomatic relations with the United States and provide military bases to the Soviet Union if the Whitehouse continues to spurn its overtures.

At the heart of the blunt message delivered in Tripoli last month to Undersecretary of State David Newsom is Libya's desire to purchase three Boeing 747 jumbo jets. The U.S. withdrew export licenses for the planes after Libyan forces intervened in Uganda to defend Idi Amin's government.

Newsom, in an interview, disclosed that sources from Libya stated, "If we are going to have a commercial embargo on Libya, then Libya would have to consider reciprocal gestures." The Undersecretary said there was no explicit mention of halting oil exports to the Americans.

Libyan leader, Colonel Muammar Khadafy, told a Paris-based Arabic-language weekly that unless the United States lifts its embargo, "We will stop producing oil-except for our own domestic consumption - for two years or more."

Newsom met with Khadafy's top adviser, Adb as-Salam Ahman Jallud, and conferred with him, saying, "On the delivery of the commercial aircraft, Libya's support of the Uganda operation was the chief factor in the American decision, and he didn't anticipate any early change in that policy.

Jallud replied that Libya "does not accept this as essential between its bilateral relations with us and its foreign policy. It was apparent that the Libyans would like to find a way to improve relations with us without sacrificing any of their external policies."

7-9-79
Reception of P.L.O. leader in Austria condemned by Israel
Jerusalem, Israel

Israel strongly condemned the welcome given Yasser Arafat, head of the Palestine Liberation Organization, by Austrian Chancellor Bruno Kreisky and called Israel's ambassador to Austria home for "consultations."

The director general of the Israeli Foreign Ministry called the ranking official of the Austrian Embassy, protesting the Chancellor's reception of the terrorist leader.

The Prime Minister, Menachem Begin, and the leader of the Labor Party opposition, Shimon Peres, are to address the Knesset, Israel's parliament, on the issue.

Israelis were infuriated at reports that Arafat was received in Vienna with the pomp of a state visit.

Arafat was met at the Vienna airport by Kreisky, later conferred with him and former German Chancellor Willy Brandt, Chairman of the Socialist International, and was the guest at a dinner given by Kreisky.

Israel Ambassador, Yaacov Doron, was ordered back to the State of Israel in a strong protest, falling short of a permanent withdrawal.

"On the P.L.O. there are no differences of opinion in the entire Zionist camp," Peres said. "This meeting will accord prestige to Yasser Arafat, who continues acts of terrorism and insists on the annihilation of Israel even during this hour of difficult negotiations."

In the meantime, the United States negotiator, Robert Strauss, has returned to Washington, D.C. from Saudi Arabia, reporting that the Arabian State demands that any Middle East settlement must be based on complete Israeli withdrawal from Arab lands.

7-10-79
Israeli policy of "deterrent actions" in Lebanon will continue
Jerusalem, Israel

Israeli infantry forces, operating in southern Lebanon almost on a daily basis, blew up two houses of suspected Palestinian terrorists about five miles beyond the Israeli border.

The incursion was the fourth in as many days acknowledged by the Israeli government. The Israeli army warned its policy of "deterrent actions" will continue.

Operating in tandem with Israeli-supported Christian militias led by Major Saad Haddad, the Israeli army patrols in the last week have demolished a number of houses in southern Lebanon. Several suspected terrorists have been abducted for interrogation.

Meanwhile in Alexandria, Egypt, Anwar Sadat and Prime Minister Menachem Begin three days of summitry in this Mediterranean resort, continuing their "getting-to-know-you-better" dialogue.

Both Israeli and Egyptian officials caution against expecting a dramatic breakthrough in negotiations on Palestinian autonomy at the meeting, the seventh between the two former adversaries.

"At this point, it is the process that is important, because it sets the psychological climate for the results that come later," said a close adviser to the Egyptian President.

The expansion of the original one-day schedule to 48 hours over three days prompted speculation Sadat and Israeli Prime Minister would try to capitalize on the procedural breakthrough at last weeks round of talks.

In the progress for peace and Israeli and Egyptian company have created a joint trade venture, believed to be the first partnership of companies from the two countries.

Koortrade, one of Israel's biggest manufacturing companies with sales of 480 million last year, has agreed to an import-export venture with an Egyptian company which has not been identified.

Moshe Balla, head of Koortrade, said each partner will own fifty percent. The field in which we can do the best and the most is in agriculture, including export of machinery, chemicals, and technical know-how.

7-11-79
Begin welcomed in Alexandria, Egypt
Alexandria, Egypt

Israeli Prime Minister Menachem Begin, enjoying his fourth visit to Egypt, held wide ranging talks with President Anwar Sadat, after several thousand Egyptians gave him an extra-ordinary welcome.

The two leaders conferred privately for an hour and later dined at Sadat's seaside villa in Mamoura, a resort area a few miles east of this ancient port city.

The substance of the discussions were not revealed, but an aide to Begin described them as wide-ranging and open.

Before meeting Sadat, Begin was the focus of a joyous emotional scene at Alexandria's huge Prophet Daniel Synagogue, where about 100 of the city's Jewish community of 150 persons had gathered to join him in after prayers.

Several thousand Egyptians who watched his arrival and departure in front of the synagogue chanted, "Begin . . . Begin," a cheer that Israeli reporters stated the Prime Minister has not heard since his Likud bloc campaigned for office in May, 1977.

Clearly touched by the warmth of the ovations, Begin ordered his limousine halted as it was leaving the synagogue, jumped out and plunged into the crowd, shaking dozens of outstretched people.

A heavy contingent of Sadat's presidential security guard, distraught by Begin's impulse into the boisterous crowd, cleared a path back to the limousine, but only after Begin had crossed the street and plunged into another crowd clustered by the synagogue gates did he consent to return to his car, waving and smiling to his Egyptian allies.

Earlier, when he entered the vast limestone and marble house of worship that once seated 2000 of old Alexandria's 40,000 Jews, Begin marveled, "There is not such a synagogue in our country."

7-11-79
Saudi Arabia's Two-edged sword - the oil weapon

The oil weapon is a two-edged sword. Not only can oil-exporting countries in the Middle East restrict supplies and raise prices as a way of pressing the United States to force political concessions on Israel, but the oil also gives Islamic militants in the area a lever for bringing pressure to bear on weak regimes. Hence the quiet dominant behavior of the leading exporter - Saudi Arabia.

The Saudis regularly export 8.5 million barrels of crude oil daily - double that of any other country. They can cut output to as low as 3 million barrels without suffering, and can raise it to more than 10 million barrels without straining.

But the Saudi regime is a theocratic monarchy, out of date even by the standards of the Arabian Peninsula. It has only a token military force, it depends for labor on foreigners - many of them Palestinians and Iraqis, consequently Saudi vulnerability matches Saudi riches.

This weakness has not been lost on the "rejectionist front" forces working to undo the American-sponsored peace between Egypt and Israel. At meetings in Bagdad last fall and this spring, the rejectionists won Saudi participation in their campaign to denounce the peace accords. Indications are that the Saudis are pressured by threats, from the Palestinian Liberation Organization and the Iraqi government, of trouble in the oil fields and violence against leading princes.

Under the influence of Bagdad, the Saudis agreed to the OPEC price rises of oil. To ease the anger by the Americans, Saudi officials have increased oil production by one million barrels a day for three months, perhaps more.

The tension in the Middle East will not disappear overnight, concessions by Israel to the Palestinians, divisions by Arabs in the Arab states, and the United States plans for developing its own synthetic resources, and mobilization of forces in the Indian Ocean and the Persian Gulf are future considerations and realities.

7-12-79
Summit with Sadat-Begin reveal major differences
Alexandria, Egypt

Egyptian President Anwar Sadat has failed to win a pledge from Israeli Prime Minister Menachem Begin to halt West Bank settlements, but the two leaders agreed at their summit that Lebanon should not be partitioned.

Sadat and Begin concluded two days of summitry in limited agreement on minor issues, however they have major differences on Israeli settlements in occupied Arab territory.

Officials announced at a news conference Sadat would visit Haifa, Israel at the end of next month to continue talks on Palestinian self rule in the Occupied West Bank of the Jordan River and the Gaza Strip.

The settlement issue and Israel's anti-guerilla operations in Lebanon dominated the three hours of conversation over two days. Both men described their talks on Palestinian autonomy as important, but not details were disclosed.

The news conference in the ornate ballroom of the Ras-El-Tine palace produced no dramatic effects, but reporters were cautioned by officials of both countries not to expect breakthroughs.

Sadat, speaking alternately in Arabic and English, said, "I believe progress will come as a fruit of what we are doing now to maintain the momentum of the peace process, and the agreement for full autonomy."

Egypt, Israel, and the United States agreed to set aside one year, beginning last May, to negotiate autonomy for the 1.2 million Arabs living in the West Bank and Gaza Strip.

Sadat stated, "the talks yesterday were fruitful, and we shall continue." The President of Egypt and the Prime Minister of Israel both were in accord that anti-guerilla operations in Lebanon should not lead to division of Israel's northern neighbor.

Begin said, "We do not want to see the disintegration of Lebanon into separate Christian and Moslem states."

7-12-79
Hostile regime restrict the freedom of the Egyptian President.
Alexandria, Egypt

In the summer, when the heat in Cairo is unendurable, President Anwar Sadat spends his time in Alexandria, listening to the Mediterranean surf, and he seeks guidance from Allah, and for progress and prosperity for his people. Sadat looks for answers to problems surrounding him. He has accomplished much with his daring manuevers.

Sadat bravely faces a public that is diverse, who is like an American general. He said, "The enemy has got us surrounded. Don't they know when they are defeated?" Sadat exudes tremendous confidence, but the dangers around him are real.

To the West in Libya, a population of 2.5 million people, who have a rejectionist leader, Moammar Khadafy, he employs expensive arms and munition makers. They superintend a huge arsenal of Soviet weapons, and are ready to start trouble, when Khadafi sounds an alert.

The miasma of fear, the Libyan leader exerts on his followers, and other countries in the region remain threatened in his presence.

Still Sadat is assured of his and his nation's ability to shoulder great burdens, and with the exile of the Shah of Iran, he has become the constable of the Middle East.

The President of Egypt will is tenacious. Although his freedom is restricted by the Arab regimes, he finds peace with Israel calming to his spirit. The Arab critics can do nothing without Egypt, in the world of the political realm. Anwar Sadat is a master in gaining acceptance in the United States, England, France and the European sattelites.

7-13-79
Begin agrees with Sadat on some key issues
Jerusalem, Israel

Prime Minister Menachem Begin returned to Israel ebullient about his reception in Alexandra and a series of agreements he worked out with President Anwar Sadat. "We didn't hide anything from each other," he said.

Reporting on his seventh summit with the Egyptian leader since the peace process began 20 months ago, Begin stated that Israeli-Egyptian relations have advanced to a "stage of friendship, common understanding, and cooperation."

The Prime Minister landed at Jerusalem's Atarot airport, where he strolled down a red carpet, greeting family members and government ministers. The small airport is in the half of the city annexed by Israel in 1967.

Begin claimed agreement with Sadat on several aspects of normalization, including visits to Israel by Egyptian Jews with relatives there, increased Israeli tourism in Egypt, and eventual reconstruction of the railway line that once linked Egypt and Palestine.

Begin also declared that he and the President of Egypt reached concordance over the question of Israeli equipment in the Gulf, and Egyptian oil sales to Israel were reported deadlocked.

"We will hand over the oil wells to the Egyptians on November 26, 1979." "We will buy back this oil at the market price in the world," the Prime Minister said. The oil fields are located at El Sur on the Sinai's Peninsula Gulf of Suez coast. The fields provide about 36,000 barrels of oil per day, 22 percent of Israel's needs.

On plans for Palestinian autonomy, the two leaders concurred that conditions will be created for full autonomy for the West Bank Arabs.

On Lebanon, Begin stated that he and Sadat stand for territorial integrity, but Israel will "defend her people" by striking at the P.L.O. inside Lebanon.

7-14-79
Egyptian Embassy seized by Palestinian terrorists
Ankara, Turkey

Four Palestinian terrorists raided the Egyptian Embassy, killing a policeman and a security guard and taking about 20 hostages, including the Egyptian ambassador.

Two of the hostages escaped by jumping out a ground floor window. One of the gunmen said to a Turkish reporter by telephone that they would blow up the embassy building if their comrades in Egypt are not released.

The raiders killed two Turks and wounded two other guards as they invaded the embassy compound, firing automatic weapons and grenades.

The Turkish state radio stated that Ambassador Ahmed Kamal Olema and the other hostages were unharmed. A hostage released earlier said there were many dead inside the building, but she may have been in shock and confused.

An anonymous caller to newspapers in Beirut, Lebanon said that the attack had been carried out by the "Eagles of the Palestine Revolution," as part of a campaign to punish Egypt for signing the peace treaty with Israel.

"The Eagles," linked to Saika, a Syrian-backed guerilla organization, is a faction within the Palestine Liberation Organization.

Premier Mustapha Khalil warned of serious retaliation if the diplomats of Egypt were hurt or killed.

The embassy raiders demand that Turkey sever relations with Egypt and Israel and recognize the P.L.O., in addition to freeing two Palestinian prisoners in Egypt - a Lebanese named Joseph Selm, jailed as a spy for Syria, and a Syrian named Ibrahim Daya, accused of working for "Saika."

The Egyptian Embassy raid was the latest incident in many months of political violence in Turkey, and also the most serious Palestinian insurrection against an Egyptian target since the signing of the Israeli-Egyptian treaty in March of 1979.

In one of the bloodiest assaults, Palestinian terrorists in February of 1978, assassinated an Egyptian editor and close aide of President Anwar Sadat in Cyprus. Egyptian commandos were sent to Cyprus to capture the assassins, but Cypriot forces killed 20 of them when they tried to attack an airliner held by the terrorists.

7-14-79
Israel, Constable of the Middle East
Jerusalem, Israel

When Shah Mohammed Reza Pahlavi was driven from power, the oil kingdoms of the Persian Gulf, lost their peacemaker. Strategic planners now see Israel as the cop on the beat in the Middle East.

A basic belief of the Israeli military contingent is that someday Arab monarchies will fall, and the oil reserves beneath the Palaces will be fought over by radical regimes of the Arab world.

Israel's fear is that a radical state may take over a weak neighbor, gain control over a major part of the Mideast's oil, raise prices or cut production to imperil the Western powers, and force Israel into concessions to its Arab enemies.

Iraq, for instance, has long claimed the northern part of Kuwait. Iran protected Kuwait until the Shah fell. Now, the Israelis say, only they can intervene swiftly enough to forestall or repel an Iraqi move against Kuwait.

Also, according to some experts, it is only the threat of Israeli intervention that protects Jordan and Saudi Arabia from attack by other Arab states. One Jewish strategist says:

"They know from Entebbe that we can go far, and strike boldly, with imagination."

Israeli prophets see three interlocking developments:

A crisis of stability in the Arab world, with the firebrand spread of the Islamic revolution, the unavoidable demise of the monarchies, and apparent nations like Syria deteriorating from internal disarray.

A rise in the importance to the West of Israel as a steady base. A danger that the United States will pressure Israel into giving up its security on the West Bank at a time when the Jewish nation can afford to show no weakness.

Dr. Eytan Gilboa, professor of international relations at a Hebrew university states, "As long as we do things in negotiations that do not hurt our national security, Israel remains an important balance in the Middle East."

7-15-79
United States denies arms sale to Saudi Arabia - oil increases
Washington, D.C.

The State Department is recommending sale of about 1.2 billion dollars in arms and military equipment to Saudi Arabia, denying that the pending arrangement is related to a recent Saudi decision to step up oil production.

If President Carter gives his approval, and Congress agrees, the Saudis will receive tanks and a wide range of arms including uniforms and equipment for four mechanized battalions.

Officials at the State Department and the Pentagon insist, contrary to several published reports, that the Saudis are being rewarded for stepping up oil production by about 13 percent. The increase of one million barrels per day will help make up the current shortages.

Hodding Carter, the State Department spokesman stated, "The arms sales are being conducted without links to Saudi Arabia's decisions on oil."

Meanwhile in Ankara, Turkey, the siege of the Palestinian guerillas has come to an end with the nine hostages freed, without a fight, and without additional bloodshed, at the Egyptian Embassy.

The Turkish Prime Minster Bulent Ecevit emphasized a peaceful solution was reached with "no concessions."

The four Palestinian prisoners, radical members of "The Red Eagles of the Revolution," will be tired under marshal law, probably charged with murder, as well as illegal possession of arms, and assault on foreign property.

Two Turkish security guards died from grenade fragments. The third victim was one of the Egyptian hostages who tried to escape by leaping from the third story window and died from his injuries.

7-17-79
Iraq President resigns because of health
Bagdad, Iraq

President Ahmed Hassan Bakr resigned and was replaced by Saddam Hussein, Vice President and chairman of the ruling Revolutionary Command Council under Bakr, the news agency from Iraq announced.

Hussein reshuffled the cabinet, and he assured Syria there were no plans to change the political-military alliance that the two nations have pledged to form in defiance of Egyptian-Israeli peace accords.

Baker, known to be suffering from a heart ailment, has made few appearances in public in recent years, during which Hussein has exercised many of the day-to-day functions of a government chief.

The President announced his resignation in a nationwide address marking the 12th anniversary of a coup reviving his "Baath Socialist Party" after five years of obscurity.

Bakr was one of the officers who overthrew the Iraqi Hashemite monarchy in July 1958. He was appointed Premier in 1963. Later on that year his Baath party was ousted from power by a military coup. The President engineered a drive that brought back his "Baath" party in 1968.

The Iraqi leader kept Iraq on a firm Arab nationalist course and followed a hard line in the Middle East conflict, ruling out any peace settlement.

Meanwhile in Lebanon, changes in the Lebanese government have occurred to bring consolidation and reduced tension between Christians and Moslems. The Prime Minister, Salim el Hoss has formed a 12 member cabinet made up of seven members of Parliament and five technocrats. His President, Elias Sarkis, has included six Christians and six Moslems for harmony in the war torn country.

7-18-79
Uprising reported against the Sultan of Oman
Beirut, Lebanon

Marxist guerillas appear to be preparing to attack the conservative Sultan of Oman, Qaboos ibn Said, ruler of an area of vital interest to the West.

Diplomats familiar with developments in the Persian Gulf stated that the Popular Front for the Liberation of Oman has begun to regroup and reorganize its forces after the departure of the Shah of Iran, Mohammed Reza Pahlavi, which changed the balance of power in the gulf last January.

Well-trained commando groups have resumed operations in several areas of Oman's southern Dhofar province, which borders on South Yemen, the Soviet's closest ally in the Arab world in the Middle East.

Oman has 1000 miles of coastline and overlooks the Strait of Hormuz, a narrow deepwater channel through which more than 100 tankers a day carry oil to the industrialized nations.

In the early 1970s, the Shah of Iran sent several thousand soldiers across the Persian Gulf to Oman to join the Sultan's army which included a contingent of British contract officers - in fighting the Dhofar Rebellion. In 1975, Qaboos declared the revolt crushed.

Since the post of policeman of the gulf is declared vacant with the exile of the Shah of Iran, fresh resistance is being felt in Oman.

Western sources in this oil rich country said the United States, already faced with a shortfall of oil supplies, is considering extending military support to Oman.

Qaboos is the only Arab ruler of the Emirates who has unqualified support for Egyptian President Anwar Sadat's peace pact with Israel. The Popular Front reports that Egypt has moved about 7000 of its troops to the frontier to prevent revolutionaries from disrupting the Oman nations.

7-19-79
Israel will agree to accept a joint African force
Tel Aviv, Israel
The Israeli radio reported that the State of Israel will agree to a joint African force to replace the U.N. peacekeepers in the Sinai Peninsula if the countries involved renew diplomatic ties with the Jewish state.

The mandate for the 4000 troops of the United Nations Emergency Force patrolling between Egyptian and Israeli troops since the end of the 1973 Mideast war expires next week.

The Soviet Union, displeased at being shunted aside by the Israel-Egypt peace treaty, is expected to veto an extension of the force's mandate. According to the treaty, a peacekeeping force is to monitor Israel's withdrawal from Sinai over three years.

Meanwhile in Monrovia, Liberia, President Anwar Sadat of Egypt defended his peace treaty with Israel before the Organization of African Unity summit, and a number of Arab and African leaders walked out. Sadat ignored the afront, and spoke for more than 45 minutes in Arabic, denouncing his Arab enemies for obstructing is peace policy and challenging them to find an alternative.

The President of Egypt formally entered into the summit record the full text of his speech to the Israeli parliament on his first visit to Jerusalem in 1977.

"As for Egypt," he stated, "We are on the path to peace. Nothing can deflect us from this path. Peace is the aspiration of every Egyptian."

Mauritanian Foreign Minister Ould Abdallah said the walkout was a "natural consequence" of the Bagdad conference of the Arab League in April, where Egypt was expelled, and most countries assented to a boycott in retaliation for the signing of the peace accords.

During his speech, Sadat invited and welcomed the Palestinians and other Arabs to join in the comprehensive negotiations, with Israel.
7-20-79
United States moves to assure Israel's oil supply

As congress grapples to produce more energy for consumption at home, it is writing into law a promise to guarantee oil supply to Israel.

In dealing with the controls on exports, the law now virtually bans the export of oil produced in Alaska, but these bills would exempt Israel from the ban.

The only opposition has come from the National Association of Arab Americans. The guarantee grew out of the Middle East peace treaty negotiations. Last March, President Carter promised to sell oil to Israel for up to 15 years to meet its "normal requirements" if she was unable to get oil on its own.

If the United States faces an oil embargo, it would not have to supply Israel directly, but could get oil through an emergency system established by the major industrialized nations.

Since the fall of the Shah of Iran, in which Israel received 50 percent of her daily consumption of oil, the State of Israel has been forced to buy most of the oil used from the spot market, paying a higher price than oil sold under contract.

7-22-79
Egypt now stronger despite sanctions
Cairo, Egypt

Despite the Arab economic and political threats that followed the Egyptian-Israeli peace treaty, Egypt and its President, Anwar Sadat are in better shape today than at any other time in the last decade.

The nation that was considered an all-but-hopeless social and financial disaster has made a surprising recovery in terms of its economy, the morale of its 41 million people, and the political power and popularity of its president.

The economy - An annual growth rate of 8-9 percent makes Egypt one of the most productive Third-World nations, according to the World Bank and International Monetary Fund sources.

A near calamitous balance-of-payments deficit of 2.5 billion dollars in 1976 has been reduced to a manageable tenth of that amount. International debts, staggering in arrears two years ago, have been restructured.

Money lenders have developed "Islands of competence" in the United Arab Republic, especially in the Egyptian airlines, Egypt Air.

Public morale - visible improvements in urban transportation, communications and food supply have lifted the spirits of overcrowded city dwellers.

A building boom in Cairo has increased the earning power of the workers by over 200 percent in the last 18 months.

Farmers, once on the verge of revolt, over disorderly policies and prices, report steady improvement in allocations and crop quotas, that once were alarmingly restrictive.

Politics - President Sadat has completed a restructuring of his government that has effectively isolated most of his critics, and left him more powerful and popular, since he assumed control after the death of Gamal Nasser in 1970.

The President of Egypt is a gentle dictator in his democratic pronouncements, and now commands a two-party parliamentary government with what he terms "responsible democracy." The two-party governing body created by Sadat is his own "National Democratic Party, and the opposition "Socialist Action Party."

With his critics stifled and denied access to a nominally free but actually state-controlled press, Sadat is riding the crest in popularity inspired by the peace treaty with Israel.

Most analysts agree that if Sadat can maintain the peace momentum that gained him and Egypt undreamed-of-world respect and if the United States and other countries will continue financing the country's development, the people of Egypt will stand behind him.

Against the background of harsh sanctions imposed by his fellow Arab leaders as punishment for the peace accords have had an impact more verbal than real.

A united Arab conference at a meeting in Bagdad last March severed diplomatic relations with Egypt, imposing an economic boycott that included the cutoff of all aid and technical assistance. Of the 20 nations in the Arab Leaque, only Sudan and Oman refused to comply with the directive. The sanctions have consolidated rather than erode Sadat's political strength.

The Arabs have threatened to stop the movement of oil tankers through the Suez Canal, and through Egypt's Sumed pipelines, but oil experts claim the threats are rhetoric, because once the oil is pumped into tankers for transit through the canal or into the pipeline, it is out of the producers hands and under the control of the companies that buy it.

Only if the sanctions continue over a long period - three to five years - will they begin to undercut the United Arab Republic. Arabs in history are noted for their disunity, and it is doubtful the present unified stance will endure to cause division of the Egyptian nation.

7-22-79
Key to Palestinian deadlock may be Jerusalem
Washington, D.C.

Middle East troubleshooter Robert Strauss suggested one way of breaking the Egyptian-Israeli deadlock over Palestinian rights. It is the complex and controversial - future status of Jerusalem.

Strauss stated, "It may make it easier for other Arab nations to join the negotiations."

Furthermore, the influential presidential adviser says Saudi Arabia, contrary to persistent reports that it wants the peace process to fail, is prepared "to come in as a key player" in the consultations with Israel once clear progress is demonstrated on the Palestinian issue.

National Security Council sources said that Strauss has ordered a special White House State Department study of the chances of achieving an early breakthrough on Jerusalem.

One important policy maker explained that it could take the form of a joint Egyptian-Israeli declaration pledging that the Holy City would not be divided, or become a battleground again, and some form of autonomy or self-governing body could be established.

In a disclosure by Strauss with his return to Washington from the Middle East two weeks ago, he said, "Saudi Arabia, who has agreed to increase oil production by one million barrels a day for the next three months, does not oppose the peace treaty, but they want it to succeed with them as a participant.

The Middle East negotiator met with Crown Prince Fahd and remarked, "The Prince of Arabia wants to play a constructive role, he has selfish and unselfish reasons." He wants to be on amicable terms with the United States, and he does not like the interference of the Soviet Union."

Strauss does not rule out an eventual meeting with the P.L.O. if they agree to the U.N. Security Council Resolution 242, which recognizes the right of the Jewish State to exist.

7-22-79

Syria, controversial Arab State, may be an avenue for negotiations

After visiting Jordan and Saudi Arabia, two kingdoms whose support for the Camp David process is essential; who apparently have resisted his overtures, Presidential adviser Robert Strauss may consider adding Damascus to his itinerary. The Syrians acute problems, since the collapse of the Shah of Iran, have caused a unity with Iraq, Libya, Algeria, and the Palestine Liberation Organization, and has put pressure on Arab moderates to adopt more militant policies. This has, in effect, deepened instability in the area.

Syrian should not be sidestepped in the pursuit of peace. The sectarian violence, directed against the regime of President Hafez al-Assad, has lead Washington officials to presume the possibility of a subtle approach, probably by the French, in Israel returning the Golan Heights to Syria, under tight security arrangements, in exchange for a pledge of peace and co-existence.

Assad is in deep difficulty, and requires a major victory capable of rallying nationalistic sentiment. His minority, the Alawite regime, drained by a civil war in Lebanon, is being challenged by the Sunni majority and the Moslem fanatics, and the possibility of a bloodbath is real. War with Israel is an option, attractive but suicidal, without Egyptian support on the southern flank, but a negotiation with Israel, focusing on a phased return of the Golan Heights, might save Assad's control by restoring national honor, provided this does not abandon the Palestinian cause in the process.

During the negotiations at Camp David and Egypt, the government of Prime Minister Menachem Begin made three major concessions in exchange for the promise of peace: Israel agreed to withdraw to the international boundary to abandon military bases, including the sophisticated air base at Etzion in the eastern Sinai, and most painful, to dismantle more than a dozen settlements.

The United States, working with the French, can negotiate with what is the strongest force in the Arab world - the force of Nationalism.

7-22-79
Arafat pledges to halt commando raids
Cairo, Egypt

Yasser Arafat, head of the Palestine Liberation Organization, has pledged to stop P.L.O. commando raids outside of Israel and Israeli-held Arab terrorists, official sources reported.

The Cairo magazine, October, states that the rejectionist leader made the pledge in writing at a meeting held earlier this month in Vienna with Austrian Chancellor Bruno Kriesky and former West German Chancellor Willy Brandt, leader of the Socialist International Organization.

The pledge was a condition set by Kreisky for the meeting with Arafat, and Brandt also promised to help the P.L.O. gain observer status at Social International. This group represents primarily leaders of the West European Socialists.

In Jerusalem, the Israeli cabinet, conferring with hospitalized Prime Minister Menachem Begin by phone, rejected a U.S.-Soviet compromise plan to move an existing United Nations force into the Sinai Peninsula to replace another U.N. force whose term is about to expire.

The mandate, which has functioned as a buffer between Israeli and Egyptian units, expires this week. The Soviet Union has stated it would veto attempts to extend the mandate.

Prime Minister Begin was reported in improved condition at a Jerusalem hospital where he is being treated for a small blood clot in a brain artery. Deputy Prime Minister Yigael Yadin has assumed some of Begin's duties.

Official sources said that Prime Minster Menachem Begin's condition was a localized, mild thrombosis that caused problems with his balance and vision. He is improving with treatment of anti-coagulants.

Yadin presided over the cabinet session on Sunday, July 22nd, which among other business denounced the U.N. Security Council's resolution calling on Israel to halt settlement activity in occupied Arab territories.

7-24-79
Tension in Israel easing over West Bank Settlement policies
Jerusalem, Israel

The Israeli government, facing pressures from abroad and within, is easing it heavy-handed treatment of those who oppose its West Bank policies.

Prime Minister Menachem Begin remains inflexible on what he calls Israel's right to settle - and ultimately to claim sovereignty - in the former Jordanian territory west of the Jordan River that Israel calls by its biblical names, Judea and Samaria.

In recent weeks the government of Israel, for a variety of reasons, has made a series of moves that have relaxed tensions in the Arab populated areas.

Some of them are
The calling off of the trial about 50 Arabs from the Nablus sector hor holding an illegal demonstration June 17, although charges against them have not been dismissed. The defendants, including the Mayor of Nablus, were protesting the establishment of the Jewish settlement of Elon Moreh nearby.
Slowing down settlement activity on the West Bank. Following a Supreme Court order temporarily halting construction of the controversial settlement, no new projects have begun.

Reopening Birzeit University near Ramallah, which was closed indefinitely on May 2nd, because of anti-Israeli demonstrations by the Palestinian student body.

Permitting the East Jerusalem office of American Friends Service Committee to resume its work, continuing legal aid to the Palestinian Arabs.

As of the end of 1978, there had been 65 settlements established on the West Bank, including 21 started under the Begin government.

7-24-79
United States criticizes veto of peacekeeping force
Washington, D.C.

State Department spokesman, Hodding Carter used strong language, speaking on behalf of Secretary of State Cyrus Vance, in defending the proposal to use an expanded United Nations Truce Supervisory Organization to enforce the Egyptian-Israeli peace treaty, made no direct reference to Israel's rejection of the plan.

The United States and the Soviet Union agreed to a compromise plan that unarmed but experienced military observers of the truce organization could serve in place of the United Nations Emergency Force to supervise the Jewish nation's withdrawal from occupied territory under the treaty.

The American officials also condemned the Israeli attacks on the coast of Lebanon. The State Department charged that the latest raids were carried out at dusk, "When the roads were filled with motorists and people returning from the beaches and mountains," with mostly women and children the victims of the attacks.

Israel's ambassador, Ephraim Evron, stated there would be no change in his government's policy. "We shall do everything possible to protect the citizens fo our country. We shall hit the bases of terrorism wherever they are."

7-25-79
In Galilee the Jews are becoming a minority
Tel Aviv, Israel

The people living in the sparsely populated area north of Israel are asking for a share of the resources now being given to promotion of Jewish settlements on occupied Arab land.

Inhabitants of the hilly Galilee region have great difficulty attracting new settlers to live in the struggling townships not far from the Lebanese border.

For Galilee the problem of development and new settlement is urgent. Demographers, (Scientists that deal in births, deaths, and diseases), estimate that within a few years Jews will become a minority in the region. Many fear this could encourage the Israeli Arabs to press for the same kind of autonomy which Prime Minister Begin has proposed for the West Bank and Gaza.

Today, in certain areas of Galilee, Jews are outnumbered seven to one by various Arab communities including the "Druze" (a secret offshoot religion of Islam), Christian Arabs, Moslems and Bedouin tribesmen.

Residents of towns like Kiryat Shimona and Safad are protesting that the government is neglecting their needs for housing, industrial development, and improved services.

Galilee must compete for government funds with settlements that are being constructed on the West Bank, in the Gaza Strip, and in the Golan Heights, and following the evacuation of settlements in Sinai under the peace treaty with Egypt.

At a recent symposium on the future of this area, the mayor of Kiryat Shmoneh, Avraham Aloni, spoke on the attention to the needs of his town. "It has taken 25 years to establish a science-based industry in our town," he told participants. Hundreds of young residents have left for training in new skills, and are unlikely to return for lack of suitable job opportunities.

Galilee consists of mostly non-arable land because of its hilly topography. Industry is composed mainly of textile and food factories which provide lower than national average per capita income.

An inter-ministerial committee has been organized to improve the quality of life in order to attract newcomers to the Galilean area, but the wheels of government bureaucracy are slow and the people must be patient and diligent inn their efforts.

7-25-79
Israel's second phase of Sinai pullback
Jerusalem, Israel

Ignoring the mandate to expire of a U.N. buffer force, Israel withdrew all but a token number of troops from a desolate western sector of the Sinai Peninsula to be returned to Egypt.

When the Israeli flag is lowered, marking the second phase of the nation's pullout from the Sinai, the Jewish military will leave a 66 by 30 mile block of desert and mountains on schedule, withdrawing eastward to a point behind a new buffer zone in which there will be no neutral forces.

No concern was expressed by the absence of a peacekeeping unit. "There are no buffer forces between Egyptian and Israelis at El Arish, and we expect no problems in the extension of the Sinai, a military official stated.

A United Nations source said troops of the Emergency Force will stay in their bases, without patrolling or manning checkpoints, until they get their orders to leave from the Security Council.

The Israelis prefer an Egyptian-Israeli force to police the peace agreement and its series of staged withdrawals, which are to continue until the entire Sinai Peninsula has been returned to Egypt in 1981.

SECOND WITHDRAWAL - FROM WESTERN SINAI

Flag of Egypt raised over West Sinai
Bir Nasseb, Egypt

With U.N. troops conspicuously absent, Egypt hoisted its flag over this desert oasis and resumed control of a 75 mile-long strip of Sinai Peninsula territory controlled by Israel since the 1967 Mideast War.

Military bands from both countries played their national anthems and honor guards stood at attention under a blazing sun during a brief ceremony marking the second phase of the five-part Israeli withdrawal from the Sinai.

An Egyptian soldier kissed the red, white and black flag, then raised it over the Suez coastal town, which was decorated with banners and giant portraits of President Anwar Sadat.

The region's only residents are about 4000 Bedouin Arabs. Sheiks from a number of tribes observe the transfer ceremony from a platform erected for their presence.

This section of the Sinai is known as the "oil corridor" because Israel's Suez wells are located off this coast. Under treaty provisions, the State of Israel keeps the wells until November, 1979. Nearby are the Abu Rodeis oil fields, which Israel returned to Egypt in 1975.

Secretary General Kurt Waldheim announced that the mandate of the peacekeeping force, which had acted as a buffer between Egypt and Israel armies, was being allowed to lapse in accordance with the Security Council.

7-26-79
Zuheir Mohsen, military Chief of Operations of P.L.O. dead
Paris, France

The Chief of Military Operations of the Palestinian Liberation Organization, Zuheir Mohsen, died from a bullet in the head, shot at close range outside his apartment in the French Rivera city of Cannes.

The P.L.O. office in Paris issued a statement charging that "the assassination could only have been the work of Israeli agents."

No arrests have been made, and the shootings have been attributed to factional strife among the Palestinian activists or to Israeli counter-intelligence operatives.

Mohsen, who at 43, had been active in Palestinian politics and terrorist operations since the early 1950s, and represented the P.L.O. at the recent summit conference of the Organization of African Unity in Monrovia, Liberia.

The P.L.O. leader was born in the town of Tulkarem in the West Bank of the Jordan River, now occupied by Israel, and early in his political life he joined the leftist Baath Party. He was expelled from Jordan for political disruption in 1957 and went to the Persian Gulf area, where he lived first in Qatar and then Kuwait.

He joined the Saika, (thunderbolt) branch of the P.L.O. in Syria in 1968. Given Mohsen's background and his high position in the Palestine Liberation Organization, he could have been the victim of either Palestinian terrorists or Israeli agents. So far there have been no clues as to the identity of the assailants.

7-26-79
Moslems begin holy month of Ramadan
Beirut, Lebanon

The world's 600 million Moslems begin their holy month of Ramadan today with the Islamic world in unrest.

The Egyptian-Israeli peace pact, the Iranian revolution, religious unrest in Syria and a trend toward Islamic fundamentalism adds tension to the dawn to dust fasting.

Sheiks in Egypt, Saudi Arabia, Lebanon, and a dozen other Mideast countries scan the skies for the luminous crescent that ushers in the holiest month in the Moslem calendar.

At dawn on July 25th, thousands of Mussaharatis (awakeners) strolled through villages and cities beating drums and singing to awaken Moslems for the Sohour, (dawn meal).

Afterward, guns boomed, marking the beginning of the first day's fast, a total prohibition of food, drink, sex, tobacco, and evil.

Government-run radio stations in the Arab world have encouraged "Islamic Unity" this week, urging Moslems to heed lessons from Ramadan and observe the Koran injunction: "And hold ye fast to the cord of God, all of you, and break not loose from it."

It was during Ramadan, 1399 years ago, that the angel Gabriel descended to the Prophet Mohammed and imparted the wisdom of the Koran, according to Moslem belief.

Since then, fasting and unity in a perennial Jihad, (Holy war), has been required of all Moslems capable of them.

In Egypt, the (unity-Jihad) theme has been re-tailored to serve the objectives of peace with Israel.

In Syria, Iraq, Libya, Algeria, and among the Palestinians, the call for Jihad underscores the theme of (war preparedness and sacrifice.)

The oil rich countries of the Persian Gulf led by Saudi Arabia have been preaching a (middle of the road approach) to unite for peace with a view to eliminating the specter of war.

The Mideast hardliners have successfully ostracized Egypt from the Arab fold, and the world Islamic community has reluctantly rebuked the Egyptian-Israeli peace process.

7-27-79
Iranian troops sent in to defend the Strait of Hormuz

Iran will send troops to the Arabian Peninsula state of Oman to help protect the Hormuz Strait, and all international tanker traffic that passes through it. This was reported by the newspaper as Siyassah of Kuwait.

Iran's decision comes after receiving a U.S. warning of potential danger to tanker hijacks in the Strait. At one point it narrows to about 25 miles wide. The Iranian soldiers will be stationed alongside Omani military, but will be used only to defend the strategic waterway, to which ships pass to the Persian Gulf.

Meanwhile in Beirut, Lebanon, the assassination of the Palestinian leader, Zuheir Mohsen, has sent the P.L.O. leadership underground, and raised fears that the Israelis are bent on wiping them out. Yasser Arafat and his second level bureaucrats are attempting to gain worldwide respect.

Major Saad Haddad, a Christian director in Lebanon, supports Israel, and has established a colony, and a safe zone for the Jews, effectively denying Arab influence in Southern Lebanon.

In another area of the Middle East, in Tel Aviv, Israel, the Jewish State has agreed fo the Egyptian president, Anwar Sadat to visit a Kibbutz, a group of Jews, in the Northern port city of Haifa. He will learn about their cooperative way of life, said Shmuel Zeira, the manager of the Yagur Kibbutz, that is located seven miles east of Haifa.

7-29-79
If Begin is unable to govern, who will assume command?
Jerusalem, Israel

A coalition government, that Europe gave to democracy, is often held together by the will of its leader. In Israel, where sometimes the pendulum swings from one extreme to the other, it is the stern paternalistic Menachem Begin, their Prime Minster, who holds his Likud coalition together. The difficulty arises, because Begin is in the hospital recovering from a blood clot in the brain artery. This has limited his ability, especially his vision. Whether it is temporary or permanent has not been announced.

The Deputy Prime Minister, Yigael Yadin will fill in for him until he recovers. Under Israel's proportionate representation, each party, a dozen of significance, listed in the 120 member Knesset of Parliament, gets a number of seats according to its share of the popular vote. In the 1977 election, Begin's Likud coalition won 43 seats to the Labor Party's 32. The Prime Minister's own Herut Party and a Liberal Party joined forces to establish plurality, with 61 votes, the amount needed for a Knesset majority.

Since then, Begin has expanded his original base to a safe margin for his coalition. His Defense Minister was Ezer Weizman, elected by popular vote.

7-30-79
Peacekeeping troops begin to leave the Sinai
Tel Aviv, Israel

The first contingents of the U.N. peacekeeping force in the Sinai Peninsula will begin leaving the oil corridor of Israel, now a republic of Egypt. A treaty calls for the United Nations to monitor compliance with the Peace Accords. In the new talks, both the Egyptians and the Israelis can demonstrate an alternative to a United Nations Emergency Force.

Continued bloodshed was rampant as a Palestinian leader was killed, Zuheir Mohsen, in Nice, France, and a Lebanese businessman was jailed after 12 hours of questioning. The wife of Mohsen stated she has witnessed two men at the time fo the murder. One was what appeared to be a sportly dressed European, about 20 years of age; The other a slight mustachioed man having the likeness of an Arabian.

In another area, in Ankara, Turkey, four Palestinian guerillas were charged with killing two Turkish guards, and seizing 18 hostages at the Egyptian Embassy.

In the end of the two-day embassy siege, the Turkish government declared no concessions to the guerillas, who had demanded Turkish severance of ties with Egypt and Israel, and safe passage out of Turkey.

7-30-79
The United States promises to Israel

To induce Israel to give back the Sinai territory to Egypt lost in the 1967 War, President Carter put in writing on March 26, 1979, a United Nations commitment to exert its utmost effort to keep in place the U.N. forces now in the Middle East, who report to the Security Council and not to a dominated Arab Secretary General.

On June 18, 1979, the American President in Vienna, Austria, persuaded President Leonid Breznev of Russia to extend the U.N. Emergency Force past its deadline of July 24, 1979, however Breznev flatly refused.

Meanwhile the American pledge with the Jewish State, led by Carter, have offered to maintain acceptable multi-national peacekeeping forces for future withdrawals. A substitute observer group, smaller in size than the original 4000 Emergency Force, was proposed to Israel. It was refused by the Jewish Parliament. The Israeli Prime Minister, Menachem Begin, expressed a clear personal preference for a multi-national force outside the United Nations, mandated by U.S. resolution 242, in compliance with "The Camp David Accords."

In Jerusalem, The Israeli Cabinet voted to send their Foreign Minister, Moshe Dayan, to Washington over who will enforce the peace plan in the Sinai Peninsula.

7-30-79
Moderate Palestinians may join the peace treaty negotiations
Washington, D.C.

U.S. envoy to the Middle East, Robert Strauss, said he has received signals indicating that moderate Palestinians will soon join the Mideast talks. Strauss said, "We have to take some risks despite the danger of assassination by radical terrorist groups. There is a good chance we can lessen the pressure in the next 60 to 90 days."

The Mideast negotiators indicated the Palestinians would eventually have to take part in the peace process, but the P.L.O. must define its role more precisely, before the guerillas participate.

Meanwhile, in Israel, the Egyptian Defense Minister, Kamal Hassan Ali, arrived in Tel Aviv for a three day series of discussions with the Jewish Defense Minister, Ezer Weizman, on future withdrawals from the Sinai Peninsula. In welcoming his counterpart at the Ben Gurion Airport, the Israeli Defense Minister pointed out that the two portions of the Sinai have been transferred without incident, and that he thought that Israel and Egypt could handle the peacekeeping problems themselves.

7-31-79
Palestinians seek real peace in Israel

Israel's Deputy Defense Minister, Mordecai Zipori, describe his government's view of Palestinian autonomy, which differs from that of Egypt and the United States. He stated, "our forces will remain in the area, and Jewish settlements will continue to exist and develop, including a number of soon to be constructed clusters of bedroom communiti9es, that will improve the quality of life in congested Jerusalem and the coastal plains. Our government will not agree to a partnership with Jordan or an Independent Palestinian State."

Egypt considers an autonomy as an intermediate step to creation of a Palestinian state.

A wave of repressive measures has been instigated against the Palestinian population, unprecedented in 12 years of occupation. A recent example is the collective punishment of the residents of Nablus for a demonstration from the new settlements. The punishment limits the amount of produce the city can export to Jordan, and to allow no visitors of the city of Nablus from joining Arab family members.

The Palestinian problem, which has been the heart of the Middle East conflict for nearly 30 years, will plague the region until a solution is found that takes the wishes of the Palestinians to heart.

8-1-79
Violations of the Egyptian-Israeli peace at El Arish denied
Jerusalem, Israel

Egypt's defense minister denies charges of some Israel leaders that the Republic of Egypt is turning El Arish airport into a military field.

"Charges of a violation are not true," stated Kamal Hassan Ali at the airport news conference, as he was ending a three-day visit here. There are no combat aircraft here."

Some members of the Israeli cabinet have accused Egypt of infringements of the treaty at El Arish, the Mediterranean coastal city returned to Egypt in May, which is the first withdrawal of the jews in the Sinai.

It had been expected that the United Nations Emergency Force would act as a buffer between the two sides, and would monitor and report any deviations in the implementing of the peace accords, but this mandate has expired. Israel is unwilling to accept the Middle East Observer Force as a substitute. A few of the cabinet officials have criticized Ezer Weizman, Israel's Defense Minister, for his statements that the two countries can manage the implementation of the peace treaty without the U.N. or any other multi-national buffer force.

8-2-79
In the Sinai, the U.N. observer force keeps peace
Egypt - Checkpoint 560

The United Nations Emergency Force will gradually reduce its strength in the Sinai over the next several months, while the United States discusses over who will police the Egyptian-Israeli peace treaty. Unarmed United Nations observers are acting as watchdogs. They have no mandate to do the policing, however seeing a vacuum, they assumed peacekeeping duties as of July 25, 1979.
    The United States, the United Nations, and the Soviet Union, with Egypt, tentatively agreed to replace the United Nations Emergency Force with a smaller truce organization, but Israel declined in fear that the U.N. Secretary-General could withdraw that force.
    U-Thant's sudden pullout of the truce observers in 1967 precipitated the Middle East war, stated Major Jorgen Jensen of Denmark, who is the Deputy chief of the observer force. In Jerusalem, Prime Minister Menachem Begin is scheduled to be released from the hospital, and allowed to resume his duties after a week's rest, the doctor reported. Statements by Sylvan Lavie, chief of Hadassah hospital's neurology department, who heads a four doctor team treating Begin, said, "the Prime Minister has impaired vision, but it will not prevent him from assuming a full work load." The relatively slight vision of his right eye has been reduced, and in all probability will not affect his mental capacity in any way.

8-3-79
In what way would the United States assert its military power?

In the United States, the Middle East is a dilemma that will, by its diplomacy, resolve the complex problems. We are dependent on oil from the Persian Gulf. An urgent priority is to develop an American presence without involvement.
    In Iran, the Ayatollah Knomaini, who brought about the revolution that unseated the Shah, is unable to control radical groups. Political and military leaders in Tehran, and in the province oppose his rule.
    The upheaval in Iran causes neighboring countries, first of all Iraq, Saudi Arabia, and the Arab states, to be concerned. The leading members of their council are Moslem, of the Sunni sect.
    There are tensions between two ethnic groups; the Kurds in the northeast, and the Moslems of the Shiite sect, who dominated Bagdad.
    The resignation of the ailing President of Iraq, Ahmed Hassan Al-Bakr, has given command to his protegee, Saddam Hussein, and as head of The Revolutionary Council, he has instituted a purge of Shiites in his regime.
    Saudi Arabia and the Sheikdoms of the Gulf, (Kuwait, Quatar, Bahrain, The United Emirates, and Oman) are equally subject to developments in Iran. All are rich, conservative monarchies, dependent on foreign labor, and vulnerable to attack by warring nations.

The right kind of presence for America would appear to be a naval task force, assigned to a permanent station, based in the Indian Ocean. Carrier base planes, cruise missiles, landing equipment, and naval gunfire, could moderate any hostilities.

8-3-79
Tension developing between Israel and U.S. over Palestinian question
Jerusalem, Israel

Israeli officials adds to a growing list of disagreements between the Jewish state and the United States.
Sources in Israel denounce what they consider a pro-Palestinian stand in the United Nations and in negotiations aimed at setting up a system of autonomy for Arab residents of the Israeli-occupied West Bank of the Jordan River.
Deputy Prime Minister, Yigael Yadin stated, "Any change in the status of U.N. Security Council Resolutions 242 and 338 on the Middle East could be a serious problem for the peace process; even an implied change is unacceptable to Israel."
Resolution 242, voted after the 1967 Middle East War, calls for Israeli withdrawal from the occupied territories and affirms the rights of all nations to exist in the area of peace.
Resolution 338, voted after the 1973 War, calls for cease-fire and urges that the stipulations of Resolutions 242 be invoked.
Issues under discussion, not acceptable to Israel, are:
Establishment of an Arab legislative body with judicial and executive powers in the Israeli-occupied territories.
The incorporation of East Jerusalem Arabs in autonomy elections.
Extension of voting rights in elections to Palestinians living as refugees outside the occupied sectors.
Interior Minister of Israel, Yosef Burg, made no official comment on U.S. maneuvers in the United Nations, but circulated a copy of a 1975 agreement between the U.S. and Israel in which the United States opposes any moves in the Security Council Resolutions 242 and 338, "in ways incompatible with their original purpose."

8-4-79
Palestine Liberation Organization may except Israel's right to exist
Washington, D.C.

A member of the P.L.O. stated that it might be able to accept the language of a proposed resolution of the United Nations recognizing the right of Israel to exist.
Zahdi Tarazy, had of the observer delegation at the United Nations, said a "working paper is evolving that contains four main points calling for:
Affirmation of the Palestinian people's right of self determination.
Affirmation of their right to have a Palestinian homeland, with the specific reference to an "independent state."
Affirming the right of all Palestinians to return to their homeland, and their right to financial compensation, if they choose not to return.

Incorporating U.N. Resolution 242, which recognizes the right of Israel to live in peace and obliges Israel to withdraw from territories occupied in the 1967 war.

Tarazy said, "If the United States wants us to reaffirm Israel's right to exist, we'll consider that."

The Israelis are opposed to the idea of any new U.N. resolution on the Palestinians." Our acceptance of any resolution as the basis for future negotiations is necessary, because we are 50 percent of the conflict," and official member of the cabinet remarked.

8-4-79
Israel will establish a new airbase in the Negev Desert
Jerusalem, Israel

A bulldozer blade is poised to descend on the land and the lifestyle of about 6000 Bedouins in Israel.

Their camps and flocks lie in the 40,000 acres of Negev Desert in southern Israel on land the government states is urgently needed for a new airbase.

Construction of the base in to begin without any legal entanglements, employing a system of expropriation that the Bedouins and civil rights groups supporting them call "arbitrary, unjust, and anti-democratic."

The Bedouins are nomadic Arabs who have lived for centuries in the Negev, wandering from semi-permanent camps in search of grass for their sheep, goats, and camels. Some of them have used the same pasture land for centuries, but few have legal documents to prove ownership.

Earlier in the week, the Knesset, Israel's parliament, by a vote of 46-44 approved legislation that gives the state the right to expropriate land in the Negev by legislative rather than administrative action. Legislative action cannot be appealed in the courts.

As Israel withdraws from the Sinai under the terms of the Israeli-Egyptian peace treaty, the Negev will become the site of extensive new development. Two other air fields are planned for future relocation. New towns will be built to house military personnel being transferred from the Sinai.

It is the desire of the Israeli government that a peaceful solution may be reached with the Bedouins, and people of the area.

God's revelation in the Middle East through Isaiah

"Thus the Lord will make Himself known to Egypt, and the Egyptians will know the Lord in that day. They will even worship with sacrifice and offering, and will make a vow to the Lord and perform it . . . In that day there will be a highway from Egypt to Assyria, and the Assyrians will come into Egypt and the Egyptians into Assyria, and the Egyptians will worship with the Assyrians. In that day Israel will be the third party with Egypt and Assyria, a blessing in the midst of the earth, whom the Lord of hosts has blessed, saying , "Blessed is Egypt my people, and Assyria the work of My hands, and Israel my inheritance." Isaiah 19:21, 23-25

The prophet Isaiah revealed to us that this would happen, and now it is coming to pass. God is pouring out a spirit of revival, and there will be harmony among these nations. The Assyrians will travel to Egypt and the Egyptians will sojourn to Assyria developing trade, travel and a spirit of cooperation with each other.

In order for this to occur, Israel must open her borders to trade and commerce with her neighbors to the north and south. A highway will link these nations together and God will receive and bless them, saying "Blessed is Egypt, My people, and Assyria, the work of My hands, and Israel, My inheritance." Isaiah 19:25

The President of Egypt, Anwar Sadat is a deep, religious, spiritual man, who has a leader has made peace with Israel. The borders between Egypt and Israel are now opening, and a highway to allow the free movement between the two countries will be built.

To the north, a new nation is emerging. Syria and Iraq, the territory of ancient Assyria, have agreed to work with one another. They have been concerned with events in Iran, and have withdrawn from Marxism and the extreme Muslim position.

This is a testimony of the faithfulness fo God, a fulfillment of his prophecy.

8-6-79
Support for Iseral turned down by the Netherlands

Secret Israel mission seeking Dutch support for repeated incursions into Lebanon and Israel's limited autonomy for the West Bank Palestinians, has not come to fruition. Israel's Foreign Minister, Moshe Dayan, left the Hague in Germany on July 27, 1979, without gaining support from Israel's best friend. The abrupt turndown by the Netherlands points to the Jewish nation's political isolation.

This isolation is intensified by the widely criticized pounding of Lebanon by air and by sea.

The Dutch officials told Dayan that the Egyptian-Israeli peace treaty cannot stand by itself alone, but must be in congruence with participation with the arab states, especially Jordan and Saudi Arabia.

The same feeling is felt in Germany, despite the trauma of the Holocaust, that has influenced Bonn's policy toward Israel since 1945. Chancellor Helmut Schmidt, has warned Israel about risks of Europe losing arab oil, and also dangers of the Soviet Union penetrating into the pro-western Arab world, if the Palestinian question is not resolved.

The P.L.O. indicated they may accept Israel's right to exist if they would change their policy, end the U.S. embargo, and embark on serious negotiations with the Palestinians.

The P.L.O. leader, Yasser Arafat, visited Austria on July 6, 1979, and this has caused consternation with the Israeli prime minister, Menachem Begin.

Since the delay in the autonomy plan for the Palestinians is blocking a wider Mideast accord, it is imperative, that strong measures be taken, step by stem, to ensure peace.

Progress on Palestinian Autonomy made at Haifa, Isreawl
Haifa, Israel

Egyptian, Israeli, and U.S. representatives have made constructive progress in their fifth meeting on proposed Palestinian autonomy in the West Bank of the Jordan River and the Gaza Strip.

Egyptian and Israeli negotiators agreed to discuss election procedures at the first full negotiating session on August 6, 1979.

The agreement is termed a success for Israel and a sign that Egyptian-Israeli relations were progressing despite tension between Israel and the United States.

"Resolutions were adopted empowering the Foreign Minister Moshe Dayan to provide guidelines to the Israeli Ambassador, in the United States, for continuing the contacts he is conducting with the Administration there."

Israeli officials are concerned that the United States is assuming the role of "a partner" and not a participant at the talks. Ambassador Leonard, chief negotiator at the Haifa conference, of the United States, will clarify that the proposals of the American nation were only procedural in content.

Israel regards the Camp David agreements as a framework for the establishment of an administrative autonomy - but does not possess the legislative and judicial powers presented by the United States ambassador.

Haifa, Israel

Israel, Egypt, and the United States ended two days of talks on Palestinian autonomy with an agreement on an agenda for more discussions on election procedures, but no progress was made on extended issues of the Palestinians political future.

In Cairo, it was reported that Egyptian President Anwar Sadat would come to Haifa and hold further talks September 5, 1979, with Israeli Prime Minister Menachem Begin on the issue of the Palestinians - on which the two leaders failed to agree at their summit in July. Begin was released from a hospital in Jerusalem last week where he was recovering from a minor stroke.

The Camp David accords which led the Israeli-Egyptian peace treaty predicted "autonomy" for Palestinians living in territory occupied by Israel since the 1967 Mideast war, but Israel and Egypt have widely different views and are trying to work out ways to put the concept into effect.

Israel is adamant in rejecting an amendment that will change the wording of the U.N. Security Council resolutions 242 and 338, because it includes a declaration supporting Palestinian rights.

8-7-79

The representatives of the local Palestinians and of Jordan, former ruler of the West Bank, were invited to join the talks, but to date are boycotting them. "The door is still open," Khalil, the chief negotiator of Egypt stated, "whenever they come, the delegates will be willing to hear their point of view, and take them into consideration."

Although the agenda does not mention East Jerusalem, which Israel says is not to be considered part of the West Bank, it is possible that East Jerusalem can be discussed under the heading of "constituencies." No mention of parties, opposed by

Israel, may be considered under the heading of "conduct and limitations of campaigning, and political expression of elections.

8-8-79
Yemen

For many years, we, in the United States, have recognized the strategic importance of the Persian Gulf, and we have a deep interest in and are committed to the Security of Saudi Arabia. Saudi Arabia's stability is directly affected by the situation in neighboring Northern Yemen, and Arabian Republic, who supplies perhaps a million people to the Saudi work force. The focus of our initial assistance to the YAR, Yemen Arab Republic, is economic aid.

This aid is a catalyst to the Arab region. Since the restoration of relations in 1972, the United States has supplied over $75 million in development, with Saudi Arabia giving nearly one billion dollars in aid.

The Soviet Union has supported South Yemen, and given them military arms and equipment, as well as domestic needs. There is a serious imbalance in the military capabilities of North Yemen.

Last June, the President of North Yemen was assassinated, and the Arab League found South Yemen terrorists to be responsible. A few days later, a pro-faction Soviet regime ousted and killed the head of state of the South, People's Democratic Republic of Yemen.

Tension was in the air. The United States Deployment Force interceded. Planes, tanks, and armored personnel carriers supplied North Yemen, beating back an attack from the South Yemen forces. A cease fire, was ordered, emphasizing a withdrawal of the South Yemeni forces, which was accepted, after several skirmishes. A warning control system was set up to prevent further attacks.

The President of the United States also has ordered a carrier task force - headed by the aircraft carrier Constellation - from the seventh fleet into the western Indian Ocean to demonstrate our concern for the security of the Arab Peninsula.

These responses indicate the seriousness with which we view the danger of unwarranted attacks, and our determination to meet the legitimate defense needs of moderate governments in the Middle East. Our military responses are designed to reinforce the prospect for cessation of hostilities, withdrawal from occupied territories, and an end to violence in the Arabian Peninsula.

8-9-79
Shift in U.S. policy denied by Vance in Israel

Secretary of State Cyrus Vance denies that the United States is shifting policy against Israel to secure more oil from Arab producers.

He stated, "Our relationship with Israel is unshakable." The Israeli ambassador Ephraim Evron, standing at the side of the Secretary of State said, "Our basic friendship with the American nation prevails."

The subjects understood to have been discussed included the continuing negotiations over autonomy of the Israeli-occupied West Bank and the Gaza strip; a

United Nations resolution that could modify the future role of the Palestinians, and the linkage of oil and the possible changes in U.S. policy in the Middle East.

The meeting at the White House in Washington with the President of the United States was strained due to comments by the Foreign Minister of Israel who said, "There appears to be a real change in the Israeli-U.S. relationship," increased by the insistence that Saudi Arabia apply pressure on the signatories of the Egyptian-Israeli peace accords to create a Palestinian state on Israeli-occupied land.

Official sources in the State Department denied emphatically that there has been discussion between the Carter Administration and the Arab regime of Saudi Arabia in which oil production was linked to Israeli-Egyptian peace treaty negotiations.

Steps to normalization taken by Israel and Egypt
Jerusalem, Israel

Egypt, responding to heavy pressure from Israel, started to meet demands from her counterpart for steps toward normalization of relations.

Although full relations between Egypt and Israel are not to begin until the exchange of ambassadors next year, the two countries have agreed to take steps to speed up the process.

Some of these new developments that have occurred are:

On August 9, 1979, fifteen Egyptian university-level students from the Gaza Strip who had been studying in Egypt were allowed to cross the lines between Egyptian and Israeli forces in the Sinai unescorted. Previously, the Red Cross had brought such students over the lines.

Israeli officials were excited with the crossing, without incident, at a checkpoint on the Mediterranean coast near the city of El Arish. Israel had insisted that the border be opened without the presence of a third party, as was the practice when the two countries were technically in a state of war. There are about 6500 Gaza students studying in Egypt, and several thousand are reported wanting to return to the Gaza area for summer vacations.

Foreign Minister Moshe Dayan met with Egypt's Deputy Foreign Minister Butros Ghali, who was in Haifa, Israel for negotiations on autonomy for the Palestinian Arabs, stated that for full implementation of the treaty accords, the two nations should begin now to make transfers to back their words with action.

The Director General of Education for Gaza - employed by the military government in the formerly Egyptian-controlled enclave - made the transfer and all parties agreed on the compromise.

8-11-79
Pledge given Israel to block U.N. Palestinian modification
Tel Aviv, Israel

President Carter has promised Israel he will attempt to block a new United Nations move on Palestinian statehood, not agreed to by Israel. A top Egyptian diplomat suggested, however, that a fresh U.N. resolution may be the impetus to bring the Palestinians to the negotiating table.

Resolution 242, passed in 1967, could be amended or replaced in a Security Council debate beginning August 23, 1979. Israel objects to any tampering with the resolution, which refers to the Palestinians as a refugee problem, and fears that the United States might support a move to strengthen the position of the Palestinians for government control and eventual establishment of a state of their own.

This is a tender subject to the Israelis. They do not want the Palestine Liberation Organization, recognized a terrorist group who is dedicated to destroying the (Zionist), Jewish people, who migrated out of area surrounding Mount Zion in Israel, involved in the negotiations, in which their survival is at stake.

8-12-79
Fascination in Egypt

In Luxor, Egypt, a graceful sail of a felucca, a small sail boat, billowed in the cool evening breeze, as birds flew over the Nile River. A lonely kingfisher hovered above the water, then darted down to pluck a tiny perch fish near the surface.

In the modern town of Luxor, on the sight of the ancient Thebes, the feluccas are a pleasant change from the tortuous labor in the villages. Horse-drawn carriages are seen with tourists visiting the majestic 3500 year old stone temples, still beautifully carved with scenes of their gods and royalty. The kingdoms of the Pharaohs ruled the empire, when civilization was centered in the area, with sculptors and architects building structures that survive today.

In the Valley of the Kings, was the world's largest treasures in gold and precious stones. The walls of the tombs showed scenes of farm workers sowing and reaping grain, interspersed with graceful maidens dancing, and royal families boating in the Nile River.

Underground tombs include that the King Tutankamen, where the boy Pharaoh's tomb was discovered in 1922, encased in gold, alabaster, and precious jewels.

A cruise upriver brings you to the Aswan Dam. It was built during the reign of Gamal Nassar. At the Sudanese border is the Temple of Rameses, at Abu Simel, the most colossal of all Egypt's temples.

Ordered by Rameses, workman quarried over 200 feet into the sandstone cliffs, along the banks of the Nile, to create three inner chambers. A remarkable achievement. During the vernal and spring equinoxes, the sun's rays penetrate into the dark inner sanctuary, and they illuminate the statue of Rameses.

A fascinating city of Cairo along the Mediterranean is rich in ancient and modern culture. A mouski, (marketplace) of narrow lanes twist through old Cairo, is enticing with an array of copper and brass vases and trays, gold and silver jewelry; leather, perfumes and antiquities, and artifacts.

Cairo's mosques, the oldest is the ninth century "Ibn Toulun Mosque," recognized by its spiral minaret, along with the fourteenth century Mosque of Sultan Hassan are majestic in splendor, and demonstrate Arabic architecture in Egypt.

The Pyramids of Egypt, are less than ten miles from Cairo's Liberation Square, and Cheops, the largest, has stood in defiance of nature for more than 4500 years.

The Egyptians are polite and friendly, and they have a sense of humor compared to that of Americans. Peace with the nations of the world is a desire of their people with exchange and freedom.

8-13-79
Palestinian Liberation Organization demands statehood
Damascus, Syria

The Palestine Liberation Organization decided on a collision course with the United States, rejecting any United Nations resolution that does not explicitly recognize "Palestinian Rights" to an independent state.

The 57-member Palestine Central Council, meeting for nine hours with P.L.O. Chairman Yasser Arafat in attendance, agreed that U.S. hints of dialogue were merely "maneuvers" aimed at alienating P.L.O. radicals from moderates.

"The council decided to refuse any resolution that does not stipulate the need to establish an independent Palestinian state, and that the P.L.O. is the sole and legitimate representative of the people, and the Palestinians have the right of self-determination.

In Jerusalem, Prime Minister Menachem Begin presided over cabinet in his first day back at work after a mild thrombosis (heart) attack. Foreign Minister Moshe Dayan was also present after undergoing minor surgery on his vocal chord.

Deputy Prime Minister Yadin will fly to Washington, D.C. on August 15, 1979, to clarify Israel's position on the agenda meeting with the U.N. Security Council on August 23, and attempt to improve U.S. relations.

The confidence requires stabilization on few issues including:
Israeli use of American-made equipment in attacks in Lebanon.

United States sales of new tanks to Jordan.

Possible changes in United Nations Security Council Resolution 242 to recognize "Palestinian Rights."

Lack of U.S. support for establishing a multinational peacekeeping force to replace a phased-out U.N. presence in the Sinai Peninsula.

8-14-79
U.S. Peace Negotiator, Robert Strauss, returns to Israel and Egypt.

The United States will not submit to pressure in formulating Mideast peace proposals. Robert Strauss served notice to his conferees that the President, Jimmie Carter, and his administration, will oppose any change in the U.N. Security Council resolution that does not recognize Israel's right to exist within defensible borders.

Robert Strauss will fly to Israel for talks with Prime Minister, Menachem Begin, with a follow-up to Egypt, to confer with President Anwar Sadat. He said, "the feeling we reject or are insensitive to the legitimate rights of the Palestinians is equally false." The Security Council is to meet on August 23, 1979.

Ambassador Andrew Young was accused of a rendevous with the P.L.O. and this has brought harsh criticism from the Israelis. Although, it was reported, he violated a sacred trust, meeting with a P.L.O. official, Young said he did not reveal any secrets that would lead to problems for the United States. Ambassador Young resigned his post, rather than create a further embarrassment for America.

Schlesinger warns of Soviet Mideast entrenchment

Soviet military power continues to grow - most ominously in the form of increased strategic mobility and strength of its airborne divisions, "stated Schlesinger, who was once the director of the Central Intelligence Agency, departing from his post as Secretary of Energy."

The Secretary said, "We must maintain a strong military position in the Indian Ocean, and close surveillance on all shipping and air reconnaissance."

In Cairo, Egypt, U.S. Middle East envoy Robert Strauss told Israel that, despite its strenuous objections, the United States has tentatively decided to propose a new United Nations Security Council resolution aimed to bring Palestinians into the peace process.

The clear enunciation of American intentions on the resolution appears on the surface to increase the strain that has marked U.S.-Israeli relations since the dissolving the peacekeeping force in the buffer zone of the Sinai.

Under consideration in the Security Council of the United Nations is an Arab sponsored resolution that restates the basic formula of resolution 242, and adds to it a reference to Palestinian rights to self-determination, including a Palestinian state.

Strauss said that the United States might approve "rewording" that would give Palestinian Arabs and ability to determine their own future.

A key factor in the Palestinian boycott has been a lack of trust that the Americans will use its influence on Israel to produce an acceptable form of autonomy in the negotiations. Israel has been firm in demanding a limited self-administration on the West Bank and in Gaza, with the Israeli army retaining authority to promote Jewish settlements.

8-21-79
Black leaders seek accords with Israel and the Palestinians

The Southern Christian Leadership Conference of black supporters want Israeli endorsement of the rights of Palestinians, as well as Jews, to a national home, and Palestinian acceptance of Israel's right to exist within defensible borders.

Campaigning for Israeli-Palestinian reapprochment in the wake of Ambassador Young's resignation, officials of the SCLC met with Ambassador Yehuda Blum of Israel at his mission.

The Rev. Joseph E. Lowery, SCLC president, lead a party of 12 into the Israeli mission, after meeting with representatives of the Palestine Liberation Organization, stated the "Goal of mutual acceptance of a Palestinian Homeland, and Israeli Nationhood."

The leader of the SCLC communicated with Zendi Terzi, the P.L.O. observer in the United Nations, for support for the human rights of all Palestinians, including the right of self-determination. Mr. Lowery urged Chairman Yasser Arafat to "give consideration to the recognition of Israel as a nation, whereby steps can be taken that would lead to peace and reconciliation."

The Ambassador of the United Nations resignation was a catalyst in which the Southern Christian Leadership is attempting to bring the Israelis and the Palestinians together.

8-23-79
Austrian Chancellor says contacts with U.S.-P.L.O. will continue

Contacts between Western governments and the Palestine Liberation Organization will "inevitably" continue, Bruno Kreisky of Austria stated in an interview with reporters in Vienna, but it is unlikely that Austria will be used for secret rendezvous.

The United States Ambassador to Austria, Milton A. Wolf, who met with ranking representatives of the P.L.O., was unavailable for comment.

Kreisky, who welcomed Yasser Arafat, head of the guerilla organization, last month was instrumental in bringing Wolf together with an aide to Arafat, Issa Sartawi, on June 12, of this year.

The encounter took place aboard a chartered aircraft on a flight from Paris to Vienna. The Ambassador to Vienna was a former Cleveland contractor and successful fund raiser for the Democratic party and a staunch supporter for Jewish causes.

Meanwhile, in Jordan in the Middle East, Yasser Arafat and King Hussein announced agreement on "practical steps" toward more cooperation on unity to resist the policies of Israel in setting up Jewish settlements on occupied Arab territories.

In 1970, Hussein defeated the terrorist organization in a bloody coup, and ostracized them from Jordan in a campaign that cost the lives of over 25,000 Palestinians. The guerillas have unsuccessfully requested a chance to return to Jordan to resume cross-border raids against Israel.

8-24-79
Terzi of the P.L.O. invited to sit in with the Security Council
United Nations

When the United States Ambassador Andrew Young opened the 2,164 meeting of the Security Council on August 23, 1979, and invited the observer from the Palestine Liberation Organization to take a seat in the chamber, no on offered a protest.

Less than four years ago, however, the presence of a P.L.O. representative at Security Council debates was bitterly opposed by Young's predecessor, Daniel Patrick Moynihan. Twelve members of the fifteen nation body voted to admit a Palestine Liberation Organization spokesman to debate on the Mideast. America voted in opposition and Britain, France and Italy abstained. The United States veto power, conclusive in substantive matters, had no effect in a procedural protocol such as the admission of a speaker.

Farouk Kaddoumi, the senior P.L.O. official called for recognition of a Palestinian Arab state in 1976, a demand that has been voiced with growing insistence by Arab delegates ever since.

The General Assembly had invited the guerilla group to sit in on its debates two years earlier, starting with the appearance of the terrorist leader, Yasser Arafat, in November of 1974. While thousands of pro-Israel demonstrators protesting outside the United Nations headquarters, Arafat, wearing a pistol, declared from the assembly rostrum that he "carried both an olive branch and a freedom fighter's gun." The implication was that unless a Palestinian state were created, he would continue warfare against Israel.

Shortly afterward, the Arab delegates proposed that the P.L.O. be given the status of an official observer at the United Nations. This was granted in 1975. Observer status is short of full membership, permitting the representatives to speak and participate in the Assembly and the Security Council, but without a vote.

The permanent observer of the Palestine Liberation Organization has been Zehdi Labib Terzi, a native of Jerusalem, who travels on a Tunisian passport. He is a civil servant in Palestine, the government of the British mandate, and he became a Palestinian militant when the mandate ended in 1948 when Palestine was divided between Israel and Jordan.

8-26-79
The Arab oil dependency in the United States is real

Our best protection against being both closed down for want of energy and bankrupted by its cost is to steadily increase our energy at home until we break the oil cartel by reducing our imports. This is a task that America - with its vast natural resources, technological competence, public spirit and can-do mentality has failed to accomplish.

The cities in the United States are struggling to stave off decay and bankruptcy, while the Middle East is laughing by building large metropolitan complexes in the desert sands.

The North American nation has become enslaved to a group of Arab rulers only a generation removed from tribal feudalism.

In the Arab world there has been a yearning for renaissance, a striving toward unity that the Arabs call (Nahda). A growing undercurrent for a generation, today Nahda is bursting through the dams and divisions that have walled it in, sweeping the Islamic crescent from Afghanistan to Morocco. Its "spirit is anti-Western, its soul anti-Israel."

The great prophet of Nadha - and of the contemporary relationship between Islam and the West - was Gamal Nasser, who rose to power in Egypt in the reaction against Israel's victory in the 1948-49 war. Preaching the unification of the Arab world, the crushing of Israel, and the expropriation of what the industrial countries had taken from Islam, Nasser mobilized a new Arab generation with vision for utopia.

Nasser's challenge to the nations of the world in the industrial society became real in 1956 when he closed down the Suez Canal. His disciples, the radical Arabs, are today the driving force of aggressive Islam. Foremost among them is Libya's Colonel Muammar Qaddafi - picturesque, puritanical, intolerant, a devotee of purposeful suffering. As he would close down Tripoli's bars or sever a hand in theft, so he would sacrifice wealth, safety, convenience, pleasure, life itself - to pursue "Nahda." His tempestuous 10 year career exemplifies the vulnerability of the mighty, cautious industrial nations before the objective of the powerful zealot.

8-26-79

Reversing the traditional Arab request for more oil production to increase revenue, Khadafi threatens to cut off the supply altogether if his demands for greater profits are not met. People who have lived for 5000 years without petroleum, are able to live many more years without it.

Early in 1973, in Saudi Arabia, King Faisal attempted to pressure the United States to reverse its Mideast policy, and abandon Israel, using oil as their weapon. The U.S. diplomatically refused to become embroiled in the controversy.

In the past, America was not dependent on imported oil. Only about 5% was shipped to the United States. The incomparable discovery of the black gold in Saudi Arabia made King Fasial supreme ruler of the oil kingdom. The Arab states formed a "Cartel" to raise the price of oil to what the world would accept, and they grew in power and strength at each meeting of the Cartel.

The oil embargo of 1973 was a sign for the Cartel to quadruple the price of the black gold.

Although prices were raised periodically, other nations began resisting buying oil, and some started using synthetic fuels, and conserved, and the tide of dependency fell to a low level. The Cartel cut back on their prices to prevent a mass exodus, nations boycotting the Arab Cartel called "OPEC."

Countries will resist a monopoly, and the forces of evil. When they are threatened, they will find a way to escape, with inventive minds finding a substitute to take the place of evil conspirers.

8-27-79
Cease fire in Lebanon temporary
Beirut, Lebanon

Renewed artillery duels broke out on south Lebanon hours after the United Nations announced a dawn cease-fire between Palestinian guerillas and Lebanese Christian forces aligned with Israel. Lebanon's right-wing Phalange radio said U.N. peacekeepers were trying to salvage the shattered truce even as shells rained down on the ancient port of Tyre, the market town of Nabatiyeh, and six other locations in the embattled region near the southern frontier with Israel.

The Phalange radio stated that the Palestinians and their leftist allies shelled Israeli border regions and the Lebanese right-wing Christian strong-hold of Marjayoun. Major Saad Haddad, commander of Israeli-backed Christian military said, "The shelling was very heavy and quick from many guns at the same time."

In Jerusalem, a spokesman for Prime Minister Menachem Begin's government said Israel would continue to strike at Palestinian terrorists based in southern Lebanon despite American objections to Israeli raids north of the border. Arieh Naor, cabinet secretary in the Jewish government, stated that "Israel was launching counterattacks to prevent civilian casualties."

Israel's military command has consistently denied taking part in the barrages that wracked the areas along the countries borders, but it returned fire after Soviet-made Katyusha rockets fell on Northern Israeli settlements on August 25, 1979.

8-23-8-79
Policy to invite the P.L.O. in negotiations negative

The policy to include the Palestinian Liberation Organization in the United Nations has not received the desired results - to have them agree in writing to recognize the State of Israel, and their right to exist.

The reason the initiative could not succeed lies in the basic political scene in the Middle East. This area is dominated by the Egyptian-Israeli peace accords, which as set in motion an ongoing process of political, diplomatic, and commercial ties.

Continuous progress in one area - achieving autonomy for the Palestinian Arabs - has been slow. The Israelis and the Egyptians have found it difficult to define their version of autonomy. The local Arabs, in keeping with the contention of the P.L.O. that the treaty sells out their rights, have boycotted the negotiations.

Still the talks continue. Some Palestinians may join the talks. An offer of territory on the West Bank of the Jordan River might prompt King Hussein to enter the negotiations as a surrogate for the Palestinians. These possibilities depend less on Israel and Egypt than on the staying power of the Arabs banded together against the peace treaty in the "rejectionist front."

The "rejectionist front" has a new incentive to continue its challenge to Israel and Egypt by using guerilla tactics to convince Saudi Arabia and the Mideast oil kingdoms that the Palestinian Liberation Organization must be a part of any Arab coalition for freedom and right to govern their own destiny.

8-29-79
Lebanese villagers caught in a crossfire
Hasbaya, Lebanon

Living on an international firing range is not easy. Bullets, artillery shells, and Jet fighters fly overhead daily, yet this village and other southeast Lebanon people manage to carry on. Within 15 miles of the city, are no fewer than 10 foreign armies, private militia groups. A short distance to the north, on a road lined with olive trees is a checkpoint of the Syrian peacekeeping force stationed in Lebanon. The Israeli occupied Golan Heights is only half an hour driving away.

Major Saad Haddad's Christian Militia, who is allied with Israel , occupies the town of Marjayoun, 6 miles to the west. Between them and Hasbaya, are Nepalese and Norwegian peacekeeping forces of the United Nations.

Bands of Palestinian guerillas live in the village, or camp in the surrounding hills and valleys. People here pray to Allah, faithfully to protect them from intruders. Hasbaya is heavily populated with members of the "Druze" religion, who are loyal to the Jewish State.

The guerilla commandos are a normal feature in the village. They frequent cafes, and their jeeps are often met on winding roads, and posters and slogans cover most of available wall space. Although sympathetic to the guerillas, the villagers realize the deadly undeclared war they bring. The "Fatah," or guerilla headquarters has been established in Hasbaya, and the people are at their mercy.

8-30-79
Jewish Foreign Minister, Moshe Dayan, meets P.L.O. sympathizer
Jerusalem, Israel

Israel Foreign Minister Moshe Dayan held a two-hour meeting with a prominent supporter of the Palestine Liberation Organization in the Israeli-occupied Gaza Strip.

Dayan went to Gaza to meet with Hader Abdul Shafi, a physician and outspoken sympathizer of the P.L.O., which opposes the state of Israel.

Dayan stated that the meeting was conceived in an effort to understand the Arab revolutionaries, and to hear their ideas of co-existence with the Jewish people.

Meanwhile, Ambassador Young of the United States in his last official recognition as chairman of the Security Council of the United Nations, rebuked Israel for its preemptive bombardment of Palestinian targets in Lebanon equating the attacks with the terrorism they are designed to quell. They are painfully at variance with the values Israel has traditionally espoused.

Young said, "It is important to assure that the legitimate rights of the Palestinians are included in a comprehensive settlement, but their objectives cannot be achieved through violence and terrorism."

8-31-79
Moral responsibility rests with Israel on raids in Lebanon

There is no evading the fact that a great many noncombatants, including children and women, have been killed and wounded in southern Lebanon in recent months by Israeli land, air and naval bombardment. The burden of these assaults have been prompted by the Palestine Liberation Organization's use of Lebanon as a launching base for terrorist raids into Israel that have taken the lives of many civilians. The political spokesmen of the two sides debate the morality of cause and effect of these actions. There is no morality, however, in killing and maiming the innocent.

The Israeli government candidly acknowledges that the purpose of its assaults is preemptive, to keep the radical Arabs off balance and prevent it from mounting terrorist operations across the border, or by sea. The objective has not been without success. Terrorist bombs continue from time to time to explode in Israeli cities, but since the intensified strikes began there has no Palestine Liberation Organization infiltration from Lebanon into Israel.

The right of Israel to protect itself against marauders operating from neighboring territory is not in question. The government of Lebanon has been unable to control the P.L.O. The 30,000-man Syrian army in Lebanon or the United Nations peacekeeping force have not prevented the terrorist attacks. Israel is not obligated to wait until the gunmen are within its borders before acting.

The tragedy lies in the method. High explosives are not precision weapons. Civilians have been among its victims. An Israeli bomb or artillery shill that lands off target in Lebanon can have the same consequences as a machine gun fired by a P.L.O. radical into a schoolhouse or bus. It is the outcome, and not the intent, that must be considered.

In the absence of the P.L.O.'s giving up southern Lebanon as a base for terrorist activities, or in the absence of other forces preventing it from doing so, can Israel put its civilian population at risk by halting its strikes? It is a moral and political problem, and the ultimate responsibility for what has been happening falls heavily on the Palestine Liberation Organization. The cycle of terror started with the Arab radical group, and it can end it whenever they plan to negotiate seriously, recognizing that Israel has a right to live as a free nation within defensible borders.

Palestinian Liberation Organization proclaims moderate negotiating position.
Beirut, Lebanon

Encouraged by a windfall of respectability after the resignation of Ambassador Andrew Young of the United States, the Palestine Liberation Organization has, for the moment, forgotten guerilla war against Israel, and agreed that terrorist tactics will not bring a moderation of the refugee problem.

P.L.O. Chairman, Yasser Arafat, is openly seeking a dialogue with the American nation, and his aides say he is prepared to tacitly recognize Israel in exchange for a United States commitment to support a Palestinian homeland.

A ranking member of Arafat's "Fatah" group stated that "sooner or later we will have to recognize Israel," but we will have to have the right terms."

The Palestinian radical organization has veered toward moderation before, only to return to its more familiar rhetoric and the use of force.

The resignation of the American ambassador has been a great victory for the refugees. The Palestinian cause is now an American domestic issue.

In Western Europe, the P.L.O.'s diplomatic fortunes are higher then ever before. Turkey has granted the guerillas diplomatic recognition and Greece may soon follow. The Palestinians are working on more official contacts with France, Great Britain, and West Germany.

The military action against Israel has almost been eliminated by the Jewish State's constant shelling of the south Lebanon refugee camps that served as the guerilla bases. The United Nations who guard the buffer zone between the Palestinians and the Israeli-controlled southern border states that the P.L.O. has been unable to mount anything but "symbolic" attacks for months.

9-3-79
Anwar Sadat of Egypt to visit Haifa, Israel

Anwar Sadat will make his third visit to Israel this week, sailing aboard the Egyptian presidential yacht to Haifa for a two day "Peace Festival" and a summit with Prime Minister Menachem Begin on the tough issues facing their peace drive.

The President of Egypt is scheduled to arrive at the northern Israeli port city of September 4, 1979. He will find Haifa decked out in black-white-and-red Egyptian flags, and will meet municipal leaders anxious to point out good relations between its mixed population of Arabs and Jews.

The Israelis have also arranged a special program for Jihan Sadat, the Egyptian leaders' wife, who will be making her first visit to Israel. Officials stated that a program will be tailored to her special interests in physical rehabilitation and children's hospitals.

Beyond the pageantry, Sadat and Begin, who have met several times since the signing of the accords at Camp David, Maryland, in the United States, have some serious issues to discuss at a luxury hotel atop Mount Carmel, overlooking the Mediterranean port.

"There will be time to discuss everything," an Israeli official said of the two working sessions scheduled before Sadat's departure.

Problems have been piling up since the Israeli Prime Minister and the President of Egypt met in Alexandria in July. Little progress has been made in the talks on Palestinians autonomy.

Besides the autonomy discussion, the informal agenda is crowded with such topics as Egyptian oil sales to Israel, continued normalization of relations, an early Israeli withdrawal from the Mount Sinai sector of the Sinai Peninsula.

Israel and Egypt were both disturbed with the abortive attempt of the Carter administration to write Palestinian rights in the basic United Nations Security Council guidelines for peace in the Middle East. Egypt feared the plan might torpedo the autonomy talks, while the Israelis claimed it represented a U.S. policy shift toward the Arabs. The tough decisions still remain, including an answer of Palestinian home rule.

9-4-79
Jews victimized by blacks and the Palestine Liberation Organization

Selected black leaders are now negotiating with the Palestine Liberation Organization. There is apparent resentment and hostility that is dividing blacks from Jewish minorities.

Jewish success in every walk of life mocks the excuse of victimhood. Most recently, blacks were slaves, Jews were victims from programs, limited civil rights and Nazi concentration camps.

There are three features about the P.L.O. that make it improbable for the State Department, Andrew Young, Ambassador to the United Nations, who tendered his resignation, or the black Southern Leadership Conference, pledged to non-violence, to force Israel to negotiate with the terrorists.

No state should be coerced to negotiate with a body sworn to annihilate it. Survival is not subject to negotiation.

The Palestine Liberation Organization is not a representative body or even a shadow government

The P.L.O. is not an independent force. It has no financial base of its own. Various foreign nations fund it.

Among the 100 million political refugees since World War II, the Palestinians have been refused welcome by those who say they are friends and united kin. They have been deliberately kept by Arab nations in refugee camps. Jordan controlled the West Bank from 1948 to 1967 and did not set up a Palestinian state.

Many Arabs import hundreds of thousands of workers. The Middle East has plenty of land, much of it potentially fertile. Why aren't the Palestinians welcome? Jordan is their homeland.

It is not in the interest of human rights or of the United States to empower the P.L.O. The P.L.O. is a puppet organization hostile to Israel's existence.

9-4-79
Sadat arrives in Haifa, Israel
Haifa, Israel

Egypt's Anwar Sadat sailed into Haifa harbor aboard a presidential yacht today for his first meeting with Israeli Prime Minister Menachem Begin in two months, and he declared Egypt has a "moral commitment" to resolve the Palestinian issue. Sadat stated he would insist on a comprehensive settlement by the end of the year.

Setting an optimistic and friendly greeting from the outset, the Egyptian leader told a cheering crowd of Israelis that he regarded Begin as "my friend."

Israeli jet fighters saluted the president of Egypt's 475 foot-long yacht Horreya, with a fly-over as it entered the breakwater and docked, escorted by Israeli and Egyptian warships.

Balloons and doves were released into the sky as the Egyptian president spoke a welcoming ceremony. Thousands of schoolchildren lined the streets and others perched on rooftops to catch a glimpse of Sadat as he rode through the streets festooned with Egyptian and Israeli flags.

Israel's president, Yitzhak Navon, described Sadat's visit as "an additional link in the golden chain of peace."

The President of Egypt responded, "We have to consolidate the gains we have made on the road to peace." Sadat affirmed that Egypt felt a strong commitment to solve the problem of the Palestinian people . . . a moral commitment to which we will remain faithful.

9-5-79
Arab cause supported by Sadat

Egyptian President Anwar Sadat met with Prime Minster Menachem Begin for a new round of summitry and declared, "The recognition of Palestinian rights is the only guarantee for co-existence in the Middle East.

"The realization of the legitimate rights of the Palestinian people is not incompatible with Israeli interests," Sadat told a state dinner audience, after his first formal session with Begin.

The President of Egypt said his goal was a comprehensive Mideast, not a "tactical accommodation with Israel."

An advisor to Sadat said, "It is almost certain the result of the Haifa discussions would entertain a three-sided summit with President Carter of the United States in November."

The collaboration produced a tentative agreement on replacing a United Nations peacekeeping force in the Sinai Peninsula with a joint Israeli-Egyptian patrol.

In the meantime, Israel's Foreign Minister, Moshe Dayan, revealed to the people of Israel that he plans to have additional meetings with Palestinian leaders in the West Bank of the Jordan River and the Gaza Strip. Defending his previous meetings with supporters of the Palestine Liberation Organization, he stated, "There is a distinction between sympathizers and representatives." He endorsed the continued Israeli refusal to speak to the P.L.O. directly because of its murder of civilians and its persistent call for the destruction of Israel.

9-5-79
Black reversal linked to approval of P.L.O.

Amid the heated controversy generated by the resignation of Andrew Young as the United Nation's delegate, some black people have suddenly embraced the Palestine Liberation Organization.

A few black leaders have turned to the P.L.O. in an effort to act as conciliators between Israeli and the Palestinians. Other blacks are demonstrating their independence from official United States policy.

Regardless of motivation, black people and minorities must understand the moral issued involved here.

There are monumental risks which will cause division of the people, forfeiture of moral prestige, and the noble tradition of non-violence, and unwitting accomplices of an organization committed to the destruction of Israel - indeed of the Jewish people.

The history of the Palestine Liberation Organization, from the day of its creation has not uttered a word in support of non-violent resistence, peaceful relations between Israelis and Palestinians, or a political solution to the complex problems in the Middle East.

By contrast, black leaders in America, especially central figures like Dr. Martin Luther King and Phillip Randolph, never once in the long history of the civil rights struggle countenanced violence or terrorism.

The Palestine Liberation Organization espouses violence, hatred, and racism. It scorns reconciliation.

Any link with the P.L.O., no matter how limited, would give legitimacy and tacit approval to the rule of the gun.

9-6-79
United States is committed to the articles of Resolution 242

The resignation of U.S. Ambassador, Andrew Young, over his Palestine Liberation Organization contact, has caused serious undermining of consistency in our Foreign Policy.

Security Council Resolution 242 properly is the basic commitment of the United States and all nations genuinely seeing peace in the area of the Middle East. It is equally balanced between "withdrawal" of Israeli forces from territories "occupied" in the 1967 War, and respect for the acknowledgment of the sovereignty, integrity, and political independence of nations rights, to live in peace within recognized boundaries, free from all threats or acts of force.

The Palestinians are not excluded under the present arrangement, from determining the ultimate status of the West Bank and the Gaza Strip. The Camp David Accords states that there will be a permanent solution for government of the Palestinian people. The Palestinian leaders will have a voice in the negotiations regarding the West Bank cities.

This can be accomplished by giving consideration to the 24 Mayors and principals of the towns and cities of the West Bank, that were duly elected under the provisions of Jordanian Law, that is still administered there.

Hussein criticizes Egypt, Israel accords
Havana, Cuba

Jordan's King Hussein attacked Egypt and the Camp David accords at the sixth summit of non-aligned nations, apparently diminishing prospects that Jordan may be drawn into the agreement.

Hussein's criticism of Egypt came more in sorrow than in anger, but his speech was interpreted as a clear signal that Jordan would remain solidly aligned with the other Arab countries against Camp David and a separate Egyptian-Israeli peace treaty.

In Haifa, Israel, where Egyptian President Anwar Sadat and Israeli Prime Minister Menachem Begin are continuing their peace efforts, official sources of Sadat predicted that Hussein would join the peace negotiations this year.

In his speech with the non-aligned nations, the King of Jordan declared: "The whole Arab nation stands with the Palestinian people and its right of self-determination and national ingathering and with the right of repatriation for those who were forced out of their homeland.

The Arab nation finds no possible solution outside complete Israeli withdrawal from all occupied Arab territories and the exercise of the Palestinian people of the right of free self-determination on their national soil.

Jordan shares deep pain at the departure of the Egyptian leadership from common national feelings, interests, and commitments.

9-9-79
Genuine affection manifested between family of Sadat and Begin
Haifa, Israel

Egyptian President Anwar Sadat made a simple gesture last week that may be more significant than anything he and Israeli Prime Minister Menachem Begin achieved in their summit meetings.

Although it went largely unremarked here and in the rest of the world, the presence of Mrs. Sadat and their youngest daughter cemented what increasingly appears to be Sadat's genuine conviction that the Jews, technically enemies of Egypt less than six months ago, are now members of a family, with binding interests. It was no accident that both the Egyptian President and his wife addressed their hosts and hostesses in Haifa, Israel as cousins.

In his gestures and pronouncements the President of Egypt made it clear that Israeli-Egyptian friendship is here to stay, no matter how difficult the differences remain, or how vigorously other Arabs may object. Sadat has offered to pipe water from the Nile River across the Sinai desert into Israel's Negev Desert.

Although the Egyptian President stressed the importance of solving the questions of autonomy and Jerusalem, he did it without harsh words, and he appeared completely relaxed about the outcome.

In addressing the Jewish audience on the morning of his departure, Sadat angrily criticized his Arab opponents and described case by case the disarray that has overtaken the so-called rejectionist states since the gathering at Bagdad in late March 1979, condemning the President of Egypt's overtures.

The meeting in Haifa was truly a performance designed to underline to the rest of the Arab world that his course of peace and comradeship with Israel will not change.

9-10-79
Strauss confident Palestinian autonomy will be successful
Cairo, Egypt

United States envoy Robert Strauss said he was "absolutely confident" that Israeli-Egyptian negotiations on Palestinian autonomy will be successful.

The optimistic appraisal was made after briefing Egyptian President Anwar Sadat on his summit meeting with Prime Minister Menachem Begin.

After a 90 minute session with Sadat, Strauss said none of his previous trips to Egypt "has been as constructive, non as informative, none as positive or encouraging as his latest with the leader of the Arab Republic."

The U.S. mediator, on his third visit to Egypt, met with Sadat in a villa across from the Great Pyramid.

The peace process, started by three courageous leaders, Sadat, Begin, and Carter, will conclude successfully, but it will be a long and tedious road with many difficult problems ahead.

Sadat stated that the United States should begin a dialogue with the P.L.O., but assurances must be granted in writing that the radical organization will recognize that Israel will be given national status in world affairs, and accepted by the United Nations.

Meanwhile Israeli Foreign Minister, Moshe Dayan, arrived in Bonn, Germany for a three day tour seeking assurances that West Germany is not shifting toward the Arab position in the Middle East. There have been reports that the Bonn government was moving closer to Arab demands for Palestinian statehood, although this is officially denied.

9-10-79
Independence from major power bloc affirmed by non-aligned nations
Havana, Cuba

The non-aligned summit conference ended with the reaffirmation of the movement's independence from major power countries after a bitter battle over a proposal to suspend Egypt because of its peace treaty with Israel.

In a marathon session, the summit left Egypt's status unchanged, but called into question its future membership in the 95-member movement, that Cairo help establish 18 years ago.

P.L.O. leader Yasser Arafat said, "It was enough," that the delegates condemned the Israeli-Egyptian peace accords without expelling Egypt from the non-aligned movement.

Conference sources stated there was a debate between the Arabs and a group of 15 largely pro-Western African states led by Liberia and Senegal. The Africans argued that a member nation should not be suspended for waging peace. Underlying the dispute was growing resentment from the poorer oil-consuming nations in Africa over higher prices imposed by the Arab led cartel.

A pledge from an oil-rich state made a compromise with the African states possible.

The commission will reconvene in New Delhi, India, in 1981.

9-11-79
American Lebanese driven away by shelling
Tibnin, Lebanon

Around a mud-brown village atop a rocky southern Lebanon hill, Mike Kassem is known as - the last of the Americans.

More than a hundred United States citizens have emigrated to America, fleeing because of guerilla raids and artillery barrages.

Tibnin had more than 8000 inhabitants before Israel and the Palestinian terrorists turned the scrubby hills and arid tobacco fields into a battleground.

Since the Israeli invasion in March 1978, Tibnin and a dozen other villages have been occupied by U.N. peacekeeping troops. To the south, along the Israeli border, is a five-mile deep buffer zone held by the militia-men of Major Saad Haddad, a renegade Lebanese officer who hwas allied himself with Israel. To the West and North is land held by the Palestinians and their leftist Lebanese comrades

The United Nations forces have been caught in the middle - shelled by Haddad's contingent, kidnaped by radical Palestinians, and powerless to halt Israel's "preventive attacks."

Official sources said it was clear that the Palestinians have taken significant losses in the hit and run war, and are incapable - at least for the moment - of mounting any far reaching attacks on Haddad's border zone or on northern Israel.

The result has been the exodus of Lebanese civilians. Thousands have fled to Sidon and Beirut, where they are building new refugee camps of tin-roofed huts and squatting in unoccupied houses and apartments.

9-12-79
Strauss meets with West Bank Arab Mayor
Jerusalem, Israel

Special Middle East Ambassador Robert Strauss of the United States met with Israeli leaders and discussed ways to speed up the Palestinian autonomy talks. He later visited with a prominent West Bank Arab.

Strauss said his meeting with Bethlehem Mayor, Elias Freij concerned suggestions to form a federation between the West Bank of the Jordan River and Jordan. It was the first meeting by an American official of Strauss' standing with a West Bank leader in the area.

Before the Camp David summit, Freij was regarded by the Israeli government as a moderate major, but he hardened his position dramatically last fall, becoming one of the treaty's most outspoken critics, predicting no Palestinian political figure would participate in the autonomy discussions.

Earlier today, Freij, a Christian who was re-elected Mayor of Bethlehem in 1976 stated, "I do not think the people will accept autonomy," but they might accept a federation with Jordan. The Mayor has maintained close ties since Jordan lost control of the West Bank in the 1967 Six-Day War.

The Jordanian monarch, King Hussein, has officially supported the idea of an independent Palestinian state since the Arab summit conference in Rabat, Morocco, in 1974. A federation has no support of Jordanian officials.

U.S. envoy to Middle East accelerates autonomy talks
Jerusalem, Israel

Special ambassador to the Middle East, Robert Strauss, said the stepped up talks with Palestinian autonomy will cover a "far broader set of issues."

After discussions in Cairo and Jerusalem, the Mideast negotiator said he wanted to break down Egyptian-Israeli-U.S. working groups into small committees to study technicalities for electing an autonomous Palestinian council and to decide what powers that council will have. "It is time to intensify our discussions," he said.

The political future of Jerusalem's 100,000 Arabs, Israeli settlements in occupied territories, and whether the Palestinian council will have legislative or only administrative controls, will be decided in future agendas.

In the West Bank, Arab owners complained of a new Israeli order sequestering about 4,000 acres of land for military purposes. The land, southwest of Nablus, was to be used as a training area, adding that farmers would need permission to enter the zone, but still could work their fields.

It is these groups that Strauss wants to break up into small committees to work on specific problems.

9-14-79
Expansionism versus conservatism in Israel

There are divisions within Prime Minster Menachem Begin's coalition government over the political actions that Israel is pursuing on the occupied West Bank.

Deputy Prime Minster Yigael Yadin, who heads a small party in the coalition, is debating what he charges is disguised and "deceitful" expansionism in settlements on the West Bank of the Jordan River. The conflict offers reassurance that some moderate leaders are not inclined to follow the hardliners, such as Begin and his Likud party. The Prime Minister endorses the view that Israeli Jews have the historical right to live anywhere in Biblical Palestine, but to live in areas outside proper de facto boundaries is reality; to imply or claim the right of sovereignty over those areas, politically and morally, is illusion.

The distinction made by Begin between possible future civil autonomy for Palestinian Arabs resident on the West Bank and in the Gaza Strip, is indicative of that land.

Religious claims aside, the rationale for the settlement policy is security. The largely civilian outposts are to serve as early warning stations and tactical barriers against future Arab attacks, either by guerillas or by regular armed forces. That purpose was put to a test in 1973, when Syrian forces struck on the Golan Heights in massive strength. The settlements worked neither as alerting stations nor as delaying points. As war began, the government's first action was to evacuate civilians from the Heights to the relative safety of Israel.

Creation or enlargement of a settlement, whether in the name of religious right or additional security need only serves to postpone political adjustments that must be faced.

9-15-79
Jewish renewal of Rosh Hashanah, Yom Kipper

Beginning at sundown on September 21, the Jewish people around the world will pray for repentance of their sins of the past twelve months and look ahead to the future when Rosh Hashanah, the Jewish New Year 5740 begins.

Rosh Hashanah, literally "head of the year," begins the annual 10-day period devoted to penance and prayer and concludes with the 24-hour fast of Yom Kipper, the day of atonement.

It is also known as the day of Awe, a period devoted to spiritual inventory of the individual, the weighing of sins and virtues of the past year.

It is a chance to reflect, correct, pray, and renew. Family and community traditions will characterize the holidays with ancient and modern prayers as well as blasts on the "shofar" (a hollow ram's horn) during the opening and closing of worship services.

The blowing of the shofar is unique in history. Its special call is to remind the people of the story of Abraham in the Bible in which the ram was sacrificed instead of the man, Issac, Abraham's son.

Symbolically, some traditions in the faith include the lighting of candles, eating of special foods, and recitation of special blessings.

A devout Jewish family says, "We dip apples in honey hoping the new year is as sweet as the taste." A daughter of a Rabbi stated that the members of their synagogue will also eat of a new fruit, one in which they have not eaten in the past year - to make their senses aware of the good things of the earth."

The lighting of candles and a memorial service is observed to recall those who have passed away, and for remembrance of the six million people of Jewish faith who died in the Holocaust in Germany. Yom Kipper ends with a single blast of the shofar.

The State of Israel has made great progress in the peace process with the Arab Republic of Egypt. With the Rosh Hashanah appeal, more can be accomplished in bringing peace t the Middle East, to include other Arabian nations within the framework of a comprehensive peace.

At the present time the autonomy for the Palestinians in the West Bank and the Gaza Strip is the most pressing issue. They should have the right of self determination, with political independence, and the right to live in peace within the framework of United Nations resolution 242 and the peace accords signed at Camp David, Maryland, in the United States. Within due course, with caution, the military troops of the Israelis can be withdrawn. This is a period of reflection, correction, and renewal.

Yasser Arafat praises stand of Spanish Government
Madrid, Spain

Ending a three day visit to Madrid, Spain, the radical Palestinian leader Yasser Arafat, praised the "progressive" stand of the Spanish government on the Middle East, called the former American diplomat Andrew Young "a good friend," and compared "the unjust and barbaric treatment" of American blacks with the travails of the Palestinians.

Arafat's stay in Spain is a centerpiece in the P.L.O.'s concerted effort to win friends and sympathy in Western Europe ended on an ambiguous diplomatic trend. Instead of a joint communique, the Spanish Foreign Ministry issued a press statement which declared simply that Arafat and a P.L.O. delegation had visited Madrid "in the context of its contacts with European leaders" and had met with Prime Minister Adoplho Suarez and Foreign Minister Marcelino Oreja.

The Spanish dignitaries made clear to their guests "the will to continue maintaining and developing the special ties of friendship and cooperation that unite Spain with the Arab world, to the benefit of both peoples, expressing the conviction that the desire for peace in the Mideast cannot be reached without a just, overall, and lasting solution, based on the principles and resolutions of the United Nations and the exercise of the inalienable national rights of the Palestinians and all others concerned.

9-17-79
Israeli cabinet approves of West Bank Arab land sales
Jerusalem, Israel

The Israeli government rescinded a 12 year prohibition against purchase of private Arab property in the occupied West Bank and the Gaza Strip by Israeli citizens and companies.

The decision is certain to exacerbate tension between Israel and the United States over expanding Jewish presence in the occupied land. The cabinet voted to allow private Israeli citizens and corporations to purchase and register title to Arab land and then, with the approval of the West Bank or Gaza military forces, settle on it.

The move was couched in moral terms as eliminating a regulation that had discriminated against Jews since the lands were captured during the 1967 war, but political overtones were highly significant as further evidence of Prime Minister Menachem Begin's determination even while negotiating "autonomy" to bind them in the future to Israeli interests and controls. How many Arabs willing to sell to Jews is an open question. Some purchases have already occurred, with Jewish principals using Arabs as front men for the purchase, and registering of deeds.

The main deterrent to open sales is expected to be the Arab owners fear for their personal safety. A Jordanian Law, enacted after the Israeli occupation in 1967, makes the sale of land to Jewish people a crime punishable by death, and although Jordan is in no position to enforce the law, the P.L.O. is assumed to have assassins able to carry out the effects and results of the law.

9-19-79
Israeli West Bank Settlers bypass Arab villagers
Al Auja, Israeli occupied West Bank

There is a cruel contrast of poverty and plenty in an area around this mud-thatched ghost town on the West Bank of the Jordan River.

The once verdant valley north of Jericho is dotted with dying fields with acres of farmland parched beyond hope of crops this fall and winter. Citrus trees that will require a minimum of five years to replace have died. Banana plants that must be carefully nurtured for a year and a half before maturity have shriveled like old corn stalks.

Despite the devastating drought, lush fields and groves mark the six major Jewish settlements that occupy a large portion of the farmland near Al Auja. The fields and orchards of the settlements, fed by a network of underground water pipes and mechanized wells, show virtually no drought damage.

At a well-established Israeli settlement of Gilgal, the abundant land that sweeps to the edge of the Jordan River fifteen miles north of Jericho was being tilled, planted and watered by sprinkler and drip irrigation systems for fall and winter vegetable crops. Citrus trees and banana plant trees appeared healthy, and thousands of factory-bred turkeys were being fattened for market.

The West Bank Arabs believe the imbalance in water allocation is part of a deliberate strategy to drive them from their land and force them to sell it at a reduced price to Israelis, whose cabinet approved a new policy of permitting individuals to buy private Arab property on the West Bank.

9-20-79
Syrian Jews are not allowed to emigrate
Damascus, Syria

Damascus is less than 30 miles from the Israeli border, but for the 3500 Jews left in the Syrian capital, they live in an Arab country that is antagonistic both to them and to the neighboring Jewish state. The Jewish people in Syria are denied the right to emigrate to Israel or anywhere else.

Despite their diverse ages and occupations, Jews want to leave Syria. A prominent Jewish businessman said, "If my family and I could move to Israel, or the United States, I would give up my home, my store and my friends, to be free from this oppression." Others voice similar feelings.

Some do escape illegally, but those who have been caught have been imprisoned, and extra restrictions applied to their families.

During the past recent months, some restrictions have been removed. Most of the Jewish identification cards no longer have "Mussawi" written on them, a special red mark of followers of Mosaic faith was written across Syrian Jews driver's licenses, bank accounts, and identify cards. The people can travel freely within the city and other areas of the country if they report their trips to the authorities.

The Damascus Jewish community is still closely watched. A plain clothes Syrian policeman walks around the quarter, visiting the synagogues during services; The Jewish day schools are co-directed by a Rabbi and a representative of the Syrian government, who checks the school's activities.

American Jewish citizens are allowed to travel in Syria with relative ease, and they have an important human right, a freedom to pick up and leave a place where their security might be threatened, a freedom denied by the Jewish quarter of Damascus.

9-20-79
Accord reached on Sinai force by Egypt, Israel and the U.S.
Washington, D.C.

The Carter administration reached tentative agreement with Egypt and Israel to continue the U.S. manned listening posts in the Sinai Peninsula as part of a peacekeeping force to monitor the Israeli-Egyptian peace accords during its first three years.

The agreement, decided after two days of three-sided talks at the State Department, in effect, ratifies a previous acknowledgment between Egypt and Israel to join forces in carrying out the main task of monitoring the demilitarized buffer zone to be formed as Israel withdrawn its troops from the Sinai.

The confirmation to keep the 200 man Sinai Field Mission - consisting entirely of civilian volunteers - on station in the Sinai passes coincides with tacit agreement to abandon the United Nations Truce Supervision Organization.

Secretary of State Cyrus Vance, described for reporters the expanded role for the U.S. until April 1982, stating that reconnaissance flights over the Sinai will increase. These flights now occur once every 10 days.

All the members of the three sided conference conceded from their original stand some sacrifice.

Hassan Ali of the Egyptian delegation refrained from requiring that a U.N. presence should be in operation in the Sinai.

Israel's main concession was to accept a temporary arrangement for monitoring the Sinai until April in 1982.

The United States agreed to keep observer posts in the Sinai to augment reconnaissance flights keeping the American peacekeeping force active.

9-20-79
Saudi Arabia does not want to be a military satellite of U.S.
Washington, D.C.

An influential member of Saudi Arabia's ruling family warned the United States to avoid any high-visibility military presence in the oil-rich Persian Gulf.

"Necessary military training assistance and defense purchases can be accomplished on a mutually useful basis without an ostentatious foreign presence, said Bandar bin Sultan, Prince and brother-in-law of Foreign Minister, Prince Saud al Faisal.

The capital of Saudi Arabia, Riyadh, is satisfied with its current military relationship with the United States, but it is concerned that the Pentagon may overplay its hand in attempting to guarantee the security of the strategic region.

The Saudis do not want to be perceived as a military satellite of the American country.

The gulf states are determined to avoid an escalation of superpower rivalries, and they need to have the natural and primary responsibility for assuring the safety and stability within their own boundaries. Prince Bandar bin Sultan stressed the issues that divide our two nations. He was particularly critical of the United States for failing to bring pressure on Israel to make concessions on the Palestinian refugees.

9-21-79
Mayor Kollek of Jerusalem will meet Rev. Jesse Jackson
Jerusalem, Israel

The mayor of Jerusalem, Ted Kolled, declining to accept the government of Israel's advice of refusing to discuss moderation of the P.L.O.'s plan to recognize the right for Israel to exist, will meet with the Rev. Jesse Jackson at the Jerusalem City Hall, and will introduce him to the local Christian clergyman and Israel representatives.

The lack of recognition of the black minister has caused a sub rose debate in Israeli government circles. Many officials feel that relations between American blacks and Israel are still suffering from the aftermath of Ambassador Andrew Young's resignation, and a modest welcome should be accorded the pastor of the United States.

One official of the Jewish government says, "Jackson has prejudged the issues in the Middle East before his visit. It would have been only fair for him to reserve his comments on what Israel does, and on the justice of the Palestinian cause."

As an elected official, Kollok does not consider himself bound by orders from the national government's miniseries. The mayor of Jerusalem is proud of the fact that Jews and Arabs can live together in his city without friction. He cabled Jackson to say, "I believe that we have built a city where all persons of all beliefs can live peacefully and worship freely."

The leader of People United to Save Humanity, (PUSH) said the goal of his trip to mediate the P.L.O. leader's (Arafat) view of Israel.

9-21-79
Invitation of "Shalom, Salaam" to Israelis by Alexandria
Alexandria, Egypt

A visitor from Israel is still a rarity in Egypt's second largest city. Billboards of the likeness of President Anwar Sadat have a white dove of peace painted on his presidential uniform. A cabbie of Arab background says, "One day I will drive to Tel Aviv, if God wishes."

This trip can happen for the citizens of Egypt after the "normalization of relations" take place next year, if the course of peace between Israel and Egypt goes as expected.

The Egyptian visitor will note some differences in driving habits, such as the Israeli way of honking horns before a light turns green at intersections of streets. In Egypt the honking never stops, but seems less anxious.

On the other hand, Israelis hardly ever drive on the wrong side of the road, a practice recognized here.

An Israeli visiting in Alexandria said, as he was gathering courage to cross the "corniche," an unofficial raceway that follows the Mediterranean sea front; "How do I get to the nearest hospital?" The answer was, "Close your eyes and step off the curb."

At the Pyramids, the mention of Israel brings another welcome from the camel guide, "Shalom, Salaam," using the Arabic and Hebrew words for peace. Others are wary about the end to hostility. A young college graduate states, "The accords are happening too fast. Every family has its martyr, and the memories cannot be erased."

It has been about two years since Sadat went to Jerusalem to start the peace process. It used to be that the Israeli flag was removed after visiting dignitaries left, but now the blue-and-white star of David remains.

9-21-79
Arafat embraces blacks, but rejects non-violence
Beirut, Lebanon

Palestinian guerilla chief Yasser Arafat, with a pistol strapped to his waist, embraced a group of American blacks, but rejected the message of non-violence they carried to the war-ravaged Middle East. The meeting ended with the signing of "We Shall Overcome."

Arafat, with his head swathed in a traditional black and white checked Kafiyeh, headdress of an Arab chieftain, and wearing his familiar khaki fatigues, greeted the black movement.

"We are no terrorists, but we will not stop our struggle . . . and our confrontation with the enemy inside occupied territories," Arafat was quoted as saying.

The black organization had hoped to visit Israel to convey their plea for non-violence to Prime Minister Begin, but the Israeli Embassy in Washington refused to admit them officially.

9-21-79
Invitation of "Shalom, Salaam" to Israelis by Alexandria
Alexandria, Egypt

A visitor from Israel is still a rarity in Egypt's second largest city. Billboards of the likeness of President Anwar Sadat have a white dove of peace painted on his presidential uniform. A cabbie of Arab background says, "One day I will drive to Tel Aviv, if God wishes."

This trip can happen for the citizens of Egypt after the "normalization of relations" take place next year, if the course of peace between Israel and Egypt goes as expected.

The Egyptian visitor will note some differences in driving habits, such as the Israeli way of honking horns before a light turns green at intersections of streets. In Egypt the honking never stops, but seems less anxious.

On the other hand, Israelis hardly ever drive on the wrong side of the road, a practice recognized here.

An Israeli visiting in Alexandria said, as he was gathering courage to cross the "corniche," an unofficial raceway that follows the Mediterranean sea front; "How do I get to the nearest hospital?" The answer was, "Close your eyes and step off the curb."

At the Pyramids, the mention of Israel brings another welcome from the camel guide, "Shalom, Salaam," using the Arabic and Hebrew words for peace. Others are wary about the end to hostility. A young college graduate states, "The accords are happening too fast. Every family has its martyr, and the memories cannot be erased."

It has been about two years since Sadat went to Jerusalem to start the peace process. It used to be that the Israeli flag was removed after visiting dignitaries left, but now the blue-and-white star of David remains.

9-21-79
Arafat embraces blacks, but rejects non-violence
Beirut, Lebanon

Palestinian guerilla chief Yasser Arafat, with a pistol strapped to his waist, embraced a group of American blacks, but rejected the message of non-violence they carried to the war-ravaged Middle East. The meeting ended with the signing of "We Shall Overcome."

Arafat, with his head swathed in a traditional black and white checked Kafiyeh, headdress of an Arab chieftain, and wearing his familiar khaki fatigues, greeted the black movement.

"We are no terrorists, but we will not stop our struggle . . . and our confrontation with the enemy inside occupied territories," Arafat was quoted as saying.

The black organization had hoped to visit Israel to convey their plea for non-violence to Prime Minister Begin, but the Israeli Embassy in Washington refused to admit them officially.

from its stated goals, of dismantling the Jewish State, and the Arab group will settle for self-determination and co-existence.

The Chicago civil rights leader was greeted by a large contingent of Israeli reporters. He is leading a small, interracial group of aides and friends on an eight-day visit to three Arab countries, as well as Israel, with the avowed purpose of persuading the P.L.O. to abandon its opposition to the existence of Israel. Later this week, the plans to meet with Yasser Arafat in Beirut, Lebanon, and with President Anwar Sadat of Egypt.

"The Palestinians are close to achieving a homeland," Jackson stated, and we must evaluate the two remaining obstacles carefully, that of terrorist tactics and the P.L.O.'s refusal to recognize the Jewish State, and its right to live in peace within the United Nations and the world.

Jackson is a private citizen whose trip has no official sanction, however he is recognized as a leader with a desire to save humanity from the ravages of distrust and illusion. After a two hour discussion with mayor Ted Kollek of Jerusalem, he visited a half-dozen hospital patients wounded by terrorist bombs and said, "Dr. Martin Luther King made a statement that unearned suffering is redemptive, and forgiveness is pre-requisite to conciliation."

9-25-79
Egypt and Israel vie against rejectionist front

The Middle East goes beyond the narrow focus of Israel and the Palestinians, to include far more important developments taking place in Iran, Iraq, Syria and the oil states of the Persian Gulf.

The two countries of Egypt and Israel have a strong foundation. By working together they remove a dangerous source of conflict. Egypt, with its size, strength, and geographic position, provides a cover behind which other Arab states - notably Jordan and the conservative regimes of the Arab peninsula - can settle their differences.

In the two years since President Anwar Sadat visited Jerusalem, the Egyptians and Israelis have developed a program of peace with powerful momentum. It is built around the return of Israeli-occupied territory to Egypt over a schedule, with three more years to run. It features growing cooperation with business, culture, transportation, and friendship.

The Palestinians have not yet joined the peace accords, but there is a sense of urgency within the negotiations, that if the P.L.O. compromises and withdraws objections, recognizing the statehood of Israel, the peace process will proceed.

The rejectionist front was formed in 1977 to counter the peace movement, centering around the P.L.O., with terrorist forces and three radical regimes - those of Iran's Ayatollah Khomaini, Saddam Hussein of Iraq, and Hafez Assad in Syria. They have the support of the Soviet Union, and have kept Jordan, as well as the Palestinians living in the Israeli-occupied territory, aloof from the peace process. Last spring they exacted from Saudi Arabia and other oil states a pledge to use maximum economic power against Egypt and Israel.

Since the spring, the rejectionist front has been unraveling. In Iran submerged minorities are now asserting themselves against the Khomaini dictatorship. There has been communal strife in neighboring Iraq, a coup in Syria has poisoned relations with Hussein in Bagdad, and religious contention rocks the regime of Assad.

Apart from the Palestinian issue, the rejectionist front cannot take even the first step to dismantle the peace movement. The Saudis, in addition to supplying more oil to the United States, is quietly paying for purchases of American weapons to Egypt.

The best strategy for the United States, at this juncture, is to give strong support and cooperation in the peace process.

THIRD WITHDRAWAL - FROM SOUTHERN SINAI

9-26-79
Israel's third Sinai withdrawal returned to Egypt
Tel Aviv, Israel

Israel returned over 2600 square miles of the southern Sinai Peninsula to Egypt on September 25, 1979, under the two nations' peace accords.

"Both sides are contributing to a lasting peace, and are making sacrifices," Israeli Brigadier General Dov Sion said as be turned over control of a triangular section of south-central Sinai to Egyptian Brigadier General Saf-el-Din Avu Shnaf.

"We have achieved more in peace than in all our wars," Sion stated. This sentiment was expressed by Prime Minister Menachem Begin. "It never occurred to us . . . that we should sign a peace treaty and say, "enough," the Prime Minister reported in a speech. He repeated his calls to Jordan and Syria to join the peace talks on Palestinian autonomy, which resumes today.

Israeli and Egyptian honor guards and bands accompanied a brief military ceremony at Abu Durba, a desert outpost on the Gulf of Suez. Israel lowered its flag at the site, and the Egyptian flag was raided over the area.

Israeli and Egyptian negotiators will discuss in Alexandria the issue of autonomy for the more than a million Arabs living under Israeli occupation on the West Bank of the Jordan River and in the Gaza Strip. The government of Israel has accepted several U.S. proposals for accelerating the talks, including the establishment of technical committees to work out details concerning agriculture, education, and finance for the West Bank government.

Israel is to turn over Mount Sinai - and the strategic mountain passes in the Sinai - in November, two months ahead of schedule, to mark the second anniversary of President Anwar Sadat's triumphant trip to Jerusalem.

9-26-79
Rev. Jackson relates to Palestinians
Nablus, Occupied West Bank

The leader of People United to Save Humanity fired up a Palestinian crowd with black pride chants in the heart of Israeli occupied West Bank of the Jordan River. The Arabs carried him on their shoulders chanting, Jackson and Arafat.

"Do not put symbols over substance, do not allow acts of terror to divert you from a homeland," the black leader said after receiving a tumultuous welcome from an overflow crowd of hundreds at the Nablus town hall.

The people chanted, "Palestine is Arabic," and raised V for victory in a contrasted cold shoulder given by the Israeli government to the American pastor.

Jackson said to the Palestinians, "You are very close to freedom and liberation." Someone must break the cycle of murder and pain." He spoke to the people telling them that "they are somebody," they can win."

Jackson will meet P.L.O. Chief Yasser Arafat when he goes to Lebanon after visiting Jordan and he will appeal to his organization to stop their tactics of terrorism and to recognize Israel's right and need to exist; to articulate its own goal for self-determination, and a homeland to fight for peace with all nations.

9-27-79
Palestinian state will provide Russian base
Jerusalem, Israel

Prime Minister Menachem Begin warned the West that the creation of a Palestinian state will provide the Soviet Union with a valuable base in the heart of the Middle East, giving Moscow a strategic advantage and presenting a great danger for the "free world."

The Prime Minister expressed satisfaction with the progress made with Egypt in the last two years, and optimism that Arab participation in the peace process will spread, that relations between Israel and the Palestinians may improve, and that the Camp David formula for autonomy in Israeli-occupied territories will be the first step toward reconciliation. Begin regrets military actions in southern Lebanon, and his government is taking precautions to prevent civilian causalities.

In regard to the P.L.O. in Israeli leader stated that "whoever recognizes the P.L.O. recognizes genocide." We have certificates from schools of officers in the P.L.O. who are from the Soviet Union. Also most of the weapons of the terrorist organization come from the Soviets.

To avoid creating an embryo of communists in a Palestinian state, the Prime Minister is determined to limit the scope of autonomy granted in the Camp David agreements, which he signed with President Sadat of Egypt and President Carter of the United States.

Although Egypt has called for an elected authority with legislative and judicial powers, Begin points out that the Camp David documents specify that it would have only administrative authority.

9-29-79
Russian Soviet atheists infiltrate Iran
Bukhara, Soviet Union

A century ago, a Christian traveler who braved the deserts of Central Asia to reach this holy Moslem city stood a chance of being a martyr for his faith.

For hundreds of years, feudal kings and Khans, renown for their cruelty and religious fantacism held control over Bukhara and the nearby city of Samarkand.

Now, as men and women die in the name of Islam in Iran and Afghanistan, the throne of the last emir stands empty in his Bukhara citadel, a symbol of long ended despotism.

The ancient cities of Central Asia, admired by Alexandria the Great, plundered by Genghis Khan, and visited by Marco Polo, now are part of the atheist Soviet State and part of the large Republic of Uzbekistan.

Religion survives here, as in other Asian lands conquered in the 19th century by the Czar's army, but there are few echoes of the resurgence of Islam.

Thousands of believers still attend the surviving mosques, and old customs are strong among the 9 million Uzbek people, descendants of Turkish tribes in the Khan era.

The borders of Iran have been virtually sealed off from the rest of the world, with the exception of the Soviet Union, who have provided this region with modern apartment houses, factories, schools emphasizing the Socialist way of life, and huge cotton irrigation projects testifying to Uzbekistan's new prosperity.

Russian party officials are members of the officially sanctioned Islamic community, whose leaders make no public statements critical of the state.

After six decades of Communist rule, which brought intensive campaigns to eradicate religious belief, the number of practicing worshipers has dropped only minimally. There are about 300 Mosques, located mainly in the suburbs, and out of the way streets, however the most significant religious buildings have been taken over by the State, and restored as museums.

The position of believers, who theoretically are guaranteed to worship under the Soviet Constitution, is slightly better than in the 1917 Revolution, when 27,000 Mosques were closed, and hudreds of "Madrassahs," theological colleges were disbanded. Only two are operating now; one in Tashkent, the Uzbek capital, and the other in Bukhara.

Russian dominance is a fact to be reckoned with in the Middle East, and throughout the world. Only strong defiance and unity will prevail in a free society, and constant surveillance has to be administered to prevent Russian expansion.

10-1-79
Jewish people observe "Day of Atonement"

The sound of the "Shofar" or ram's horn echoes in synagogues throughout the world as Jews celebrate their most sacred holiday of the year, "Yom Kipper."

Yom Kipper is called "the day of atonement," closing out the ten high holy days that begins with "Rosh Hashana," the Jewish New Year.

For those who follow the ancient tradition of Jewry, it means a day of fasting, praying, meditation and examination.

The theme is repentance, and those who repent reflect on their weaknesses and their capacity to improve their lives, in short, moral regeneration. A Rabbi regarded as an example states that, "this period brings us spiritual cleansing, closer to God, endowing our people to rise above everyday trivialties."

In Israel, all manner of work ceases for 25 hours for fasting and prayer. Orthodox law prohibits all work, eating, drinking, washing, and the wearing of leather shoes during the fast. Road traffic stops at the airport in Tel Aviv, radio stations cease broadcasting, restaurants and places of entertainment throughout the country are shut down during this period.

Volunteer armed guards are posted at synagogues, and police are on alert to any possible terrorist attack.

10-2-79
Egyptian Foreign Minister attacks Arab critics of peace accords
United Nations

4Egypt's deputy foreign Minister, in a bitter denunciation of Arab critics of the Camp David peace agreements, declared that Egypt had fought four wars for the Palestinians, and that his government has regarded the Palestinian problem as the "crux" of the conflict in the Middle East, and the Arab Republic was determined to resolve it by negotiating with Israel.

The Camp David summit represents the first time that Israel has agreed to "represent" the legitimate rights of the Palestinians," and to withdraw its armed forces and civilian government from occupied territories of the West Bank and the Gaza Strip.

Although Butros Ghali did not mention the Arab critics by name, he made it clear that he included Jordan and Syria in his attacks when he condemned "massacres" of Palestinians in "certain Arab countries."

The deputy foreign minister stated that, Egypt has not sought to speak for the Palestinians, nor to divide them into factions, as other states in the Arab world have." He requested that Israel halt the establishment of settlements in the occupied territory and cease violations of Lebanese territory.

The Egyptian delegation pledged that they will continue its pursuit of a peace agreement in harmony with other nations in the Middle East.

10-3-79
Civil rights leader unofficial envoy of Sadat
Cairo, Egypt

The Rev. Jesse Jackson, the American civil rights leader, left for Beirut, Lebanon with a message from the President of Egypt, Anwar Sadat, urging Palestinian leader Yasser Arafat to call a halt to violence against Israel.

After an unexpected second meeting with Jackson, Sadat provided his personal jetliner for the flight to Lebanon for the American evangelist and his 17 member delegation of clergymen.

A number of points were agreed upon including:
"The terror tactics and the disrespect of Israel" (by the P.L.O.) at this moment are the main impediments to negotiation, and this is the time for agreement of a cease fire.

Diplomatic persuasion will advance the cause of the Palestinians more than guerilla attacks; a tremendous momentum is building for self-determination of the Arab refugees.

Egypt will not initiate contact with the P.L.O., but the Egyptian government is open to communicate with them.

Sadat stated that the Palestinians should attend any Mideast peace conference because, "no one is more entitled to decide their fate than they themselves."

10-5-79
Religious Jews driven from West Bank Arab land
Jerusalem, Israel

Israeli soldiers forced a group of religious Jews off Arab land adjacent to the settlement of "Ofra" on the occupied West Bank of the Jordan River.

The settlers, angered by a cabinet committee's refusal to expropriate Arab land to expand Israeli settlements, sought to extend Ofra's borders by setting up squatters' camp on a hill next to the settlement.

The settlers moved a bulldozer onto the hill, set up a shed that they designated a synagogue, and fenced off the area. Troops of Israel's military occupation government were sent to the location, and after hours of negotiations, convinced the settlers to withdraw. An appeal was sent to Defense Minister Ezer Weizman to discuss the expansion of the boundaries of Ofra.

In a further protest, the enraged religious sect began dismantling the fence around their own settlement. The military forces halted this move also. Every West Bank Israeli settlement is surrounded by a tall, chain linked fence, topped with barbed wire, and lit at night with flood lights as protection against intruders.

The National Religious Party, which favors the expansion of the West Bank settlements, hinted it might withdraw from the Likud coalition headed by Prime Minister Menachem Begin, if the cabinet does not approve plans of expansion. Without the religious party's 12 votes, the Likud bloc would lose its majority in the Knesset (parliament), and the government of Begin will fall.

In a related development, former Prime Minister Yitzhak Rabin proposed establishment of an Israeli-Jordanian trusteeship over the West Bank and the Gaza Strip, a departure from the policy of his opposition Labor Party.

10-5-79
Research center in Sinai may be imperiled
Eilat, Israel

A marine research center that in a single decade has spawned dramatic discoveries in solar power, commercial fishing breeding and oceanography may soon be in peril from the Israeli-Egyptian peace treaty.

Israeli scientists at the Heinz Steinitz Marine Biology Laboratory are rushing to complete valuable research projects in the Gulf of Aquaba before the Sinai Peninsula, including their productive stretch of shoreline, is returned to Egypt in 1982.

Among the projects that are threatened are studies that could unlock the mysteries of how oil was formed in the earth, and how oceans take shape between drifting continents.

Potentially rich commercial developments involving fish and oysters and the harvesting of industrial and pharmaceutical chemicals from the sea will also be affected if Egypt denies Israeli scientists access to what is to become Egyptian territory.

A leading Israeli marine biologist, Dr. Francis Dov Por, said he contacted an Egyptian counterpart, Dr. Said el Said of the University of Alexandria, with the desire to start a joint program, that will keep research efforts alive.

"In 10 years we have brought the Gulf of Aqaba into the center of oceanographic research," Dr. Por of the Hebrew University in Jerusalem stated. "It will be a great loss to both of our countries and to the world science if our projects are discarded.

One of the greatest assets is an inconspicuous one-acre pond of saltwater on the Egyptian side, that is a source of major advance in solar energy. The pond is a natural heat trap whose waters a few feet below the surface reach temperatures high enough to power a turbine engine and remain at that level year-round.

Research into the properties of the solar pond, supervised by Dr. Yehuda Cohen, have led to development of commercially successful artificial solar ponds that are providing power and hot water to an Israeli hotel at Sodom on the Dead Sea.

The organic life of the pond has revealed scientific surprises, including a possible model in subsurface algae of one of evolution's basic missing links, how life, evolved through photosynthesis, (energy in which plant cells make carbohydrates from carbon dioxide and water) in an atmosphere devoid of oxygen, breathe in plant and animal life today.

Commercial fishing is enhanced by producing giant oysters, raised entirely on food wastes washed through their beds from adjacent farm ponds of gilthead sea bream fish.

Shrimp are also fattened on the waste, and simultaneously purify the water for return to the Gulf of Aqaba, making a closed circle of fish production.

10-7-79
Bedouin tribes of Jordan migrate to cities
Amman, Jordan

The Bedouin, proud of their heritage in roaming the Arabian desert for centuries, are disappearing.

Threatened by diminishing grazing land for their flocks of sheep, goats and camels, they are taking down their goat-haired tents and migrating to the cities.

The Bedouin population has shrunk from 200,000 in the 1950s to less than 60,000 now. Unless the government of Jordan and the surrounding states works fast to produce a comprehensive rural development plan, the Bedouin may become a Middle East romantic legend.

This trend poses a serious economic threat to Jordan, which relies heavily on the Arab's livestock for fresh meat.

A director of research at the university states, "We believe it is vital from cultural and economics to halt this migration and help the Bedouin improve his standard of living through modern farming methods."

Most of these Arabian nomads belong to eight major tribes, claiming direct descent from the prophet Mohammad.

The Badia (Bedouin regions), range over large tracts of desolate scrub land, where only the nomads can survive.

The conservative Sunni Moslem tribesmen have gained an honored place in Jordanian history as loyal subjects and excellent soldiers for the Hashemite dynasty of King Hussein. Most of the desert camel corps, that hunt down gunrunners and smugglers in the border regions, is drawn from the Bedouin community.

A tentative start to reversing the migration has been accomplished with development of underground water reservoirs to farmlands beneath the barren mud flats of southern Jordan.

10-7-79
Program for American aid in Egypt a success
Cairo, Egypt

Nine hundred railroad cars, built for the U.S. Navy in preparation for the Allied invasion of Europe in World War II, are now carrying coal, molasses, and other freight in Egypt. The 2.5 million dollar purchase is being hailed by Egyptian and American officials as one of the success stories of the century in economic assistance in Egypt. The cost includes transportation by ship to the United Arab Republican state, and repairs of parts that have deteriorated. The gondolas, tankers, and boxcars were European gauge, and could not be used in the United States.

Most of the fleet is rolling across the deserts and farmlands of Egypt.

The United States is currently engaging in a variety of projects, including grain silos, sewage treatment facilities, cement and power production and port expansion.

Time is a key factor for President Sadat of Egypt, who is under pressure to meet public expectations that peace with Israel will bring prosperity.

The Minister of State for Economic Cooperation, Gamal Nazer, says that, "with the assurance of aid by the American government and other Western nations we can show the Arab rejectionists that we can survive without them." He stated its economy toward free enterprise and committed itself to peace with Israel after 30 years of war.

10-7-79
Orders await Americans in Sinai Peninsula
Jerusalem, Israel

While Israel discusses whether to accept the services of the listening post crew in the Sinai Desert, Americans are anxious to learn the details of their job as keepers of the Egyptian-Israeli peace.

Under an American-Egyptian plan worked out last month in Washington, the task of keeping the peace in the barren peninsula will fall largely on the Sinai Field Mission forces, who are primarily electronic technicians, civilian in status. The Sinai Mission has an authorized strength of 200, and there are no plans for expansion.

Their stated operation is to monitor traffic through the strategic Giddi and Mitla passes in the U.N. buffer zone. On January 25, 1980, the Israeli army will withdraw from the passes and the region will become Egyptian, phasing out the need for the listening post operation.

If the Americans stay at UMM Khaseiba, 26 miles east of the Suez Canal, and there is no multinational military force in the Sinai, the Israelis will remain in the buffer zone C, strategic outpost, until the Camp David accords can be verified.

The Camp David Accords, signed last year by Egypt, Israel and the United States, call for the supervision of the peace by the United Nations Emergency Force, which the U.N. failed to reassign to duties in the Sinai when its truce mandate expired.

Spokesman for the Israel cabinet, Moshe Dayan, is assigned to seek amendments and clarifications to a plan to police the Sinai Peninsula region. Among the requests the Israeli government made of the United States are:

The peace plan be upgraded to an official document signed in the same manner as the original treaty.

A pledge from the United States to create an international supervision force.

10-11-79
Israel and Egypt critical over arrangements of Israeli withdrawal
Strasbourg, France

Israel and Egypt were at odds over who was holding up a solution to the Palestinian question, whether Israel could re-occupy Arab land after it became autonomous and whether Europe should help solve the Mideast conflict.

Israeli Foreign Minister Moshe Dayan warned that the Israeli army would re-invade the West Bank of the Jordan River and the Gaza Strip if the areas turned into Palestinian guerilla strongholds after becoming autonomous.

The Egyptian Foreign Affairs Butros Ghali stated that the Israeli forces could not return once the one million Arabs in the territories elect their own leaders.

The two leaders were meeting together with a 21 nation Council of Europe post war institution, which promotes cooperation in many fields. There was an exchange of recriminations: By Dayan, "If the territories become bases for terrorism in our own backyard, we will not tolerate it. We will send troops in to break up the strongholds." Countered Ghali, "Once you are out, you do not have the right to come back. The Israeli withdrawal is definitive and no Palestinian group will accept any form of protectorate."

Ghali charged that Israeli settlements and land purchases were deterring the Palestinians from joining the peace talks. Deep divisions exist between the two countries on how to handle the Palestinian question.

10-12-79
Workable Framework for Mideast accord

Tensions which threaten the Middle East span our entire world. "As long as the central issues in the Arab-Israeli dispute - namely, the disposition of the West Bank, Golan Heights, East Jerusalem, and the Palestinian question go unresolved, peace will elude us. All our efforts to create greater global stability and to manage interdependence among nations will be decimated. The endless war and economic disruption is invading the United States. The anxiety between Black and Jewish peoples are growing more intense, with some favoring Prime Minister Begin's policies, and others willing to compromise to secure a permanent peaceful solution.

The balance for a Middle East settlement must meet Israel's requirements for peace and security within recognized borders, and Arab requests for the evacuation of their territories occupied in the 1967 War, and some form of Palestinian self-determination.

The criteria of United Nation Security Council Resolution 242j of November 1967 state, "Inadmissability of acquisition of territory by war, withdrawal of Israeli armed forces from territory occupied in the conflict, recognition of the sovereignty, territorial integrity, and political independence of every state in the area," and the right of all nations to live in secure and recognized boundaries; in addition the military occupation by Israel over the Palestinians must end.

A framework for peace can be successful if the following conditions occur: Israel withdraw from the West Bank, Gaza, and Golan Heights, with the Jewish state permitted to maintain military strong points for an agreed period of time, and have access to these points.

Withdrawal of civilian settlements of Israelis, phased out in stages, all owing the Palestinians to recognize their right of self-determination and self-government as an independent entity, or within the kingdom of Jordan.

Under any arrangement, however, there must be iron-clad provisions barring significant military forces which would threaten Israel.

Jerusalem's religious significance to Jews, Moslems, and Christians, and the city's tragic past is an issue of symbolic importance. No solution will fully satisfy the demands of all parties. The ultimate solution should meet the following standards:

Unimpeded access to all the holy places with each under the custodianship of its own faith.

No barriers dividing the city which would prevent free circulation throughout it.

Substantial political autonomy for each of the national groups within the city in the area where it predominates.

The issue of sovereignty with passports of Israel or Jordanian recognition.

A customs union between Israel, the Palestinian homeland, and other Arab states should be established as part of the final settlement, ensuring the free flow of goods, and people, and integrate the region economically to the advantage of all.

The United States should organize a new treaty alliance to cover the Middle East, to protect regional oil fields and shipping lanes from outside influence and terrorist interference.

Military and economic stability in the Middle East is a prerequisite to a permanent peace, which translates into the survival of Israel.

The critical key is the United States must maintain a strong military presence in this area, air and sea capability, in defending any intervention of guerilla tactics to destroy the accords.

Policy of Israeli government is to settle on State owned land
Jerusalem, Israel

The Israeli government, trying to defuse an explosive domestic dispute, decided to allocate more state land for Jewish settlements in the occupied West Bank of the Jordan River, but firmly rejected settlers demands to seize private Arab property.

"The principle is not to confiscate, or requisition, or expropriate, or seize any privately owned land unless it is absolutely necessary for security reasons," stated Aryeh Naor, cabinet secretary, announcing the compromise.

Prime Minister Menachem Begin and his cabinet preview an expansion of at least five new settlements and the construction of a Jewish city in a predominately Arab region. The city, populated in part by Jewish people from New York City in the United States, will be called "Erfat."

The decision of the Israeli cabinet was a set-back for "Gush Emunim" a fanatic religious sect movement that advocates annexation of the West Bank by the Jewish state. The Hebrews for "Loyalists Bloc" said the compromise did not answer the national problem, and urged the government to expropriate thousands of acres for widespread settlement expansion. The struggle for recognition will continue and crucial issues will have to be solved before Israel can proceed with steps to a comprehensive peace with Egypt and other Arabian countries.

10-17-79
Mounting anxiety in Israel with inflation the prime factor
Jerusalem, Israel

Against mounting anxiety, Israel's government is fighting for its survival and may collapse under the countries dire economic problems and political chaos enveloping Prime Minister Menachem Begin's coalition.

The crisis has overshadowed the peace treaty of Egypt and Israel, and has pinpointed the inability of the Likud governing body to arrest inflation, expected to reach on e hundred percent this year, and in addition political infighting of the settlement issues on the West Bank of the Jordan River.

Israeli newspapers are attacking Begin for his failure to apply a firm hand. Foreign Minister Moshe Dayan, assailing the Cabinet's paralysis, has called the government "A walking corpse," and there is talk of early general elections.
Compounding the Likud coalition is the health of the Prime Minister, Begin, who has had two heart attacks, a minor stroke, and inflamation of the coronary artery. He appears to be less willing to assert his control over his cabinet.

Amid the uncertainty, Israeli businessmen are finding projection for planning in the future, dark, and the president of Koor Industries, Israel's largest company, has stated that foreign and domestic investment has taken a downturn.

Since the signing of the Israeli-Egyptian treaty last march, Begin's cabinet has split into hard and moderate factions over the issue of Palestinian autonomy. The doves, led by Defense Minister Ezer Weizman, oppose seizure of private Arab land for expanded Jewish settlements. The hawks, headed by Ariel Sharon, include all the ministers of the National Religious Party, the second largest partner in the Prime Minister's coalition have said they will withdraw their 12 seats in the cabinet if Begin does not allocate more land for expansion of the settlements. Their departure would force a new election and divide the present government.

The cabinet rift has brought the Israeli negotiations on the autonomy issue to a standstill.

The speculation now is - what will come first - a breakdown of the talks on autonomy, or a default in the government. There are hard choices to be made. It seems like a compromise is in the future, with both sides giving to promote a peaceful solution.

10-21-79
Persian Gulf accelerates spread of Islam
Tehran, Iran

The Arab Emirates of the Persian Gulf have become the main target of the campaign by Iran's ruling clergy to spread their Islamic (submission to the will of God), revolution.

In the seven months since the overthrow of the Shah, Iran's religious sect has launched appeals and threats on behalf of Shia Moslems, (one of the Moslem sects, centered in Iran, that regard Ali, the son-in-law of Mohammed as his true successor) - in the United Arab Emirates, Kuwait, and Bahrain.

The campaign against the orthodox Sunni rulers of the Gulf states have been led by Ayatollah Sadegh Rouhani, believed to be the senior member of the ruling Council of the Revolution.

The unofficial head of state, who has confined his statements on exporting the revolution to generalized calls for the spread of Islamic rule and overthrow of anti-Moslem despots, has not disowned his family clergy Shia offensive.

The clergymen have extended their complaints against the gulf leaders to Saudi Arabia, the country in which Islam was founded.

The minority Shia sect of Islam has been thrust into the limelight throughout the Moslem world by the triumphant overthrow of the Shah. The split with the Sunni followers occurred over the succession to the Caliph after the death of Mohammad. The Shias are militant in behavior while the Sunnis are more passive.

The 12th Immam of the Shia sect disappeared some 1100 years ago, and the members believe he will return to restore justice to our world. Representatives are being sent into the Middle East to proclaim this revival.

10-22-79
Jerusalem, Israel

Israel's Foreign Minister, Moshe Dayan resigned his post, angered by the Prime Minister Menachem Begin's continued tough line on the Palestinian issue, which Dayan calls "the key question in our lives."

In a letter, read by Arieh Naor, Cabinet Secretary, Dayan expressed his reservations in the way the Palestinian autonomy is being conducted, and stated that under the present conditions he could no longer serve as the Foreign Minister.

A solution, envisioned by Dayan, who was Israel's chief negotiator in the treaty talks with Egypt, is coexistence on an equal level. He explained that the negotiating stand does not go far enough in outlining a partnership with the Arabs on the West Bank of the Jordan River.

Begin will temporarily take over the task of the foreign minister until another appointment is approved by Parliament.

Dayan was an army general in the 1956 Arab-Israeli war and defense Minister in the 1967 and 1973 wars, and indicated he would keep his parliament seat, but announced no other personal plans. He underwent surgery this year to remove a cancerous intestinal tumor and again to repair his vocal cords, which were damaged in a 1968 cave-in at an archeological excavation. He lost an eye fighting for the British government in World War II.

The resignation, that took most of the Israeli Cabinet by surprise and stunned an unsuspecting nation, may be a fatal blow to the Prime Minister Begin's coalition, or it may be an opening for Begin to resolve serious disputes within his Likud government.

10-22-79
Libya's leader has uncanny instinct for survival
Tripoli, Libya

The character and personality of Libya's chieftain, Moammar Khadafy, form a two-sided puzzle - Naive at one extreme and calculating at the other.

The Naivete emerges with the rejectionist leader's justification of support of organizations such as the Irish Republican Army, whose goals are far removed from the national interest of Libya. "Minorities are nations in search of their nationhood," Khadafy said, and he feels morally bound to advance them wherever they are.

The paradox of this clever Moslem has been visible to the world, in a former Italian colony, as an army lieutenant, dethroned King Idris of Libya a decade ago.

Khadafy supported deposed African dictator Idi Amin and Emperor Bokassa of the central African Empire. He had a plan of influencing and converting black Africa to Moslem ideology; of unifying countries to destroying Israel.

The two sides of the Libyan dictator appear to have their roots in the society of Bedouin herdsmen, in which he grew up as the only son of an illiterate family with only a goatskin tent for shelter. Both his father, who was wounded while fighting the Italians, and his grandfather, who was killed in the same struggle, were devoutly religious men of simple tastes; fiercely independent and tough.

After completing military studies, young signal corp officer plotted a coup d'etat with a handful of former high school friends, urging them to join the army and on September 1, 1969 overthrew the Libyan government in an overnight "Putsch," (uprising, insurrection), that would have been bloodless, except for an apparently accidental shooting of one soldier. Khadafy remains an enigma today.

10-23-79
Expropriated land of Arabs negated by Israeli government
Jerusalem, Israel.

They range from cities to outposts, from the edge of the Red Sea to the cool slopes of the Golan Heights. There are more than a hundred of them - Israeli settlements in the occupied territories.

A few are flourishing truck gardens, and some are bedroom communities for nearby locations in Israel proper. They can appear in the desert, surrounded by tall chain linked fences topped with barbed wire outside.

The settlements have one thing in common: They are all beyond what is called the "green line." When the cease-fire of 1949 ended Israel's war of independence, the peacemakers established the armistice line between Israel and its Arab neighbors with a green marker. Inside was Israel; everything beyond was "over the green line."

It was the Six-Day war that provided new ground for Israeli occupation and settlements in 1967. The Jewish people learned in that war that settlements reinforce their claim to land and help by arming themselves to hold them. They were to be the Jewish early-warning stations.

The first settlement was the "Gush Etzion," the children of defenders who had been massacred by Jordanian troops and local Arabs in 1948, returned in 1967 to rebuild their father's Kibbutz.

Three kinds of settlements were built:

Kibbutzim - communal groups in which the land is worked in common, profits are shared, children are reared in a "children's house" rather than in parental quarters.

Moshavim - cooperative projects in which families are assigned land; marketing and purchasing are done by majority consent.

Nahals - newly staffed settlements of men and women in military service, improved into Kibbutzim or Moshavim with maturity of the Israeli gathering.

Most of the settlements were built on land that had been Jordanian crown land and became Israeli government land after the 1967 war. Occasionally a settlement was established on land expropriated from Arabs - with payment by the military as Nahal sites.

Last June, for the first time, land to which Arab farmers held title was seized as a site for the "Elon Moreh" settlement.

The Israeli Supreme Court, decided recently that it was illegal to seize Arab property, and ordered the Elon Moreh to be dismantled and abandoned within thirty days.

Cabinet Secretary, Arye Naor, said the government would accept the judgement, and implement the action.

Middle East special advisor on Peace mission
Beirut, Lebanon

An experienced American troubleshooter arrived in Beirut, Lebanon on the first leg of a mission designed to end the conflict between Palestinian guerillas and Israeli backed forces in southern Lebanon.

Phillip C. Habib, special advisor to Secretary of State Cyrus Vance, will also visit Syria, Jordan, Israel, and possibly the Vatican in Rome, Italy.

The United States is working with the United Nations to create a base for reconciliation and peace in the war-torn countries. It does not want the proposals to be identified as American in scope, that might be automatically rejected by the Palestinians or other factions. A consortium of countries, including France, Kuwait, and Saudi Arabia may be able to influence the Israelis and the Palestinians to agree to a durable truce.

The rocky brown hills of the south Lebanon's poorest region, have suffered continual bombardment since the civil war of 1975-76, when Israeli armed military and the Christian minority seized a string of villages on the border, from the P.L.O.

Arab diplomats state informal discussions at the United Nations have focused on the possibility of enlarging the 10,000 man peacekeeping force, persuading the Palestinians and the Israeli backed militia men to withdraw from the controversial areas.

10-25-79
Religious zealots growing in Israel

The right wing religious faction, Gush Emunim, has vowed to resist the Israeli Supreme Court order to dismantle a controversial West Bank settlement built on illegally seized Arab land.

The spiritual leader of Gush Emunim has devoted his life to preserving the belief that the return to the Biblical land of Israel signifies the beginning of the Messianic age.

The movement was born in 1973, after the Yom Kipper War. It began what is regarded as its holy crusade to settle and build up Judea and Samaria, the land of the ancient Hebrews now known as the West Bank. Today there are sixteen West Bank Gush Emunim settlements, with about 2,000 settlers. The movement has important enclaves of support in political and military circles.

Gush Emunim has evolved a conscious policy of violent opposition to the Palestinian self-determination, and plans a series of demonstrations throughout Israel and the West Bank to protest the peace initiative of the President of Egypt of the Camp David Accords.

The Rabbi of the Gush Emunim states, "The offered peace treaty to Israel is by Devine Providence," and the messengers of God are prophets of the present, Prime Minister Begin, and President Anwar Sadat, and the founder of the State of Israel, Herzl, - this is not mysticism, but the land of God in history.

Clearly the religious fever has penetrated into Israel political fundamental structure, and whatever the outcome of the peace efforts, will leave its mark on the future of the Jewish state.

10-26-79
South Yemen signs Treaty with Soviet Union
Moscow, Soviet Union

South Yemen signed a twenty year treaty of friendship and cooperation with the red Communist nation, consolidating economic and military influence in the strategic Arabian Peninsula.

The treaty says, "The two countries will continue to develop their ties in the military field," specifically in the interest of strengthening their defense capacity.

South Yemen remains unofficially unaligned despite the pact. There was no indication the Middle East nation had conceded base rights to Soviet naval forces in the Red Sea port of Aden Arabia.

The agreement with South Yemen appears similar to the pacts signed by seven other developing countries including Afghanistan, Angola, Mozambique, Iraq, India, Ethiopia, and Vietnam.

The Soviets have been working to recoop from the devastating denouncement of Egypt, concluding a separate accord with Israel under United States auspices last winter.

The Soviet Premier, Brezhnev, and the President of South Yemen condemned the Israeli-Egyptian treaty and called for the establishment of an independent Palestinian state in the occupied territories claimed by Israel.

Meanwhile, the Interior Minister of Israel, Yosef Burg, is taking part in a conference in London, England, with the Egyptians and the United States on the issue of Palestinian autonomy, and has an initiative which might end the boycott of the radical Arabs joining the negotiations. The Interior Minister stated that Israel would do everything it can to resolve the autonomy impasse.

Legal location sought for Israel's Elon Moreh
Jerusalem, Israel

The Israeli cabinet decided to search for a "proper legal location" on the West Bank for Elon Moreh, ordered dismantled within a thirty day period by the Israeli supreme court.

It will be necessary to look for a legal way for Jews to settle in Judes and Samari and the Gaza district without violating the peace agreement with Egypt - or promising not to introduce Israeli sovereignty during the autonomy period.

Education Minister, Zevulun Hammer, a member of the National Religious Party faction, espouses the Israeli right to claim sovereignty over the West Bank and Gaza after a proposed five-year period of autonomy for the Arab residents of those areas.

The court ruled that under the "Hague Convention," privately owned Arab land could be seized only for military purposes, and only for the period of military operation. The ruling states that Elon Moreh had been launched for political gain and must be removed within a thirty day period.

In Jerusalem, Prime Minister Menachem Begin has reshuffled his cabinet, appointing a new head for the embattled Ministry of Finance and assuming the position of Foreign Minister himself.

A self made millionaire, Yigal Hurvitz, will take over the ailing ministry, demanding the decisions on the economy be made by a four-man cabinet, and not the full cabinet, in which budget protests on inflation fighting could be reduced.

Hurvitz was a member of Begin's cabinet - as minister of energy, commerce, and tourism - until last October, when he quit to protest Israel's agreement to the Camp David accords.

11-1-79
Jordanian - Palestinian State urged by Rabin (Prime Minister 1974-77, Israel)
Jerusalem, Israel

The most complicated political roadblock now on the path to a comprehensive peace in the Mideast is the Palestinian issue. There is no ideal solution to this complicated problem; a remedy must be sought that will enable the Palestinians to live within a sovereign state.

The Begin government's position on a permanent settlement to the Palestinian issue is that full autonomy should be given to the inhabitants of the West Bank and the Gaza Strip, under Israel sovereignty. A permanent answer will be negotiated toward the conclusion of a five year transitional period specified in the Camp David accords. The legal status of these areas will not be changed, and Palestinian residents will be able to elect an administrative council empowered with running internal affairs of its people.

Yitzhak Rabin states that Jordan should be brought into the negotiations and a Palestinian-Jordanian state should be established. Israel should return most of the West Bank and Gaza, except for zones vital to Israel's security, such as portions along the Jordan Valley, and the eastern slopes of the Judea and Samarian hills, an area unpopulated by Jerusalem, the Etzion block Kibbutzim and the Southern part of the Gaza Strip.

There is room to settle thousands of refugees now encamped in Lebanon, and Syria. A Jordanian-Israeli trusteeship may be established within the five year transition period. Egypt, Jordan, and the Palestinians would retain the right to press for total Israeli withdrawal, and the Jewish state could demand security zones.

If Jordan joins the negotiations, and if the three nations signing the peace accords approach the Palestinian Arabs as a partner, a successful agreement can be formulated.

Islam extending throughout Middle East Islamabad, Pakistan.

A nation in the Mideast theater, Pakistan, has a self appointed president, Zia ul-Haq, a devoutly religious man who organizes his daily presidential routine around Moslem Islamic prayers, who led a successful military coup against Zulfikar Ali Bhutto in July 1977, promised to return Pakistan to civilian rule within 90 days.

While Zia's political confidence has grown since assuming power, his tastes remain simple. He has shunned both the president's and the prime minister's residences, preferring to remain in the Rawalpindi House - Islamic capital of Pakistan - as an army chief.

"The government can take any form," state Zia ul-Haq, "I have no fundamental structure in mind."

The direction of the government is crystal clear: toward Islam. The self appointed president talks about reorienting the political system in favor of Islamic values, and appointing a committee of scholars and academics to carry out his orders. Zia visualizes himself as a Moslem missionary, and does not regard as incompatible some combination of limited democracy and Islam rule. He has indicated a desire to end universal adult suffrage.

At no time in Pakistan's 32 year history has an elected government managed to serve its full term and hand power over peacefully to its elected successor. With the army anxious to get out of government, and the country needing to end political uncertainty, Zia will have to give the people freedom and stability in an environment that encourages opportunity and economic growth.

Religious traditionalist of Saint Catherine on Mount Sinai site optimistic
Mount Sinai, Israel

Deep in the mountainous southern reaches of the timeless desert, where religious tradition says God spoke reproachingly to Moses from a burning bush, a mortal struggle of wills is beginning to unfold, out of sight of the world beyond the sandy horizon.

For centuries, the Greek Orthodox monastery of St. Catherine, in the shadows of the legendary Moses Mountain, has withstood the marauding nomadic tribes, flash floods, earthquakes, and adventurism of Napoleon Bonaparte, among other invaders.

The outside world forced itself on the abbey, during the 1967 war between Egypt and Israel, and since then as many as 100,000 tourists have descended on the black-frocked monks each year.

With the return of this part of the Sinai to Egypt just a month away, the monks are making a bid to protect the aesthetic beauty and solitude of Mount Sinai from a great danger - man's fondness for building monuments to his own achievements.

President Anwar Sadat has a tentative plan of building a shrine of "Three Faiths" atop Mount Sinai - and his wish to be buried there.

The monastery has weathered difficulties before, and the monks are very optimistic that the Holy site will remain as is.

The main attraction of the monastery is its ancient character. The Byzantine emperor, Justinian the Great, ordered the high walled fortress built in the sixth century to protect pilgrims who had braved the journey to the granite mountains of the Sinai wilderness.

In 1975, a fragment of an ancient Bible manuscript called the "Codex Sinaiticus" written in Greek in the fourth century was found near the Monastery, the oldest known text until the discovery of "The Dead Sea Scrolls."

Israeli court decision may lead to confrontation
Elon Moreh, Israeli occupied West Bank

The supreme court of the Jewish government has ruled that the Elon Moreh settlement must be dismantled by November 22, 1979, and the Gush Emunim (Faith Bloc) movement is refusing to leave. The residents state that they are not going to make it easy for the Israeli military. Many settlers are armed, and there have been hints of bloodshed if they are forcibly removed.

The government of Prime Minister Menachem Begin, shaken by the court ruling, Moshe Dayan's resignation, and threats of revolt in the coalition could cause a rift in the present leadership.
Gush Emunim has many followers in Israel, and it has the philosophical backing of the powerful National Religious Party and a new right-wing addition called the "Renascence Movement." It has a simple credo, it believes that Jews should be allowed to settle anywhere in what they call "Eretz Israel."

The Elon Moreh location was a battleground in the Bible called "Shechem" and the Patriarch Abraham came and settled in an area around Nablus.

After the 1973 war, many people realized that the only way the Jewish state could survive was to go back to Zionism - giving up comforts and ease - (Zionists were the Israelites exiled from the Holy land) waiting for an opportunity to return to Jerusalem, their heavenly city.

The Gush Emunim faction is a representative of loyal Zionists who are firm in their convictions, and will fight to retain their freedom, even their national government.

11-8-79
In Syria - Islamic Brotherhood calls for change

The leader of Syria's outlawed Brotherhood is calling on his countrymen to overthrow the government in Damascus, and accuses President Hafez Assad of "barbaric torture and repression."

The country has been wracked recently by political violence. Three members of Assad's minority Alawite, (one of the Moslem sects that record Ali as the Son-in-law of Mohammed as the true successor of the prophet) group were assassinated, and in June of this year 50 army cadets were shot to death in Aleppo after apparently being lured into an assembly hall by a dissident officer. The government blamed the massacre on the Moslem brotherhood.

Isam Attar, the appointed director of the Brotherhood says, "All dictatorship, whether it is built up around a single person, sect party, or the military, must be ended. "We are against communism as well as colonialism and social injustice. We believe the Arab world should be dominated neither by any of the two big power systems."

The ultra-conservative Moslem alliance was founded in Egypt in 1928 to combat Western influences considered to be corrupting Islam. President Gamal Nasser dissolved the Brotherhood in 1954, but it emerged after Nasser's death in 1970, when the present President of Egypt, Anwar Sadat, declared an amnesty to the sect.

A senior diplomat in Beirut, Lebanon, stated that it would be overdramatizing the situation to say that civil war was imminent, but recent attacks on the Alwaite power structure were the most serious threat to date to Assad of Syria.

11-9-79
Combat troops changing in Egypt

Less than a month after Egypt and Israel agreed on the basics of a peace treaty, the Egyptian army changed the color of its combat uniforms from desert Khaki to jungle green. This was a fundamental change in President Anwar Sadat's strategic thinking.

The threat to Egypt has been minimized as coming from the Eastern desert, where despite peaceful withdrawals Israel retains an armed presence, but the unsettled regions on the African continent to the south remain.

A major reorganization is underway for a quick-strike, air-mobile unit capable of ranging as far south as Zaire, where Sadat sent air force technicians to assist President Mobuto Sese Seko in 1977.

According to military sources, a growing airlift capacity, including more than two dozen C-130 cargo planes, and heavy emphasis on training new commando units, has enhanced Sadat's ability to move quickly to the aid of friendly regimes under threat from a growing Soviet presence on the African continent and the Arabian Peninsula.

The immediate concern is the Sudan, where President Jaafar Numeiri has survived three attempted coups in his decade of power; that faces serious internal problems, in addition to sporadic pressures from Libya and Ethiopia both Soviet client states.

Sadat has a moral and political commitment to protect the states of Sudan, Oman and Somalia from outside intervention because they were the only Arab League nations that did not break relations with Egypt over the peace treaty with Israel. Sudan is vital to Egypt strategically, because it is the pathway of the Nile River, the bloodstream of the United Arab Republic, and any hostile forces threatening the flow of the river could hold life or death power over the country.

11-12-79
Mayor of Nablus, West Bank jailed by Israel army

The Israeli army jailed without charge the Arab mayor of Nablus, a Palestinian leader opposed to Jewish settlement policy and autonomy plans in the West Bank of the Jordan River.

The arrest of mayor Bassam Shakaa, pending legal procedures to deport him, touched off angry protests in the region, occupied by Israel since 1967.

A development expected to heighten the tension is the Jewish Cabinet adopted a general proposal to allow more settlements and enlarge existing outposts in the Golan Heights, Gaza Strip, and the West Bank. Cabinet Secretary Arieh Naor said the government is considering a Defense Department plan for 31 new settlements and a rival agriculture proposal for additional sites.

After Shakaa was taken to the maximum-security Ramla Prison near Tel Aviv, the Nablus town council and a group of West Bank mayors resigned in protest. Scattered demonstrations of school and businesses were reported throughout the area, inhabited by more than 700,000 Palestinians.

The mayor's arrest was believed to be from a remark he made in a private meeting in which he stated, "Israel could expect terror operations like the 1978 coastal massacre as long as the occupation of Arab lands continue."

11-14-79
Attention should be directed to past performance of P.L.O. leader

When Yasser Arafat was one of a group of Palestinian terrorists operating in Egypt, one of his colleagues was accused of being an informer. Arafat calmly drew his gun and blew the man's brains out. On investigation, the man was found innocent, but the terrorist leader never apologized for his brutal act.

This exploit, as well as continual guerilla attacks against women and children in Israel - and against his own people who do not agree with him - do not appear to influence the Jesse Jackson's and the Walter Fauntroy's of America.

Arafat and his Palestinian organization levies tribute from Saudi Arabia and Libya to the tune of some 700 million dollars a year, and has made terrorist activities, training and supplying arms to the Irish provisional army, to deadly Baader - Meinhof groups in Germany, and to Latin American guerilla groups.

The Saudis and other moderate Arab states are more fearful of the P.L.O. than they are of Israel, who have seen the terrorist group destroy Lebanon by joining with Marxist and other left-wing elements to provoke and sustain a murderous civil war in what was once among the most advanced of Arab countries.

Arafat has threatened Anwar Sadat, President of Egypt, with assassination because he signed the Camp David Accords with Israel and the United States. Palestinian rights is not the sole reason for the guerilla element to be recognized, but control of the entire Arab world, and with the Soviet Union behind them, this may be a possibility. If they succeed, it would mean delivering the Mediterranean region to their control, virtually making the NATO alliance powerless.

FOURTH WITHDRAWAL FROM MOUNT SINAI

11-16-79
Fourth step of Israeli-Egyptian peace treaty consummated
Mount Sinai, Egypt

Israel ended its 12 year occupation of this region and returned it to Egypt, whose soldiers hoisted their black-white-red flag near the mountain where Moses received the Ten Commandments.

In ceremonies at an air field within view of the 2,285 foot peak, Israeli militia men lowered the Star of David banner two months ahead of schedule at the request of Egyptian President Anwar Sadat.

This is a fourth of a six-phase Jewish withdrawal that will leave Egypt with two-thirds of the desert peninsula. The land was lost by Egypt in the 1967 Mideast War, and the remaining property is to be returned in 1982 under the peace accords.

Sadat will agree to an Israeli request to allow tourists to continue to visit the area. "Here for the first time there will be a meeting between Arabs, Jews, and Egyptians," stated General Dov Sion of Israel. "In this natural workshop, youth will learn to live and work together."

Meanwhile in Jerusalem, under intense hardline pressure, the Israeli government adopted a wide-range settlement program that would triple the population of Jews in the occupied West Bank by 1981 and give Prime Minister Menachem Begin a temporary respite from his coalition crisis.

According to Cabinet Secretary Arye Naor, the proposal calls for extension of 19 settlement points, paramilitary to civilian status, within five settlement blocs. The program will involve 10,000 to 15,000 new housing units. The blocs affect Maale Adumim, east of Jerusalem; Givon, to the north of the capital; Karnai Shomron, between Tel Aviv and the West Bank town of Nablus; Gush Etzion, south of Jerusalem; and Rechan, west of the West Bank town of Jenin.

11-19-79
Last compromise for settlement Elon Moreh
Jerusalem, Israel

The Israeli government, in what was called "its last compromise," sought to avert a confrontation with pro-settlement zealots by calling for a two-stage evacuation of an illegal Jewish settlement near Nablus on the West Bank of the Jordan River.

The effect of the cabinet action was to delay from four to six weeks any forceful removal of the Gush Emunim (Faith Bloc). The Supreme Court ordered Elon Moreh removed, as demanded by Arab landowners holding title to 31 acres of the 1717 seized for the site. Prime Minister Begin voted to remove all traces of the settlement's 31 acres by the court deadline of November 22. None of the settlers' homes are in this area.

A new site is being prepared for the Faith Bloc a few miles from their present location.

Legal experts provided Begin's cabinet with a loophole needed for the two-stage withdrawal: the high court ruling technically to only the Arab land of the petitioners.

The Jewish government's most pressing problem on the West Bank is the protests of the Palestinian deportation of Nablus Mayor Bassam Shakaa, who has begun on a hunger strike at Ramla prison. Stores, businesses, and schools were closed in Ramallah and Nablus, municipal workers staged a sit-in at the Hebron City Hall, and their were sporadic incidents of violence in protest of the jailing of the Nablus Mayor.

Egypt's president celebrates peace with Israel at Mount Sinai

President Anwar Sadat, after his epochal journey to Jerusalem, has proclaimed Mount Sinai as a region where peace and love might triumph in the world. The companion measure, the agreement on the political future of the Israeli-occupied West Bank and the Gaza Strip, has not come to fruition to date.

The bargaining on the means for losing the Jewish hold of these territories and giving greater self-government to the Palestinian Arabs has made no discernible progress. Sadat professes that by the target date of May, 1980, success will be achieved.

At St. Catherine's Monastery Israel relinquished its control of the territory to the Egyptian President, the second anniversary of his peace initiative. In a mountain-rimmed valley where Moses and the children of Israel were sequestered near Mount Sinai, and where the prophet of God received the ten commandments in stone tablets, Sadat called for the three faiths of Moslem, Christian, and Jews to unite in brotherhood.

Sadat stated at the sixth century Greek Orthodox monastery, "In the name of the Egyptian people, who believe in the three Devine religions, I declare the Mount Sinai location open to followers of the three faiths, without any limitations or formalities."

11-23-79
Communist minority party emerges from revolution in Iran

The self-proclaimed leader of the Shiite Moslem sect is engineering a frenzy against the United States to conceal the mounting failure of his inept government.

The ferocity of the Ayatollah Khomeini attack on the United States measure the instability of his tottering regime. There are clear indications the Kremlin of the Soviet Union believes the Moslem regime of Iran is on the verge of collapse and is preparing to exploit it. The Soviet Union, under a 1921 treaty, has the right to intervene in Iran, should there constitute a threat to the Russian state. This provides a legal entrance of armed forces to stabilize the Iranian turmoil.

The "Brezhnev Doctrine" gives the Soviet Union the "right" to enter any Communist state to preserve its socialism should it be challenged externally or internally. The advance of Soviet power since the Cuban Crisis of 1962, with Americans, revolutionizes the balance of power in the Indian Ocean. The Russians have a superiority of military might along the Northern Frontier: Iran, Afghanistan, and Pakistan.

In addition to the surface tremors of the Kremlin's Iranian policy, attention is being centered on the rising militant nationism of Iraq. The Iraqis, until recently have been the most favored clients of the Middle East, but they have renounced its mutual assistance pact. It is apparent that the government of Iraq want no part of Soviet occupation.

The fall of the Khomeini leadership is foreseeable. President Anwar Sadat of Egypt stated, "Ayatollah Khomeini is a fanatic, consumed with hatred against the Shah Pahlavi, dethroned last year, to the point of seizing innocent Embassy Americans as hostages for his revenge."

11-26-79
Israel negotiating with Mayors of West Bank for Shakaa's release

The Israeli government is apparently planning a settlement with the Palestinian mayors of the West Bank for the release of the imprisoned mayor of Nablus, Bassam Shakaa, and an end to the deportation proceedings against him.

Mayor Elias Freij said that in exchange for Shakaa's release, Shakaa would denounce terrorist acts and Palestinian villagers would not press legal proceedings for the early evacuation of Elon Moreh, the Jewish settlement near Nablus.

Meanwhile in Tel Aviv, Israel, the newspaper Maariv reported the another section of about 865 square miles of desert in which the Alma oil fields are located that has provided Israel with over 25 percent of domestic consumption, a loss in dollars amounting to nearly a million a day. Two thirds of the Sinai Peninsula will be given to Egypt by January 25, 1980. The remainder will be surrendered in a three year agreement of the Camp David Accord of the Israeli-Egyptian peace treaty.

On December 5, 1979, Major General Benjamin Ben-Eliezer, military governor of the West Bank cancelled the deportation order for the Nablus mayor, Bassam Shakaa, and released him from the criminal charges; cautioned the Palestinians to reduce their political activity, and demonstrations against the Israelis.

The administrative body, mayors of nearby cities of the West Bank, who had resigned their posts returned to operate in the intervening towns and cities, withdrawing their resignations. The deportation was condemned by the United States, Egypt, and the General Assembly.

12-13-79
Sinai pullout of Israelis has mixed emotions
Beersheba, Israel

When the (Arye), Lion battalion withdrew from the Sinai last month, it left behind a sign explaining the reason for the departure. "We, the Israelis, left for peace."

This is the withdrawal, under the Egyptian-Israeli peace accords, from the desert peninsula conquered by the Jewish army in the 1967 War. Most of the units like the Ayre Battalion are being relocated in the Negev, the desert southern region of

Israel. New camps, many built from materials salvaged from the old bases in the Sinai, are springing up on the Jewish pre-1967 border.

Along the desert roadways, convoys of Israeli trucks are loading material for the new bases.

The members of the Jewish army and Air force have turned the Sinai Desert into one of the world's finest training areas. Israel is scheduled to leave the Refidim region, east of the strategic Giddi and Mitla passes by January 26, 1980. Some troop facilities are being temporarily relocated in the Eastern Sinai, across the line of the final pullback in March, 1982.

The Israeli defense forces have already removed several dozen camps from the Western Sinai, maintaining combat readiness, in case of an uprising. If the Israeli military has to return to the Sinai, they are better prepared than the Egyptians for fighting in the desert, but peace is the hope and future for the two nations, planning the day-to-day operations with caution and confidence.

12-26-79
Arabs of Israel becoming more aggressive
Umm El Fahm, Israel

Israel's Arab minority, still seeking a national identity, is changing its image from timidity to militancy.

The defeated, frightened Palestinians, refugees of 1948, has given way to a new generation which openly speaks out against Israel and seeks to be reunited with brothers locked behind foreign borders over three decades of violent dispute.

After almost thirty years of living in Israel, many of the 500,000 Arabs of the Jewish state talk of a long struggle ahead in coffee shops of a future of local autonomy.

The majority of Palestinian electuals in the British-ruled Palestine fled during the 1948 war. Most of the people who stayed belonged to the uneducated peasant class which was left without significant leadership.

Until the 1967 war, Israeli Arabs were cut off from the Arab world, and Palestinian refugees, abroad in particular, but the 12 years since the West Bank and Gaza with their 1,200,000 Palestinian people came under Israeli rule, have changed the way of thinking for many of the inhabitants.

The struggle against the mass expropriation of Arab land has ceased to be the ultimate objective. The populace are now looking for leadership to the P.L.O.

Habib Kahwagi, a member of the Palestine Executive Council in Damascus left Israel after his attempt to establish an Arab extremist Arab party that failed in 1967, is returning to form a coalition in support of an independent Palestinian state alongside Israel.

The P.L.O. policy calls for replacing Israel with a Socialist - secular country where Jews and Arabs would live together.

1-12-80

Balance of Religious and nationalistic forces in Israel necessary for Prime Minister Menachem Begin's coalition to remain.

Religion and nationalistic factions with Begin's ruling Likud party in the Knesset have found a common cause - a focal point bringing balance to the Israeli form of government.

Most of the people who played key roles in the creation of Israel were secular men and women for whom Zionism meant a return to a Jewish State. About 20 percent on the Israelis are Orthodox Jews, and the (Agudat), a religious sect, represents about a fifth of the 20 percent. The Agudat made a pact with the Prime Minister to support him if he would encourage change and bring religious law into the lives of the citizens.

Begin honored the Agudat by establishing a (Halacha), the religious Law of Judaism. For example: rules covering compulsory service for women have been eased so that young women who claim to be religious is exempt. The more liberal conditions of the Jewish abortion law have been removed, and pending autonomy law can virtually end post mortems.

The laws covering marriage and divorce are in the hands of the rabbinate. There is no civil marriage or divorce in Israel.

The Agudat, which has only four seats in the 120 seat Knesset, gains power by working within the government.

Other groups who make up the religious membership are the (Neturei Karta) Orthodox zealots of Zionism, and the (Gush Enumim), a faith bloc favoring Jewish settlements in the Arab populated Israeli occupied West Bank.

Israel is far from being a theocracy, - a government by religious leaders claiming to rule by Devine authority. Officially Israel does not have a state religion. It recognizes the rights of several - Muslim, the Druze, and the Christians - only tenets of Jewish religion have been written into Israeli law.

FIFTH WITHDRAWAL -
FROM REFIDIM (MITLA AND GIDDI PASSES)

Area of Israel Sinai returned to Egypt
Refidim, Israeli occupied Sinai

In accordance of peace to Egypt, Israel returns a vast stretch of desert is won and held in the battles of three bitter campaigns. Egypt formally takes over the fifth section, more than 5600 square miles on the 26th of January, 1980.

Refidim was the scene of a giant Jewish air force base and armored corp training center. Located near the mouth of the Mitla and Giddi passes, crucial westward accesses to the Suez Canal, Refidim was a strategic area in the battles of 1956, 1967, and 1973 Arab-Israeli wars.

A desert wind whipped the Israeli flags on a makeshift parade field, once an air base taxi-way. The base had been leveled, except for the runways and roadways, and a movie theater for the incoming Egyptian forces. The Republic of Egypt will rename the base "Bir Bafgafa."

As the military band played, a woman soldier sang a song written after the 1973 war: "It is the end of summer - The end of the way - Let them come home safely - Let it be."

At the end of the ceremony the band played the Israel national anthem, "Hatikva." The Egyptians will have gained two-thirds fo the Sinai up the interim line from El Arish, south of Ras Muhammed. The Jewish State will withdraw to the permanent international border in March 1982.

Behind them the Israeli military left a sign: "We're not retreating. We're leaving for peace."

Ovda replaces Etzion Air base in Sinai Desert

One of the billion dollar air bases in the Negev Desert will replace the ones Israel is surrendering to the Egyptians in the Sinai Peninsula.

Scores of air-conditioned white prefab buildings in which 1300 foreign workers live are being raised to be completed within a time frame of three years.

The facility is one of the three bases under construction in Southern Israel's Negev Desert. Ovda replaces the Etzion base in the Southwest section of the Sinai to be returned to Egypt in March, 1982.

Another base - being built with American help - is in progress at Ramon, southwest of Beersheba. A third, being built by Israel is East of Beersheba at Tel Mahata.

The first work at Ovda was the building of roads, temporary housing at headquarter facilities, and a rough air strip. A concrete plant, an asphalt plant, a steel prefabricating structure, and permanent living quarters for workers are proceeding in due course.

More than 800 Portugese laborers are at work at the Ramon base. They work six days a week, and although they take outings to Israeli resorts, they mingle little with the local population.

1-31-80
Hashemite Kingdom threatens Palestinian unity
Jerusalem, Israel

The Arab leaders in the Israeli-occupied territories call "Palestinian Unity" is being threatened by a resurgence of Jordanian influence and the reawakening of Islamic fever.

King Hussein is making subtle, studied moves to increase his influence on the West Bank of the Jordan River, which was won by Jordan in the 1948 Arab-Israeli war and lost in 1967.

Hussein has put his representatives on a committee that distributes large sums of Arab petrodollars to the West Bank and the Gaza Strip, while denying any interest in returning the region to Jordan sovereignty.

Since the Bagdad summit meeting last fall, the Arab league has prohibited direct aid from nations and "Sister Cities" to the West Bank municipalities, channeling the funds through the capital of Jordan, Amman. City officials, who used to go to Saudi Arabia or Libya seeking aid for a school or power plant must approach Amman for their request.

Despite the rule that money is to be approved by a joint committee, the Muktars, many have received direct grants from Jordan officials for projects such as wells and community centers.

Jordan has announced plans to open a series of medical clinics in the West Bank, staffed by doctors and nurses on the Jordan payroll. Most of the Hussein paid medical personnel hold jobs assigned to the Israeli military government. Under the Israeli proposal for autonomy, these services would be turned over to local Palestinians.

Egypt wants the occupied areas to have legislative and judicial powers, and capacity to proclaim eventual independence.

1-29-80
Sadat of Egypt says the United States is a source of security

President Anwar Sadat said, "Egypt will give immediate facilities to the American nation to help a Persian Gulf country faced with an external attack.

Sadat's pledge was an endorsement of President Carter's newly announced policy to use military force if necessary to protect oil supplies vital to the West, which was unveiled in his State of the Union message last week.

The President of Egypt gave credence to the fact that the United States is a security for the Arab regimes surrounding the Indian Ocean and the Islamic countries should know "who their true friends are."

Sadat has reduced the number of people at his Moscow embassy in retaliation of the Russian intervention in Afghanistan, and may break relations entirely with the Kremlin if it proceeds with their plans to extend the thrust of their armored divisions and air bombings into Pakistan.

Meanwhile reports from Jerusalem, Israel were, there appeared that Syrian armored troops in Lebanon moved within a few miles of the Israeli border. Major

Saad Haddad, leader of the enclave of "Free Lebanon, said that the Syrians had shifted an armored brigade of several thousand men from the coastal towns of Sidon and Damour to an area near Lake Qarawn, north of the border town of Metulla.

U.N. peacekeeping forces are deployed between the Syrian units and the Israeli supported Christians.

Israeli government opens door for Jews in the West Bank

The government of Israel said there is no impediment to Jewish people settling in the West Bank Arab city of Hebron.

Since the 1967 Middle East war, the Israeli military governors of the occupied territories surrounding the Jordan River and the Gaza Strip have barred the Jews from settling in the urban areas populated by Palestinian Arabs. At the same time, however, the Israeli cabinet has proclaimed that their citizens have the right to settle anywhere in the biblical "Eretz Israel" territory.

Nationalistic settlers movements have been pressing the government for permission to allow Jews to move into the West Bank cities of Nablus Ramallah, and Hebron.

Nearly a year ago the Gush-Emunim (Faith Bloc) women and children illegally occupied an abandoned Jewish hospital in Hebron's city center. They refused to leave when ordered out and have remained, under military guard, ever since.

Israeli Housing Minister, David Levy, dedicated the cornerstone of a new Jewish settlement at Efrat, north of Hebron on the road to Jerusalem, and stated, "5,000 citizens of the Jewish State will move into the West Bank complex in the near future." Efrat is an apartment development - Jewish suburb in Arab populated Judea - and part of the Etzion kibbutz dating back to the early 1940s.

Egypt and Israel exchange diplomatic ambassadors

Arabs marched, staged protest strikes, and clashed with riot police as Egypt and Israel began normalization of relations with each other and completed the establishment of diplomatic exchange of ambassadors.

Egyptian Ambassador, Saad Murtada, presented his credentials at the Jerusalem residence of Israel's President, Yitzhak Navon, and a Star of David honor guard, present with an Israel band, played the national anthem of Egypt.

The Ambassador said, "We can provide a good example of coexistence in peace between the people of the United Arab Republic and the residents of the Jewish state, reducing the threat of each nation's security, ensuring a just and lasting peace."

Meanwhile, the ambassador of Israel, Eliahu Ben-Elissar, presented his credentials to President Anwar Sadat at Abnine Palace in Cairo, Egypt, and stated, "Peace is unavoidable, and Sadat will live throughout history as the man who courageously braved the onslaught of criticism in the Arab world to bring an olive branch to the Jewish people at Jerusalem."

Sadat responded by saying "another chapter" has been opened in the history of the two-former adversaries. "Let us vow, on this historic occasion, to complete our sacred mission and make the peace process irreversible."

3-20-80

A Summit conference in April announced between Begin, Carter and Sadat that Israeli Prime Minister Menachem Begin and Egyptian President Anwar Sadat will come to Washington next month for separate conferences with President Carter aimed at increasing an agreement for the Palestinians on the West Bank and Gaza Strip that is workable.

For nine months, talks have been underway with Israel and Egypt to establish a self-governing authority for the Arab Palestinians, as stipulated in the Camp David Accords.

The President of the United States extended an invitation to the two leaders in personal telephone calls, but left the timing of the visits open. It is expected that Sadat and Begin will come to the American capital in mid-April and that King Hussein of Jordan, whose country lost control over the West Bank in the 1967 Arab-Israeli war, will follow them here at the end of the month.

The negotiations are stalled on fundamental questions that go to the heart of the 32 year old conflict: Whose sovereignty, and how much, shall prevail in territories claimed by both Israelis and Palestinians?

Egypt's position is: there should be a combination of legislative, executive, and judicial authority with control over land ownership, water distribution, and police power. Israel resists any definition of autonomy that would confer on the Palestinian inhabitants of the territories any governmental trappings of a state or sovereignty.

The main areas of disagreement are:

Governmental authority - Egypt in keeping with its broad definition of autonomy, calls for establishment of a 100 member Palestinian parliament with legislative powers, a 15 member executive council, and a separate judiciary. Israel wants an administrative council of 10 to 15 members. The military government of Israel must be withdrawn within 5 years.

Palestinian State proposed by Arab backers to United Nations

A Palestinian independent state was proposed to the Security Council by Arab leaders, and is certain to bring an American veto.

The draft resolution referred to previous General Assembly declarations and the committee's finding is the Palestinian question is the heart of the Mideast problem. It declared that the people of the area in the Gaza Strip should be able to exercise national self-determination, including the right to establish an independent state in Palestine, and that Israel should withdraw its forces from all Arab territories occupied since the 1967 Mideast War.

Security Council Resolution 242, adopted after the 1967 conflict, makes no mention of Palestinian rights, other than urging a "just settlement of the refugee problem."

Ambassador Falilou Kane of Senegal, chairman of the 23-nation committee of the Palestinians, pointed to growing support for Palestinian rights and warned the Mideast peace requires recognition of the problem. Kane denied any hostility by the committee toward Israel, although the proposed resolution makes no mention of Israel's right to exist.

The Ambassador of Israel, Yehuda Blum, attacked the committee as a pliant tool in the hands of Yasser Arafat, who in an interview published February 11, 1980 in Venezuela, said, "We shall not rest until the day we return to our homeland, and we destroy the state of Israel."

Blum charged that the debate was timed deliberately to "frustrate the ongoing peace accords," under the year-old Camp David agreements.

Involvement of Palestinian Arabs

An American initiative for a Palestinian homeland that provides security for, recognition of an normal relations with Israel, is now what many observers consider minimal. The Camp David accords can be the essential vehicle to build trust required for Israeli-Palestinian coexistence. Full autonomy for the Arabs in the West Bank and Gaza Strip is viable, provided that self-governing authority is endowed with adequate powers to give the Palestinians a sense of political power. Control over the security and administrative council are no less important as basic issues than are Israeli settlements, the status fo East Jerusalem, and the role of the P.L.O.

The crisis of the Middle East severely inhibits the United States to win the release of the American hostages in Iran and to check Soviet adventurism in the satellite countries surrounding this explosive area of the world.

For the Western super power, the Palestinian problem is a portent of things to come. The United States foreign-policy problems will continue to erupt in the developing nations, whose struggle for self-sufficiency and self-determination often causes political dislocation that directly affects imperial interests and rivalry.

If the Carter administration shrinks from its responsibility in the Persian Gulf region, there are others who are ready to fill the vacuum. Fulfilling the requirements of the Camp David Accords may be a determining factor of America's future as a global power.

Defense Minister of Israel resigns

In Jerusalem, Ezer Weizman submitted his resignation to the Israeli Cabinet, expressing his displeasure of Prime Minister Menachem Begin's stalling of the peace accords.

The Prime Minister quickly assigned Yitzhak Shamir, his Foreign Minister to fill the vacancy. Shamir was leader of the Jewish underground in the early 1940s, and spent more than a decade as a high official of Mossad, the Israeli secret police and intelligence service. He supports settlements in Palestinian regions.

Yitzhak Modai was appointed Foreign Minister to succeed Shamir. He is a middle-of-the-road Liberal in the Likud coalition and a strong supporter of Begin's right wing causes.

Ezer Weizman remains in the Knesset and in the Prime Minister's party but is in disrepute, and assigned as consultant and advisor in military matters.

November, 1982
Israeli debates over security and concessions of territory

More than fifteen years after the Israeli lighting victory in the Six-Day War that brought the West Bank and the Gaza Strip under its military control, the Jewish State has begun one of its periodic "great debates" over the future of the occupied territories.
    Prime Minister Menachem Begin, speaking for the government, and leaders of the opposition Labor Party repeated their plans for ending the military occupation that has been a constant source of friction among Israelis, Western Europe, and the United States.
    Begin repeated his announcement for giving Palestinians living on the West Bank of the Jordan River and in Gaza a limited form of autonomy that would allow them to handle their own administration of political matters, but would retain Israeli control over foreign policy, security and most important, land use. It would keep the hundred or more Jewish settlements scattered throughout the two territories under exclusive jurisdiction of Israeli law.
    The Labor Party calls for returning the population centers of the West Bank to Jordan, while retaining the Arab sector of Jerusalem, and maintaining a Jewish military presence in the Jordan Rift Valley, and along the mountain ridges.
    Palestinians are unwilling to pay the high political price demanded for either plan. To accept autonomy or partial return of the territory to Jordan, the Arabs would have to agree that Israel has the right to all the rest.
    The two factions will have to face reality, perhaps by compromising by negotiation with the Moslem Arab League.

11-1-82

Today, peace in the Middle East is an aspiring hope. Egyptians and Israelis differ in the implementation of an autonomy for the Palestinian people, however they want to coexist with the Arabs, and give them the right to form their own government, justice department, civil and municipal authority, with Israel remaining military in charge.
    In our Holy Bible, Christian believers are promised in God's revelation to Isaiah, that the Lord will make himself known to Egypt, Israel, and the surrounding Arabian countries, and they will worship together, and a highway will be built that will travel through their nations, and they shall live in peace, developing trade, travel, and a spirit of cooperation.
    Step by step, negotiations must continue if a full permanent and secure peace is to be had in the Middle East region. The land, called Mesopotamia, is the melting pot of the world, primarily Moslem, Christian, and Jewish faiths. They are suspicious and distrustful of one another.
    With diplomatic precision, problems can be solved, and they can bring an end to hostilities, and a revival of friendship and accord.

May 9, 1986

Americans in the Middle East requested to return to safer lands that can be protected from Arab Terrorists.

The United States assault of Libya has caused consternation in the civilized world. In a series of bravado: the Americans have transformed the image of a friendly ally to a power hungry antagonist of the Moslem nation, instead of using negotiations and peace maneuvers.

After nine years of very little progress, in the Arab eyes, instead of quiet diplomacy in solving the Palestinian problem of autonomy, there has been only confrontation.

The Middle East is an area where there is wisdom in the views of those determined to fight terrorism and those anxious to move the peace process. History of the Israelis and the Moslems in Palestine tells us that there is a struggle of two people, warring for the same piece of land. If terrorism is to recede, the Palestinian hope must be revived as a nation or provided with a homeland.

The Reagan administration can redeem a five-year record of sterility by seizing this opportunity of moderating resolution #242 of the United Nations charter, with the King of Jordan leading the negotiations. The P.L.O. is dependent on Egypt and Jordan, Syria has its hands full with Lebanon, the Soviet Union is not in a position to play spoilers; what a better time than now?

12-14-88
Middle East Controversy Moderates

After nearly a decade of inaction, the Palestinians are moderating their feelings toward Israel. Yasser Arafat, Chairman of the P.L.O., stated in clear and concise terms, that he deplores terrorism. The organization he represents will honor the United Nations resolutions, 242, 238, implying that the Jewish nation deserves the right to exist as a separate entity, with defined borders.

President George Bush of the United States, declared and authorized a beginning of a diplomatic dialogue, intimating the Palestinians have finally met conditions for direct talks. Simultaneously, the Secretary of State, George Shultz, designated Robert H. Pelletreau, in Tunisia, to direct operations with the P.L.O.

Shultz stated, "A wide gulf remains for settlement, with the Palestinians declaring they will not agree to less than a Palestinian State."

Behind the scene is a Swedish master of diplomacy, Sten Sture Andersson, was able t get all of the combatants together on main issues. A chief spokesman for the Swedish Democratic Party, Lief Gustafson, said Andersson combines an unerring political instinct with a warm, personable nature, to cover delicate diplomatic ground. The Foreign Minister visited the Israeli-occupied West Bank last year, and there met prominent P.L.O. supporters.

Andersson's crucial event was his meeting with the Jewish Parliament, who were opposed to the negotiations of land for peace.

In the Security Council, the English, France, China, the Soviet Union, and the United States, are members in good standing, and a solution to the Mideast problem will be thoroughly weighed by them.

12-16-88
Ambassador Pelletureau Talks Directly with P.L.O.

The first official meeting with the P.L.O. of the American Ambassador ended in a long boycott. "It is our hope that this dialogue, as it develops, will help bring about direct negotiations that will lead to a comprehensive peace," Pelletreau told reporters after meeting with a four man delegation."
    The meeting took place in an official Tunisian government guest house in suburban Carthage. Yassar Abd Rabbou, a delegate from the P.L.O., was chief negotiator. The first session was practical and useful, with the expectations of more concrete initiatives in the next several weeks.

    Pelletreau is a quiet diplomat who is committed to the survival of the Jewish State. In negotiations on the future of the occupied territories of Israel, the ambassador would hold free elections in Gaza, for the Palestinians. A source of the Israeli government stated extreme measures must be taken to prevent a Palestinian State, which could be a launch pad for war.
    The Jewish government desires to conserve its historical heritage, allow freedom of worship, and free access to all the holy places of all faiths. There will be guarantee rights for all religions and nationalities in the city of Jerusalem. These rights were denied when Jordan ruled Jerusalem from 1948 to 1967.

12-20-88
Prime Minister, Shamir Forms Coalition
After six weeks of intensive negotiations, the Likud Labor Party forms a coalition government in which the hawkish Yitshak Shamir remains Prime Minister, and the Labor's more dovish Shimon Peres, leaves the Foreign Minister position, but keep abreast of key questions on war and peace.
    Yitzhak Rabin will stay on as Defense Minister. Moshe Arens will be chosen as Foreign Minister. He is the former ambassador to the United States.
    Clauses in an accord include a ban on talking with the P.L.O., and a compromise plan to build a limited number of new settlements in the occupied West Bank and the Gaza Strip. Each of the major parties will hold ten cabinet positions. Beside the Premiership and Foreign Ministry, the Likud Party will control Housing, Industry, Transportation, Justice, Tourism and two positions without portfolio.
    Communications, Health, Agriculture, Education, Police, and two cabinet positions without portfolio.
    Optimists and cynic aside, this government has every chance of being the most important in Israel's history. The Soviet Union is stressing recognition in Middle East policy, and Egypt is shifting its position to support the Jewish nation.
    A lawyer by training, Shamir was born in Czarist Poland in 1915. The Nazis killed many of his family in World War II. Shamir immigrated to Palestine in 1935. Born by the name of Yitzhak Yzernitsky, he adopted the name of Shamir, meaning "Thorn." He joined the Irgum, a branch of Jewish fighters, in which he was captured and imprisoned in Ethiopia, but he escaped and returned to the Middle East in a hull of a ship. In the 1950s Shamir became a member of the "Mossad," the country's

secret service. Under the tutelage of Premier Menachem Begin, he was chosen as a speaker of the Knesset, the Jewish Parliament.

The Prime Minister states, "First we will put down the uprisings; the Intifada, to protect our security, and then negotiate. The result will be peace we bought, but peace with power.

3-26-89

What Progress has Occurred in Ten Years Since the Signing of the Camp David Treaty?

Today, a full decade after the three main contributors of the Peace Accords, President Jimmie Carter, Israeli Prime Minister, Menachem Begin, and President Anwar Sadad of Egypt, reflect that Sadat spoke prematurely when he said, "Today a new dawn is emerging from the darkness of the past. A new chapter is being opened in history of coexistence among nations." The chapter of harmony is ahead.

The peace treaty has proven amazingly durable, withstanding the shock of events as the President of Egypt, Anwar Sadat was assassinated by Muslim extremists in 1981. There was been an invasion of Israel into Lebanon in 1982, and a Palestinian uprising in the West Bank and the Gaza Strip.

The disappointment of the Jewish people is the lack of full normalization of relations in culture, commerce, tourism, and institutions of learning.

The Egyptians are disappointed in the peace not leading to wider settlement, to solution for the plight of the Palestinians, shot and killed in confrontation with Israeli troops in the occupied territories.

From the Jewish side, the illusion was that the image of negotiations could stand alone and grow into true friendship without any real effort to implement an autonomy for the Palestinian people.

In a major victory for Sadat's successor, President Mubarak, Israel returned a tiny Red Sea resort, Taba, to Egyptians, which is the last of the Sinai territory under terms of the "Camp David Accords."

The Middle East process is still alive, thanks to Egyptian diplomacy, and the Palestinians have recognized Israel's right to exist.

Mubarak will go to Washington in the United States next month to persuade the President that the Arabs in Egypt can be trusted.

11-24-91
Prime Minister Yitzhak Shamir

The Hebrew name that Yitzhak Shamir adopted upon his arrival from his native Poland in what was then the British led Palestine, in 1935, is taken from a type of Biblical stone so hard that it can cut other stones.

Shamir is a stocky, square shouldered Israeli Prime Minister who has spent nearly all of his 75 years in pursuit of what he sees as the supreme interests of the Jewish people and the Jewish State.

In an interview in 1986, he stated, "Peace is very important, but not more important than the security of the Israelis." As a leader of the "Stern Gang," the Jewish underground, he was labeled as a fanatical terrorist. In the early days of the

Israeli State, Shamir fought as an operative for the Mossad intelligence service. More than his mentor, Menachem Begin, the Prime Minister has a reputation for taking the hard line with the Palestinians and his other Arab neighbors. He makes clear his commitment to retain sovereignty over the territories captured during the 1967 War. The West Bank of the Jordan River, the Gaza Strip, and the Golan Heights were lands taken by the Jews. According to Shamir, the Palestinians are fighting to destroy our country, not to create their own.

It is Shamir who decided to personally lead the Israeli delegation into unprecedented peace talk that has taken place in Madrid Spain with the Moslem leaders. His entire life has been given to establishing the Jewish State in the Middle East, and achieving security and recognition. If it is to be, and the Jews and the Arabs are meant to live together, not general, or theoretical, or abstract, but real peace with us, added Shamir, it will have to be with our people and our State. Settlements are part of the territorial program. The parties need to start with unilateral steps, and come to a commitment binding both sides.

12-3-91
Tough Approach Toward Israel

Prime Minister of Israel, Yitzhak Shamir says, "How can I sit with the Arabs?" George Bush, President of the United States answers, "Go sit with them. They have undergone the American Modication."

As the Moslems prepare for the second round of the peace conference with Israel, they have come to the conclusion that Washington's new get-tough approach to the Jewish nation will outlast with overture.

In a mood of cautious pessimism that seems to prevail in the Arab camp, not all the blame is being cast toward Israel. Some of the Moslems say they have made a tactical blunder by accepting U.S. Resolutions 242 and 338, as a basis for talks, recognizing the Israelis, demanding territories captured in 1967, and leaving themselves with no room for maneuvering. The Arab coalition has fallen into disarray over how best to extract concessions from Israel, and Jordan quickly accepting the American invitation to hold discussions, without holding out for guarantees, such as focusing on substantive, not procedural issues.

Egypt has been working to temper Syria, attempting to coax Damascus into attending regional talks on arms control, the environment, and water; which are viewed by United States as ways of giving the Jews confidence to make progress on territory division.

The Palestinians are riding a fence, proclaiming publicly they agree with Syria as to disposition of land, without moving on bilateral negotiations, and saying privately that the talks need to move forward on all fronts.

If the meeting gets underway this week, the Arabs are determined to halt the Jewish settlement construction in the occupied West Bank, Gaza Strip and the Golan Heights. The settlement issue is really a test of credibility of Israel's attitude, and their seriousness in wanting peace.

Can there be peace in Palestine? Will a member of the United States have the charisma and diplomacy to end the conflict between the Moslems and the Jews? James Baker, the American Secretary of State, is a brilliant strategist.

Who would have thought the Israelis and the Arabs would speak to each other, rather than sit across form one another discussing the topic of peace? Baker has brought this to pass in Madrid Spain. The Middle East conference has revealed what is possible when a victor is unable to accept the plaudits of his accomplishment; the vanquished unwilling to say they have lost, and the referee insistent on keeping the outcome to himself.

With the Arabs weakened from the "Desert Storm" debacle, they are ready to negotiate an end to their decades- old bitter dispute with the Jewish nation. In "Desert Storm," a Saudi Arabian official spoke of "The Encounter." "It is not going to be easy for the defenders of our faith, the guardians of the Holy places, to justify having to call in the Crusaders," he added.

12-9-91
Mideast Talks Resume - Test of Patience

Arab and Israel negotiators are expected to get down to real business this week. Are both sides ready to talk about the essential issues of the decades-old dispute? Only time can tell.

Secretary of State, James A. Baker III, and his top aides, have devoted most of the last eight months to the task of bringing about concrete discussion. The next test will be of their patience.

Already, Israel is objecting to what it considers American interference, and the Arabs, who now welcome an active U.S. role, will almost surely change their minds if the United States starts to suggest specific concessions they should make. Baker fully understands that the negotiations will be long and difficult, and ultimately, may fail.

Samuel L. Lewis, President of U.S. Institute for Peace, and former U.S. Ambassador to Israel under Presidents Carter and Reagan, expressed his reason for a go-slow approach. In Madrid, Spain, on November 3, a key phase of the peace process began with direct talks with Syria, Lebanon, and a joint Jordanian-Palestinian delegation. If substantive discussion do occur this week, several key points are likely to be addressed.

The Palestinians and Israel will talk about a limited self-rule for the Palestinian residents of the Israeli-occupied West Bank and the Gaza Strip.

Prime Minister Yitzhak Shamir, will attempt to embrace an autonomy plan for the Palestinians.

Israel and Syria will talk about the Golan Heights, and a way of ending a formal state of war, that has existed between Damascus and Jerusalem since 1948.

Both sides have staked out uncompromising positions, difficult to see how much progress can be made. Israel and Lebanon will discuss security.

The northern border of Israel, and the presence of Israeli troops in a narrow strip of southern Lebanon will be talked about. No one expects any solution before

Syria and the Jewish State reach an accommodation, because Syria exerts a strong influence over Lebanon's government.

8-30-92
Palestinians Will Recognize Israel

Israel is on the verge of recognizing the P.L.O. according to sources close to the action. This is a key step toward resolving decades of conflict. An Israeli cabinet member, and a Palestinian official announced both sides could sign an agreement in principle to implement Palestinian autonomy in the occupied territories.

Israel, in the past, has refused to recognize the P.L.O. branding it as a terrorist group, but informal contacts have approved of Prime Minister Rabin of Israel's government action. It remains to be seen whether the P.L.O. will delete from its charter the reference of the Jewish Nations' destruction, and its right to exist among the United Nations.

The Israeli cabinet is expected to vote on August 30, 1993 to pursue the autonomy plan. Foreign Minister, Shimon Peres, is planning to fly to Washington, D.C. this week to endorse the agreement. Rabin may seek a vote from the Knesset, Israel's parliament.

Health Minister, Chaim Ramon said, "if the people of the Palestine will talk and contribute peace, we shall respond likewise."

In Gaza and Jericho, the Israeli army will withdraw from population centers to security locations. Palestinians in Gaza and Jericho will be given full control over their internal affairs. Israel will maintain control over entry points to the autonomous areas. She will protect Jewish settlements.

8-30-93
Self Rule by Palestinians Approved

Despite a political, military, and administrative complexity, Israeli officials indicated the Jewish State will commit to working out a program for the Palestinian people to form their own government within a framework of autonomy.

There are clear differences in how to implement the agreement of self-government, especially in the holy cities of Jericho and Gaza. As outlined by Israeli's Foreign Minister, Shimon Peres, the proposal envisions an election of a Palestinian Council, which will have its headquarters in Bethlehem, south of Jerusalem, and will assume administrative responsibility for the rest of the West Bank.

Advising the Knesset, Peres, during a stormy session, said their government will have a strong police force to replace Israeli troops as they are withdrawn.

"We want to live in peace, shouted Peres, to the angry opposition of the Jewish Parliament. Thy are human beings, like ourselves. We do not want to degrade them or humiliate them. They are not put in bottles like insects. Shalom, and may God lead and guide them in their progress."

Security, and everything that impacts the nation of Israel, is not just for the settlers of the West Bank, and Gaza, but our whole country, and peace with our neighbors is imperative for our future, intimated Prime Minister Rabin.

9-9-93
From Conflict to Peace - Israel, P.L.O.

Israel and the P.L.O., through a series of secret contacts, have cleared the way for signing an accord to launch Palestinian self-rule in the Gaza Strip and the West Bank town of Jericho.

A list of events clearly does not in itself guarantee a peaceful transition, however, according to Chairman Yasser Arafat, there is an end to violence with Israel. Terrorist organizations, such as the "Hamas," have carried "The Intifada," destruction of the Jewish State, in their hearts, and change will only occur slowly.

The key dates of Israel's relation with the Palestinian organization from conflict to peace are:

1. 1964 - Founding of the P.L.O., that calls for eliminating the Jewish State, and gain control over Palestine.

2. 1965 - Founding of "Fatah" a major component that advocates armed struggle with Israel. Yasser Arafat becomes Fatah leader, and later the P.L.O. Chairman.

3. October 1974 - Arab Summit - Recognizes the P.L.O. as sole representative of the Palestinians.
4. June 1982 - Israel invades Lebanon, pushing the P.L.O. guerillas North. Fifteen thousand P.L.O. guerillas are forced out of Beirut, Lebanon.

5. August 1986 - Israel prevents its forces from meeting with P.L.O. members.

6. October 1991 - United States sponsors Middle East peace talks.

7. January 19, 1993 - Israeli Parliament overturns law in baring Israelis from meeting with P.L.O. members.

8. August 29, 1993 - Foreign Minister, Shimon Peres, tells cabinet of Israel that it has reached an agreement with the Palestinians on self-rule in the occupied lands.

The road to peace is getting wider. In the Middle East, the participant are talking, and the United States, and their ambassadors are making progress for a lasting peace.

9-10-93
P.L.O., Israel, Agree to Peace, Recognizing Each Other's Rights to Exist

In a move toward ending the Middle East's enduring conflict, the Israelis and the P.L.O. came together, declaring their intent to begin living as neighbors, not enemies.

P.L.O. leader, Yasser Arafat has been characterized for nearly 30 years as an outlaw, however he won legitimacy as Chairman of a revised Palestinian, and reaffirmed in a session with Israel Parliament, wide recognition of the Jewish State, who then approved the status of Arafat.

With the signing of a declaration of principles, the Palestinian people can take part, leading to a normalization of life, rejecting violence and terrorism. They can also shape their reconstruction, economic development, and establish autonomy.

Shimon Peres, Foreign Minister of Israel stated, "the things the Jews wanted were achieved."

Opponents of Arafat, who boycotted the committee, argued that the P.L.O. leader was selling out. The Palestinian struggle provides no guarantees for the West Bank of Jericho, nor for the crucial issues of Jerusalem and the Israeli settlements.

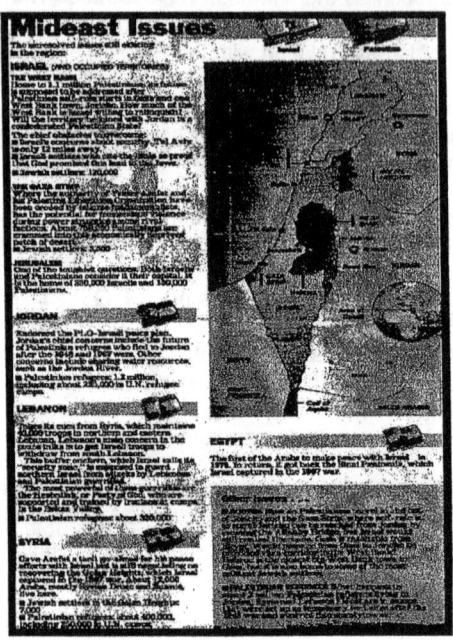

9-14-93

Israel and the P.L.O. Adopt Framework for Peace

In Washington, D.C. of the United States, with a swift stroke of the pen, the Middle East was alerted with people attempting to bury their differences, instead of resorting to bloodshed. Yitzhak Rabin, Prime Minster of Israel, declared, "we have fought against you, Palestinians, and we say to you today, in a loud and clear voice; Enough of blood and tears! Enough." The seventy-one year former general allowed a single smile to cross his face.

Yasser Arafat, the P.L.O. Chairman responded, wearing an olive drab uniform on a black Kaffiyeh, tradesmark of the P.L.O.; "It is a most difficult period of our lives. It deserves the utmost effort, because the land of peace yearns with us, and we desire a just and comprehensive peace."

Both parties recall generations of sorrow and bitter struggle, and pledge to press forward with diplomatic tasks that remain, calling upon the United States and other countries to aid in the process, and turn a theoretical framework into concrete results for Israel and the Palestinians.

Witnesses to the ceremony of history, along with President Clinton and the Democratic administration, were former presidents, Jimmie Carter and George Bush; along with Secretaries of State, James Baker, Cyrus Vance, Henry Kissinger, George Shultz, and Edmund Muskie. Scores of others were present who played an important role in diplomacy on the way to peace in the Middle East.

President Clinton indicated that the agreement of September 13, 1993, will not diminish our longstanding commitment to Israel's security.

The Prime Minister of Israel, Yitzhak Rabin, quoted the famous Bible passage in Ecclesiastes: "To everything, there is a season; and a time for every purpose in heaven; a time to be born, a time to die; a time to kill, a time to heal; a time to weep, and a time to laugh; a time to love, and a time to hate; a time of war, and a time of peace." Ladies and gentlemen, a time of peace has come.

PLO Chairman Yasser Arafat, far right, triggers a last-minute drama in Cairo at the official signing of the accord on Palestinian self-rule. From left, Israeli Foreign Minister Shimon Peres, Russian Foreign Minister Andrei V. Kozyrev, Israeli Prime Minister Yitzhak Rabin and Egyptian President Hosni Mubarak try to persuade Arafat to sign the pact. After discussions and a short recess, Arafat signed. A6

TREATY PROPOSAL WITH THE PALESTINIANS
ARAFAT AND PICTURES

9-14-93
Uncertain Handshake Seals New Relationship for Rabin and Arafat

An awkward handshake between the Prime Minister of Israel and the Chairman of the P.L.O., Yasser Arafat, may be a new beginning for peace in the Middle East. At a ceremony marking a transformation in Washington, D.C., with President Bill Clinton's encouragement, Arafat moved across the platform of the South Lawn of the Whitehouse to shake the hand of Rabin and Israel's Foreign Minister, Shimon Peres.

Visibly uncomfortable with sharing the spotlight with is previous enemy of the past, Rabin spoke of giving peace a chance. The two leaders and two peoples have taken possibly irrevocable steps for security and friendship.

With the Palestinians recognizing Israel's right to exist and live in peace, Rabin, in turn, will recognize the Palestinians as a national entity, to develop rules and regulations, with an enterprise system of government.

Hanna Ashrawi, spokeswoman for the Palestinian delegation, was buoyant with expectation, as she declared, "for the first time in many years, we have real recognition."

Rabin said he felt a certain uneasiness, indicating, "I cannot forget 30 years of Arab terror, but we have learned the hard way, that peace can come, even with your enemies, sometimes bitter enemies. In renouncing violence, Arafat has shown us we can live together in peaceful surroundings.

A jubilant Jimmie Carter, past President, stated, "We were once reviled by Jews in the Arab partisan Middle East, and I predict Israel will sign a peace treaty with Jordan, Syria, and Lebanon in the future."

> ■ MADRID II?
> U.S. envisions summit, but difficult work lies ahead. A6
>
> between Israel and an Arab state following the 1979 Israel-Egypt peace agreement.
>
> "We have gone here a long way toward a full treaty of peace and, even though our work has not yet ended, it is my hope and belief that not long from today we shall return to signing a final and a permanent treaty of peace," Rabin said.
>
> For Hussein, Monday's ceremony marked a dramatic break with Jordan's traditional determination to keep its foreign policy firmly within an Arab consensus. For years, Hussein made it clear he was interested only in a comprehensive peace agreement that would cover all Arab countries, especially Syria.
>
> To be sure, Hussein has not yet signed a peace treaty. But his declaration Monday puts Jordan far ahead of Syria and threatens to isolate Syrian President Hafez Assad. In the past, Syria has responded angrily to any suggestion of a separate peace between Israel and any Arab state. Relations between

■ **Mideast:** Historic declaration closes official state of war. Both sides pledge to move toward full peace treaty, but key details remain unresolved.

By NORMAN KEMPSTER
TIMES STAFF WRITER

WASHINGTON—Israel and Jordan drew 46 years of suspicion and hostility to a close Monday as Prime Minister Yitzhak Rabin and King Hussein, in a declaration signed on the White House lawn, pledged to "bring an end to bloodshed and sorrow."

In a ceremony that President Clinton said marks "a new chapter in the march of hope over despair," the Israeli and Jordanian leaders promised to resolve disputes peacefully and vowed not to "threaten the other by use of force, weapons or any other means."

"Out of all the days of my life, I do not believe there is one such as this," said Hussein, a once-dashing young monarch who has grown bald and gray in four decades on the Hashemite throne—all of them under the shadow of the Arab-Israeli conflict. He said the ceremony would bring both nations "security from fear, which I must admit has prevailed over all the years of our lives."

Rabin, Israel's army chief of staff in the last shooting war between Israel and Jordan in 1967, said the agreement shows the neighboring countries can "accelerate our efforts towards peace, overcome obstacles [and] achieve a breakthrough."

Despite the soaring rhetoric, their declaration merely ended the technical state of belligerency between the two countries, falling short of an official peace treaty because key details—which neither side has disclosed—remain unresolved.

Rabin and Hussein promised intensive negotiations aimed at completing the second formal treaty

• Two new border crossings will be opened, one between the twin southern cities of Aqaba, Jordan, and Eilat, Israel, and one in the north.
• Third-country tourists will be given "free access" in traveling between the countries.
• Israeli and Jordanian police will cooperate against crime, especially smuggling.
• Negotiations will be accelerated toward opening international airline routes across both countries.

Israel and Jordan also promised to prevent their territory from being used as a base for acts of terrorism against the other. And Jordan promised to urge the Arab League to end its boycott of Israel, although the kingdom did not unilaterally end its own participation in this practice.

In one provision that is potentially divisive for the Arab world, Israel agreed to respect Jordan's role "in the Muslim holy shrines" of Jerusalem. Rabin also promised that Israel "will give high priority to the Jordanian historic role in these shrines" when negotiations over the final status of Jerusalem begin between Israel and the Palestinians.

By favoring Jordan's claim to supervise Al Aqsa mosque and the Dome of the Rock on Jerusalem's Temple Mount—one of the holiest places in Islam—Israel delivered a rebuff to the PLO and its chairman, Yasser Arafat. Arafat told Christopher last week the Palestinians were proper guardians of Muslim and Christian shrines in Jerusalem.

Even as progress toward peace was being recorded in Washington, Iranian-backed guerrillas ambushed an Israeli army convoy in south Lebanon on Monday, killing an Israeli officer and wounding 10 soldiers, security sources said.

Continued from A1
Damascus and Cairo were frosty for years after Egypt made peace with Israel.

Clinton sought to smooth Assad's reaction to the Israel-Jordan declaration. In a telephone call just before the signing ceremony, Clinton assured him the United States considers Syria a major factor in the Middle East and that Washington will continue to try to mediate a peace between Syria and Israel.

U.S. Secretary of State Warren Christopher, who plans to resume his Jerusalem-Damascus shuttle diplomacy before the middle of next month, said he hopes Syria will be swept up in the momentum created by Hussein and Rabin. "Each one of these historic breakthroughs that happens makes it slightly easier for the next one to happen," Christopher said.

The ceremony—conducted at the same table used for the Israel-Egypt agreement and for the pact Israel signed last year with the Palestine Liberation Organization—marked a welcome foreign policy success for the Clinton Administration, which has been buffeted by crises in Bosnia-Herzegovina, Haiti and Somalia.

The United States served as go-between to set up Monday's meeting. In his speech, Clinton paid tribute to predecessors Jimmy Carter and George Bush for earlier Arab-Israeli peacemaking that helped make the current talks possible.

Clinton made the most of the latest Middle East accord, presiding over the ceremony and signing the document himself to demonstrate his government's support. "History is made when brave leaders find the power to escape the past and create a new future," he said.

It was the first publicly acknowledged meeting between Hussein and an Israeli prime minister. But, unlike other Arab leaders, Hussein met regularly in private with a succession of Israeli prime ministers and foreign ministers in what became the Middle East's most widely known secret.

When the Rabin-Hussein meeting was announced 10 days ago, it appeared that the most significant outcome would be to take the relationship into the sunlight. But Israel-Jordan talks in the last week produced an impressive list of substantive agreements.

Besides better relations with Israel, Jordan is looking for economic assistance from the United States, especially some relief from its $700-million debt. Although he made no promises, Christopher said the U.S. government "is committed to supporting those that take risks for peace."

Jordan and Israel, carved out of the old British mandate of Palestine, have been blocked by almost half a century of hostility from developing cooperative economic projects that their similar geography seems to demand. Hussein and Rabin pledged to heal that breach, outlining a series of steps:
• Direct telephone links will be opened.
• The countries will link their electricity grids.

Recalling the tedious 13 days of negotiations in September of 1978, the President then, Jimmie Carter, declared to an enthusiastic ovation, "Diplomacy brought about the signing of 'The Camp David Peace Treaty', with the courage of Prime Minister Menachem Begin, President Anwar Sadat of Egypt, and the dismantling of the settlements of Israel in the Sinai Desert, we have secured peace in the region. These negotiations will succeed too."

Israeli Prime Minister Yitzhak Rabin, left, shakes hands with PLO leader Yasser Arafat after the accord is signed as President Clinton looks on.

9-15-93
Jordan Inks Interim Pact with Israel

Official sources reveal the momentum building for the Jordan Arabs and other countries of the Moslem world to join in a cooperative effort, to lay a foundation and a framework for a lasting peace with Israel.
    After the historic breakthrough with the Palestinians and the Israelis, the Secretary of State, Warren Christopher, who brokered the agreement between Jordan and the Jewish State, there were calls for environmental studies, water resources, economic development, security and refugee settlements.
On his way back to Jerusalem, Prime Minister Rabin of Israel, stopped in Morocco for talks with King Hussan. They spoke of starting normal relations with each other soon. Rabin said, "I think of what happened in

    Washington, there is an opening for more Arabian Countries to join the peace process."
    Rafael Edri, A Morrocan-born member of the Jewish Parliament, from Rabin's Labor Party, organized the visit. It bolsters the Israeli Prime Minister's large community of Morrocan Jews, estimated at 120,000 people.
    Rabin and Peres met King Hussan at his seaside palace in Skhirat, Morrocco, amid tight security. Morrocan Prime Minister, Mohammed Karim, and other government leaders were also present.
    Prime Minister Abdul Salam Majali, who was Jordan's chief negotiator, and architect of the agenda, confirmed during a press conference in Amman, Jordan, that

the signing agreement permits the two nations to implement interim accords in all their five provinces, without a treaty or regional peace settlement. Jordan hopes to resolve with Israel water rights to the Jordan and Yarmouk rivers. They also would seek the return of two small tracts of land that were captured by the Israelis in the 1967 War.

5-6-94
Mideast, Gaza, Jericho, Palestinians Seek Homeland

The dynamics of peacemaking in the Middle East dramatically changed on May 4, 1994, when Israel and the P.L.O. signed an agreement on Palestinian self-rule. Peace now depends on bold moves by courageous leaders like the Israeli Prime Minister, Yitzhak Rabin, and P.L.O. Chairman, Yasser Arafat, and also the abilities of tens of thousands of people to make the process work.

    Coexistence and cooperation will replace confrontation and conflict. It is the hope of the Palestinians that life will improve for them. Believing that the political solutions will provide for common individuals to rise from impoverishment.

    With determination, Prime Minister Rabin shook hands with his former enemy, Yasser Arafat saying, "We have passed through a very difficult time to reach this day, but it has happened." "For almost a century, we have experienced blood and hatred; but today we declare peace, and we welcome you as neighbors," added Rabin.

Arafat, frustrated over months of inaction, was subdued for much of the ceremony. He intimated that the coming steps will require greater vision. A total of 6000 new Palestinian police are to arrive in Gaza and Jericho over the next several weeks, and hundreds of prisoners will be released from Israeli jails. The P.L.O. is to appoint a 24 member authority to form the government structure.

The signing ceremony was held in the presence of dignitaries; Secretary of State, Warren Christopher of the U.S., Russian Foreign Minister, Andrei Kozyrev; Japanese Minister, Koji Kakizawa; and their envoys from around the world. This event has hosted by the Egyptian President, Hosni Mubarak, on his 66th birthday.

Mubarak stated, "We live in an age of political wonder, where old hatreds give way to new hopes. Despite the obstacles, the countries long for peace."

Warren Christopher, U.S. Secretary of State, added, "Tenacity and conviction of the Jews and the Palestinians will build a bridge to peace."

All was not well for some Palestinians, wanting more, the Statehood too. Within minutes after the signing ceremony liberating his land, a Palestinian, Akil Abu Shammala, left his television set, and took to the streets. He was not happy, and he and some of his friends in Gaza spent the afternoon sun at Israel's military headquarters, protesting that they were waiting for something far more concrete, profound, and personal. Shammala came for his older brother, after nine years of imprisonment, for his release, as one of many others. Most of the 850,000 residents in the region, in defiance of army orders, had staged a prayer vigil against the autonomy accord. They still are under occupation.

For now, Shammala worries most about his brother and friends who will have difficulty adjusting after years in prison. Now will they rehabilitate? His brother has six children. How will he face his sons? Many Palestinians have hopes and fear what will happen next. Shammala repeats, "we cannot celebrate until we know the land is ours to keep."

7-25-94
Border Crossings Open Between Israel and Jordan

Israel and Jordan drew 46 years of hostility and suspicion to a close in a declaration signed at the Whitehouse in Washington, D.C. and Yitzhak Rabin, the Israeli Prime Minister stated, "we pledge to bring an end to bloodshed and sorrow."

King Hussein, a once dashing monarch, has grown bald and grey in four decades on the Hashemite throne, all of them under the Arab-Jewish conflict. "Opening up our borders will bring both nations security from fear and reprisals," was what the King of Jordan stated.

Two new border crossings will be opened, one between the twin southern cities of Aqaba, Jordan and Eilat Israel, and one in the north. Third country tourists will be given free access in traveling between the countries. Israel and Jordan will cooperate against crime, especially smuggling. Negotiations will open to forming airline routes, previously closed.

Israel and Jordan also promised to prevent their territory from being used as a base for acts of terrorism. Jordan will urge the Arab League to end its boycott with Israel.

Israel agrees to respect Jordan's role in the Muslim holy shrines of Jerusalem.

By favoring Jordan's claim to supervise Al Aqsa mosque and the Dome of the Rock on Jerusalem's Holy Mount, Israel delivered a rebuff to the P.L.O., and its Chairman, Yasser Arafat.

Jordan and Israel carved out of the old British mandate of Palestine, new conditions for friendship, blocked by almost a half century of hostility from developing economic projects which would increase trade with one another. Hussein and Rabin promised to heal the breach.

Israeli Prime Minister Yitzhak Rabin, left, President Clinton and Jordan's King Hussein during the signing ceremony of the peace treaty that ends decades of hostility between Israel and Jordan

King Hussein signs agreement on table used for the Israel-PLO pact and 1979 Egypt-Israel treaty

DECLARATION OF PEACE PROPOSAL
JORDAN

7-26-94
Declaration with Jordan and Israel May Lead to a Lasting Peace

A historic declaration of peace closes an official state of war with Jordan and Israel. There are details to be resolved in this agreement. In the United States, Prime Minister Rabin and King Hussein of Jordan promises to resolve their differences through negotiations. Israel's army chief of staff in the last shooting war in 1967, indicated with action to the Muslim nations that the two countries can overcome obstacles, and achieve a breakthrough of peace.

With Syria, before the signing of the Declaration, President Clinton called President Assad to assure him that the U.S. considers Syria a major factor of the Middle East in bringing the Arab countries together to recognizing the members of Jewish nation, and it will become part of the community of nations in the world.

Besides better relations with Israel, Jordan is looking for economic assistance from the United States, especially some relief from its $700 million debt. Although he made no promises, the Secretary of State, Warren Christopher, said the U.S. is committed to supporting those who take risks for peace.

Rabin and Hussein pledged to link electricity grids, open new border crossings, and give tourists free access in traveling and transportation.

Some Israelis expressed reservations about making territorial concessions to Jordan, or sharing its water.

Second Page

In Washington, D.C. Israel and Jordan are consolidating environmental projects intended to give their citizens a tangible dividend from 46 years of hostility.

Jordan's Crown Prince and Israelis Foreign Minister met with President Bill Clinton of the United States, at the Whitehouse on October 3, 1994, to arrange future building in the Negev Desert, to convert it into a valley for peace, agriculture, and tourism. For the economic development of Jordan, the Rift Valley is a region centered near the Red Sea, that straddles the border between the two countries.

Foreign Minister, Shimon Peres, and Jordan's Crown Prince, Hassan, agreed to establish free trade zones, and create a Red Sea marine Peace Park, and begin feasibility study of dams on the Yarmuk and Jordan rivers.

Secretary of State, Warren Christopher, will visit the Middle East this weekend to resume shuttle negotiations between Syria and Israel. In advance of this trip, President Clinton plans to meet with Syrian Foreign Minister, Farouk Shareh.

10-27-94
Israel Signs Peace Treaty with Jordan

Mideast - In a desert ceremony, Prime Minister Rabin of Israel and King Hussein of Jordan end generations of fighting and reprisals. At the Arava Crossing, a border between Jordan and Israel, on the 26th of October in 1994, a peace treaty was signed, which adds momentum for a comprehensive peace with Muslims and surrounding countries.

With soaring hopes, the two leaders declared their nations were not only at peace, but also good neighbors, interested in relationships as partners in building the region.

Jordan's King Hussein, left, and Israel's Yitzhak Rabin shake hands as President Clinton applauds.

In Arava, a sand blistered desert area, Jordan and Israel acknowledged each others sovereignty removing scores of enmity between them.

This treaty effectively shifts the balance of power across the Middle East, making it easier for other Arab states to reach peace with Israel.

President Bill Clinton of the United States praised King Hussein and Prime Minister Yitzhak Rabin as great leaders, who sees bright horizon of dawn, even while darkness lingers. He stated, "These men are taking no man's land into every man's home, taking down the barbed wire, removing land mines, and helping the wounds of war to heal."

Israel signed its first treaty with an Arab state when Anwar Sadat was President of Egypt in 1979. Last year, an interim peace agreement was signed with the P.L.O. on Palestinian self-government.

Israel will allow King Hussein and Jordan to take more water from the Yarmouk and the Jordan rivers.

They are the Yormouk and the Jordan rivers. The flow of water will be increased into the Jordan River from the Sea of Galilee to benefit Jordan farmers.

President Clinton of the U.S. has a concern of the growth of Islam and an upsurge of terrorism intended to thwart the peace movement. He approved of the handling of the deadly Hamas bombings in the cities of Tel Aviv and Jerusalem.

King Hussein is willing to move into a centrist position, shifting from a cold war to a realistic approach in today's world. With the Prime Minister Rabin, of Israel, it is easier now bridging the differences in negotiations, and the King can accept Israel's right to exist and be at peace with its neighbors.

Not far from the signing of the peace accord, people loyal to King Hussein, live in Naur, Jordan. Abdul Salam Samarneh Ajarmeh, has gazed with longing the lights of Jerusalem twinkling on the horizon. As he watched Jordan and Israel sign the peace treaty, with the leaders embrace, he will begin his first visit to the Holy City of Jerusalem. "Sure, I am going to go," he stated; "We support our King, and we welcome the prospect of peace." Naur lies 20 miles south of Amman, Jordan, and home to a mixed settlement of Bedouins. The village is organized along tribal lines, and nearly half of the people, 20,000 population are army officers. The Holy City for many has been only a dream to visit, but now they can go in peace.

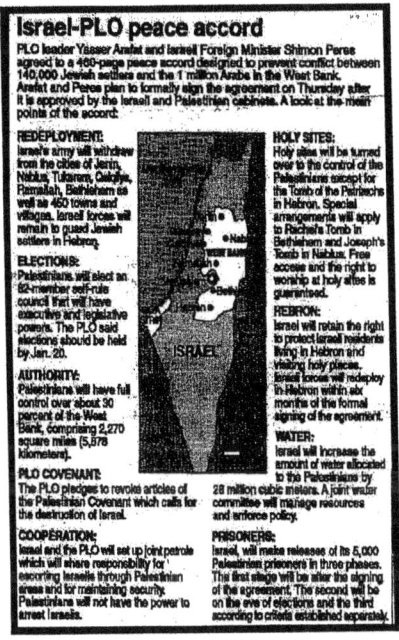

9-25-95
Israel, P.LO. Agree to a Peace Accord
West Bank, Taba, Egypt

After all night talks, and a shouting match, with angry walkouts by the P.L.O. Chieftain, Yasser Arafat, the two sides agreed Sunday, September 24, 1995, to sign a pact ending nearly three decades of Israeli occupation of the West Bank cities.

    In the Israeli-P.L.O. peace agreement, Foreign Minister, Shimon Peres, and the Palestinian leader, Arafat, will sign a 460 page accord designed to prevent conflict between 140,000 Jewish settlers and one million arabs in the region.

    Looking at the main points of the Accord:

1. Redeployment - Israel's army will withdraw from the cities of Jenin, Nablus, Tukarem, Qalqilya, Ramallah, Bethlehem, as well as 450 towns and villages. Israeli forces will remain to guard the settlers in Hebron.

2. Elections - Palestinians will elect an 82 member self-rule council that will have legislative and executive powers. The elections will be held by January 20, 1996.

3. Authority - Palestinians will have full control over 30% of the West Bank, comprising 2,270 square miles.

4. P.L.O. Covenant - The P.L.O. pledges to revoke Articles of the Palestinian declaration which calls for destruction of Israel.

5. Cooperation - Israel and the P.L.O. will set-up joint patrols who will share responsibility for escorting Israelis through Palestinian areas to main security. The Palestinian police does not have the power to arrest Israeli citizens.

Holy sites - Except for the area in which the Tombs of the Patriarchs are located, Palestinians will exercise protection of other areas on the West Bank and Gaza Strip. Special arrangements will apply to Rachel's Tomb in Bethlehem, and Joseph's Tomb in Nablus. Free access to worship is guaranteed.

6. Prisoners - Israel will release 5000 Palestinians in three phases: the first, after signing the Pact; the second, will be on the eve of the elections; and the third, separate after establishing a free exchange.
   The prisoner exchange will be discussed in detail in the United States before the signing on September 28, 1995. This accord is an attempt to bring people born in the same cradle, who are fighting on the same fronts, and agree to a new future.

11-5-95
Prime Minister, Yitzhak Rabin of Israel Dies by an Assassins Bullet
Tel Aviv, Israel

A right-wing student gunned down the Prime Minister on November 4, 1995, after he had told thousands that what we really want is peace. Rabin, a war hero who became an architect of the Arab-Israeli reconciliation, died on an operating table from gunshot wounds to his chest and back.
   The gunman was identified as a Jewish law student, Yigal Amir, age 27. The assassination of Israel's Prime Minister, Yitzhak Rabin, leaves a profound political void in the peace process for Israel and its neighbors.
   Amid outpourings of sorrow, the future of peace will move ahead, according to negotiators. Rabin's death will ignite the fires of the conservative party, but his unique credibility to convince the Jewish Nation to pay the price of land for peace will be sorely tested.
   Shimon Peres will become the interim Prime Minister, and has been a prime mover behind recent efforts for peace with the Palestinians and Jordan. The Israeli public has become polarized with the prospect of elections next year, amid opposition by some Israelis to trade land for peace. President Bill Clinton of the U.S. and

Secretary of State, Warren Christopher have been busy with Mideast leaders reaffirming support for the peace process.

A shaken P.L.O. leader, Yasser Arafat, who has escaped numerous assassinations, expressed shock and sadness, and called Rabin a great emancipator for the Israelis. Shalom, Chever, Rabin

Clinton: 'Goodbye, friend'

WASHINGTON (AP) — Visibly shaken and on the verge of tears, President Clinton mourned the death of Yitzhak Rabin on Saturday, saying the Israeli prime minister gave his life trying to bring Israel a lasting peace. "Goodbye, friend," said Clinton.

Standing in the Rose Garden, Clinton's voice choked with emotion as he said, "I admired him and I loved him very much." The flag flying above the White House was lowered to half-staff.

Clinton bade his farewell to Rabin not far from where he had stood with Rabin and PLO Leader Yasser Arafat in September 1993 when the former enemies signed a historic peace agreement and sealed it with a handshake.

In words directed to the
Please see CLINTON, A5▶

Israeli mourner sets candle before portrait of Prime Minister Yitzhak Rabin, who died of gunshot wounds Saturday.

4-26-96
P.L.O. Abandons Its Stance for Destruction of Israel

Swiftly answering the P.L.O.'s decision to end its call for annihilate of the Jewish nation and people, the Labor Party of Israel approved the plan for autonomy of the Palestinians in Israel.

With a landmark vote, discarded was recognition of the Palestinians as unable to govern themselves. The peace process, frozen since a series of suicide bombings of Hamas radicals on Jewish citizens, the Israelis have buried their dead of nearly 60 victims, and moved ahead.

The new platform abandons a Labor Party position, that of the Golan Heights, captured from Syria in 1967, and annexed to Israel in 1981, keeping it for the Jewish nation security. The strategic plateau, which Syria wants back in exchange for peace, has political importance.

In Gaza, Yasser Arafat, praised the Labor move. Talks on a final Israeli-Palestinian settlement are to begin in May, 1996, which will discuss the P.L.O. demand for statehood, and borders. Hardliners want Jerusalem to remain under Israeli protection, and they call for sovereignty over parts of the West Bank, including the Jordan Valley.

7-10-96
Israel's Prime Minister Meets with President Clinton
Washington, D.C.

The Mideast peace has been put on hold as Prime Minister Benjamin Netanyahu comes to America to meet President Bill Clinton at the Whitehouse to have a dialogue with him on Tuesday, July 9, 1996. His nation will give no ground for Mideast peace unless terrorism is halted and Israel's security is bolstered.

The statement of Netanyahu is that those on the side of peace must show complete dedication to the fight against terrorism. After more than two hours of discussion with the President, they reached an understanding. The Prime Minister made it clear he is not ready to meet with the Chairman of the P.L.O., Yasser Arafat, until he shows interest in pursuing land for peace, with protective rights of the Jewish citizens insured.

The Prime Minister will not withdraw his troops from Hebron, where more than 450 people, Israelis live, in the Jewish settlement houses, among nearly 100,000 Arabs, unless security is guaranteed for them.

For his part, Clinton declared, "There's no alternative to the peace process. Recognizing the sea of change, the President of the U.S. indicated, "We are going to have a period of adjustment, and those of us who care will attempt to minimize the negative, and maximize the positive." He added, "We will pray for a lasting peace."

8-29-96
Yasser Arafat Calls Strike on Settlements

In Israel, P.L.O. Chairman, Yasser Arafat calls for a strike to protest Jewish Settlements in Jerusalem and the West Bank. Visibly angry, he accused the Israeli government of "declared war," on Palestinians through their recent actions. The demolishment of Arab-owned buildings and a Palestinian center for studies has slowed the peace process.

Palestinians see the Prime Minister of Israel, Benjamin Netanyahu, as personal poison to them. Hanna Ashrawi, a Palestinian legislator and Cabinet Minister for Arafat said, "our people are reaching an impasse in the negotiations. The Council and the P.L.O. has passed a resolution urging a halt to all contacts with the Israeli government, and it is binding to all the members except Chairman Arafat.

The Foreign Minister of the United States, David Levy, telephoned Arafat, and spoke to him of the urgency in not creating havoc that would destroy a comprehensive peace. He stated, "Do not increase more tension, but weigh carefully your position, and to your constituents; Be wise; Think before you act, and guard your tongue."

In the Bible, the peace of God passes all understanding. He gives us judgement to act with calmness and decisiveness. Let us remember and be guided in wisdom.

Friday, August 30, 1996, is the Muslim Holy Day. As the Arabs converge on the Aqsa Mosque, with prayer and patience, their hour will come. All faiths will gather at the Holy sites in Jerusalem to pray.

9-30-96
Opening of Tunnel to the Mount in Israel by the Jews Incites Riot by Palestinians

Israeli security forces open fire in a crowd of Palestinians at the Temple Mount, which sparks confrontation on the West Bank and Gaza Strip. The incident, outside of the Aqsa Mount compound, one of the holiest sites in Islam, could plunge the peace process into war. As it is, the comprehensive peace process has slowed to a crawl.

The Clinton administration in the United States is making sure the Prime Minister of Israel and the P.L.O. Chairman, Yasser Arafat, are apprised of the situation, and action be taken to prevent further deterioration.

King Hussein of Jordan, is invited to share his thoughts in how to move the negotiations forward. In Ramallah, West Bank, in a clear message that the days of bloodshed must end, Yasser Arafat's policemen dragged away Palestinians marching to the Israeli army posts, and moving toward the Jewish settlements. General Uzi Dayan, the West Bank commander of the Israelis, stated, "we are ready to use whatever force that is necessary to quell the riots for our security and protection."

Some say the real cause of violence is intransigence of the Prime Minister, but his answer is "the Palestinians must be restrained for the security of our people."

In the Oslo Accords, there are a few simple steps that may end the violence. Netanyahu can redeploy his troops from Hebron. He can also ease closure of the Jewish borders for the Palestinians, and he may also publicly consider the closing of the tunnel in Jerusalem. The Prime Minister can also ready his team to continue the peace talks, to allow the Palestinians more latitude in organizing their government.

10-2-96
A Crisis Exists in "Eretz" Israel
As hardliners on each side of the peace process move to establish identity, negotiations came to a screeching halt. Prime Minister, Benjamin Netanyahu, and his Likud party are remaining firm. They will not give up land for peace without solid guarantees of security for the Jewish people.

For example: Israeli troops are in Hebron to safeguard 450 Jews living in the settlement houses, surrounded by 100,000 Palestinians. The center of the town is where "The Caves of the Patriarchs," a shrine believed to be the burial place of Abraham, Isaac, and Jacob are.

Arafat, the Palestinian leader, insists that the Clinton administration in the United States, hold a summit meeting, and attempt to diffuse the crisis. According to the P.L.O. leader, a date must be set to produce the Israeli army pullout of the city of Hebron and the West Bank. He fears a delay could leave the
poor in stranded groups that are desolate and mostly inhabitable.

If Netanyahu chooses not to make concessions, he
faces the option of war that both sides know will be far greater than the seven year "Intifada," or uprising against Israeli rule.

The signing of the comprehensive treaty, "The Camp David Peace Accords," in 1979, has led to the Oslo, Norway, agreement in 1993, with the previous Prime Minister of Israel, Shimon Peres. Netanyahu wants to avoid war, however both sides are preparing for it. The Israeli army has tanks and armament

poised outside of Arafat's West Bank cities, ready to disarm the Palestinian police, if necessary.

Jordan's King Hussein, left, and Israel's Yitzhak Rabin shake hands as President Clinton applauds.

1-2-97

Peace Plan Resumes for Hebron
Jerusalem, Israel

      Israel's Prime Minister, Benjamin Netanyahu, will meet P.L.O. Chairman, Yasser Arafat, to finalize a pullout of the city of Hebron, on the West Bank, which is still under occupation. According to the latest reports, both the Palestinian leader and the Prime Minister have their meeting scheduled at the Erez Border Crossing for a signing ceremony. It will be confirmed by U.S. mediator, Dennis Ross, and Egypt's envoy of President Mubarak.
      Redeployment of Israeli troops will begin. The Jewish Enclaves which are the Caves of the Patriarchs, will remain under the protection of the Israeli troops. In compliance of the Oslo Accords, Israel will withdraw, creating a buffer zone of several hundred yards in width.
      One issue that could clash with the peace process is the Palestinian demand that an Israeli-Palestinian mobile military unit be allowed to patrol near the Holy land of the Jews. The site is called Ibrahim by the Arabs.
      The Tomb of the Patriarchs is sacred because it is believed to be the burial site of Abraham, Isaac, and Jacob of the Bible. The high ground, overlooking the Jewish Settlements, must also be patrolled by a joint Palestinian-Israeli contingent.

The Palestinians are trying to get the Jews to commit to further deployments, and for release of some of their prisoners. They further add that Israel fulfill a promise to allow a Palestinian airport to open in the Gaza Strip.

Netanyahu states, "Arafat has to commit to disarming terrorists, and cease all activities in Jerusalem, that leads to a Palestinian State."

U.S. special envoy Dennis Ross, left, congratulates Yasser Arafat as Benjamin Netanyahu looks on.

1-14-97
Follow-up of the Oslo Accords
Jerusalem, Israel

After months of hard fought negotiations, and a final push from U.S. envoy, Dennis Ross, and King Hussein of Jordan, Israel and the Palestinians appear ready to sign a declaration to pull Israeli troops out of the West Bank rural areas by August, 1998.

The compromise sets the stage for the Israelis leaving Hebron, the last est Bank City under occupation. Israeli Defense Minister, Yitzhak Mordechai, and his staff will furnish details for both sides. In Gaza, P.L.O. leader,

Yasser Arafat, discussed with his cabinet, the negotiations, step by step.

Prime Minister, Benjamin Netanyahu, of Israel stated, "we will honor the Oslo Accords. For withdrawal from our Holy land in the peace treaty, it will be in a timely fashion

Convincing the 18 members of the Israeli cabinet is possible, but it will be difficult. Although votes in favor of the accord is not required, the coalition is vital for the Prime Minister when it comes to election time.

In Washington, President Bill Clinton called the agreement a step forward to a lasting Middle-East peace.

Commitments of both sides are for Chairman Arafat to give peace and security and protection for the settlements. New limits will be placed on the Palestinian police on weapons used and there will be joint patrols on the hills overlooking the Jewish enclaves.

Buffer zones several hundred yards will be created between the settlements and their Arab neighbors. Extra protection is necessary to prevent snipers from shooting at Jewish citizens. A further report commits redeployment of the Israeli military, return of Palestinian refugees, and emphasis of Moslem autonomy.

PASSING OF HEBRON ACCORD WITH PALESTINIANS

1-17-97
Hebron Accord Passes for Israel and the P.L.O.
Jerusalem, Israel

Yasser Arafat, the P.L.O. leader and his cabinet easily passed the Hebron agreement, brokered by the United States, and the U.S. Ambassador, Dennis Ross. For Prime Minister, Benjamin Netanyahu, his Likud leaders voted 11-7 for the proposal. The final decision will be made in the Jewish Knesset, consisting of 120 members.

The Prime Minister's main opposition was with the son of the late Prime Minister, Menachem Begin, who is against the Land for Peace Agreement. Despite other clashes, the opponents failed to block the Hebron accord. The persistence of the Ambassador to the U.S. and the intervention of King Hussein of Jordan, resulted in compromise that all the parties could live with, and go forward.

Israel promises to release Palestinian prisoners, and immediately resume negotiations over unresolved issues such as travel routes between the Gaza Strip and the West Bank, and the opening of an airport and a port in Gaza. The Palestinians, in turn, promise to strengthen security, prevent incitement and hostile propaganda, and apprehend and punish terrorists.

The accord leaves many unanswered questions, particularly about the extent of further pullbacks on the West Bank. The Palestinians, who now control nearly 27% of the territory, want to end up with about 90% by the end of their third deployment with the Israelis in 1998. Prime Minister, will extend time.

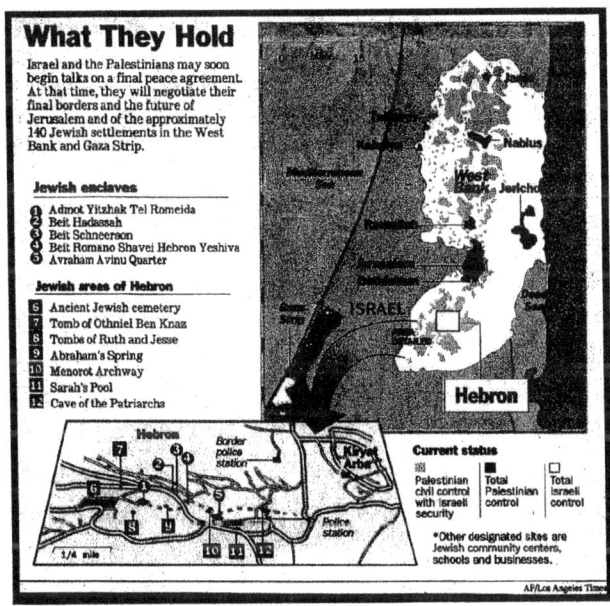

1-18-97
Israel Redeploys Its Military
Hebron, West Bank

The Israeli army ended 30 years of occupation in Hebron, on the West Bank, on January 17, 1997, handing over its hilltop headquarters to the Palestinian police, as a number of witnesses cheered. The long awaited withdrawal of this ancient city in the Holy land for Arabs, Christians, and Jews, came hours before the vote for passage of the Hebron accord by the Palestinians and the Jews.

The military headquarters was a symbol for Israel of its occupation of the 1967 War. Just before 6:00 a.m., the P.L.O. received the keys to the military compound, with only a handshake. A Palestinian flag was raised on the radio tower by a young man, and as he unfurled the red, green, white, and black emblem, a thunderous applause was registered by the people below. Some time later, the Jewish Parliament voted 87-17 for the Hebrew accord.

Israeli border guards and Palestinian police were to begin operating joint patrols the next morning. Army officers of the Jews carefully removed a Mezuza, a parchment scroll inside a small case, that by tradition, is attached to the doorway of a Jewish home or building.

A line of Israeli jeeps made their way out of the compound, followed by supply trucks, removing their belongings down the hill in advance of the redeployment.

Israel will retain control of about 1/5 of the city, including the area of the Israeli settlements or enclaves, and they will protect the caves of the Patriarchs, the burial ground of the Bible prophet, Abraham.

1-20-97
Arafat Arrives in Hebron, West Bank
Hebron, West Bank

P.L.O. leader, Yasser Arafat, lands in Hebron in a helicopter, as 60,000 Palestinians waited to honor their leader. When he emerged from the aircraft, he was wearing his black and white checked Kaffiyeh, headdress for Arab Chieftains.

The first words to be heard were "Awah," meaning yes. Arafat waved to the crowd and showed a "V" for victory sign as he was directed to the stone fortress that served as a Jewish military base, and also a prison.

To the Israeli settlers, the P.L.O. leader said, "I do not want a confrontation with you, we back a just peace." Arafat considers the occupation of Hebron a springboard that will end in Jerusalem as a capital of Palestine.

Surrounded by security guards, Arafat spoke to the Palestinians in Hebron, and vowed to continue his goal, which includes taking charge of the occupied West Bank, and establishing an independent state in East Jerusalem.

Benjamin Netanyahu, the Prime Minister of Israel repeated his promise, that his Likud Party will not cede any part of Jerusalem, nor allow sovereign rights for the Palestinians, including raising an independent army.

2-10-97
Muslims Pray as Ramadan Ends
Ramadan

In a pious conclusion to a month of fasting and self-discipline, millions of Muslims throughout the world gather on Sunday, February 9, 1997, to pray and celebrate the end of Ramadan, gratitude to God, Allah, and a sense of accomplishment of self-restraint. The people of the faith face Meca, their holy shrine, and assemble; touch their heads to the ground four times in a gesture of submission and humility, while a leader intones, "Allah Akbar, God is great."

The holiday, which is called, Eid-ul-fitr, the festival of breaking the fast, is a time for friends to gather together to share a meal, and perhaps contact relatives far away by telephone. Ramadan expresses petitions in all areas of life. It is a purging of anger, use of foul language, or other evil vices or intent. The month long fast involves abstaining during daylight hours, of food, water, and lower desires.

What is learned is the ability to disciple oneself, to know when to say no.

Over one million Muslims are in Southern California, with more than 1.3 billion throughout the globe. The spiritual aspect of this holiday is: Fasting is to remember God and his mercy. Christians, Jews, and Muslims all believe in the Prophet Abraham in their worship, which is belief in the oneness and obedience to God.

The faithful worship in bare feet or socks in the Islamic religion. Shoes are put aside to signify leaving behind worldly possessions. Many men wear Khufis, an Islamic head covering. When a service is concluded with a Muslim cleric, there are hugs and kisses of the cheek. These greetings are called, "Eid Mubarak."

Muslims bow in prayer during ceremony at Anaheim Convention Center that celebrated the end of the monthlong fast of Rama

2-14-97
Netanyahu and Clinton Discuss Peace

Prime Minister Benjamin Netanyahu of Israel and President Bill Clinton seriously discuss a renewed sense of promise for expansion of Mideast relations to include Syria.

Arriving in the United States on February 13, 1997, the Prime Minister of Israel spoke with President Clinton for nearly 3 hours on the extension of the Oslo Accords, and promises of land for peace with Syria.

Netanyahu stated that the President of the U.S. and his administration are exceptional; friends of Israel, and repeated that there is a strong possibility; lasting peace and progress in the Middle East. He intimated for Syria; show its good faith by reigning in Hezbollah terrorists in Southern Lebanon. Also Israel will not withdraw its troops from there, because, as he said, "if we simply walk away, Hezbollah and other terrorist organizations will come to the borders and attack our towns and villages."

This was Clinton's first meeting with the Prime Minister since the Israeli leader and P.L.O. Chairman, Yasser Arafat, ended a dangerous impasse last month in agreement for Israel's pullout from the city of Hebron and parts of the West Bank. Netanyahu, who took office in June of 1996, is determined to slow down the transfer of land to the Palestinians, and stay within a framework for a comprehensive peace. The Prime Minister indicated in the discussion with President Clinton that he was not interested in the process and vague promises, but in results to reach a goal of a lasting peace with the neighboring countries in the Middle East.

President Clinton answers questions as Israeli Prime Minister Benjamin Netanyahu looks on during their joint news conference Thursday. The president met with the Israeli leader to discuss future peace efforts in the Middle East.

10-8-97
Prime Minister of Israel, Netanyahu and P.L.O. Chief, Arafat Meet for Negotiations

The leaders agree to hold regular face-to-face talks. U.S. envoy, Dennis Ross, sees a new beginning for stalled peace process. In Jerusalem, the two leaders met for the first time in eight months to defuse tensions that have brought the Middle East negotiations to the brink of collapse.

The predawn summit at the Erez border crossing between Israel and the Gaza Strip, was arranged by the U.S. special envoy, Dennis Ross, who said it was a very good meeting. Shaken by incriminations from both sides, and Islamic suicide bombings, it came against a backdrop of a political storm in Israel, of botched Israeli assassination attempt of militants in Jordan.

Meanwhile, the spiritual leader of the Islamic movement, Hamas, was returned to the Gaza Strip, following eight years in an Israeli prison. Sheik Ahmed Yassin, floated a conditional proposal for a cease fire with Israel.

The Bar-Illan calls for withdrawal from the West Bank, Gaza Strip, and Jerusalem, with the dismantling of Jewish settlements, and the release of all Palestinian prisoners as totally unacceptable. The Hamas claimed they would temporarily stop military attacks and hold a cease-fire, however the movement deserves the right to continue the struggle to free all Palestinian land.

10-15-98
Can There be Peace in the Middle East?

How is it that the peace process, that was so promising with the Palestinians and the people of Israel, is in continual danger of collapse? Part of the question is of trust. The level of trust with Prime Minister Rubin, allowed both sides to make necessary concessions, and to move forward, even though there was violence along the way. This trust eroded with his death by a Jewish extremist.

With the emergence of the new Prime Minister, Benjamin Netanyahu, the Israelis have formed a hard-line government, and manages through a coalition, in which many people are ideologically opposed to the present course.

Jordan's Ambassador to Israel, Marwan Muasher, a Christian, in an overwhelming Muslim country, states, "It is Israel that threatens the Arab sense of security. During the first year, following the Oslo Accord plan, a lot was done to encourage areas of cooperation. More than 100,000 Jewish citizens visited Jordan. There were contacts between universities, the people of each religious sect, and business operators. The wars of the past still register with the Jordanians, and some have moved to the West Bank, in Palestinian held land, in hopes of finding peace and a better life.

Jordan's Ambassador intends to persuade the Palestinians to persevere, however pressure to building inside the Arab occupation. Three years ago, a Peace Treaty was signed with Israel, in an era where peace was advancing on all fronts. Stalemate has existed since Prime Minister Netanyahu became the leader. The United States is doing its best to effect an agreement, which is longstanding.

The relationship with Israel does not mean it cannot have a good and healthy relationship with the Arab world, with a spirit of partnership; not adversarial.

The decision-making process in the U.S. is unique. There are many centers, and policy is made by consensus, with the centers often converging with one another.

The centers of power in the America are congress, the president, Supreme Court, the media, Think Tanks, religious groups, and the American people as a whole.

In the meantime, President Bill Clinton, on Thursday, October 15, 1998, welcomed the Prime Minister, Benjamin Netanyahu, P.L.O. Chairman, Yasser Arafat, to Queentown, Maryland; for Summit talks, intending to break a stubborn stalemate in the Mideast process. As if in a difficult problem, neither side can expect to win 100% on every point. Concessions will be hard now, but far less important, in the light of an accord, that moves Palestinians and the Israelis closer to a lasting peace; said the president.

Netanyahu stresses the Jewish state's security demands; ironclad guarantees, and the control of Hamas and all terrorist groups. Arafat wants land; and freedom for his people, and aspires a Palestinian State.

In the quiet setting, at a resort along the shores fo Maryland, the talks are expected to last a week. Face-to-face sessions and the intervention of President Clinton may open the gates to a lasting peace. The concentrated effort will allow walks for his visitors in the woods at Wye River, and relaxing invitation to dinners, leaving them a chance to unloose the log jam.

Secretary of State, Madeleine Albright, and Peace Envoy, Dennis Ross, will be present to assist in the discussions. The purpose of the Summit meeting is to complete a long-delayed implementation of the Interim Israeli-Palestinian Peace Accord, that was negotiated in Oslo, Norway, in 1993. The Treaty was signed by the signatories; Prime Minister Rubin of Israel; PLO Chairman, Yasser Arafat; and President Bill Clinton of the United States.

To date: The final stage has not been reached. May 4, 1999, is the deadline. Arafat has threatened to issue a unilateral declaration of Palestinian Statehood, on that date, which could trigger a military response from Israel.

Benjamin Netanyahu, left, President Clinton and Yasser Arafat at White House opening ceremony for summit.

Interim Steps to a Lasting Peace

Under a new agreement with the Palestinians and Israelis, the P.L.O. is promised a sizable piece of land, needed to achieve their goal of Statehood. The package of new security measures will put the Islamic militants behind bars, and aid in preventing terror attacks. In the past, they have frayed the Jewish confidence in the peace process.

In the East Room of the Whitehouse in Washington, D.C., the leaders; Prime Minister Benjamin Netanyahu of Israel, Chairman of the P.L.O. Yasser Arafat; and the President of the United States, Bill Clinton; signed a breakthrough of land-for-peace negotiations, a stepping stone was laid to a permanent and lasting peace.

The first test will come when the Prime Minister of Israel returns home to face a political storm of defiance, the Jewish Settlers, who contend the accord amounts to "betrayal and treason." They are vowing a bitter fight to block its implementation, and bring down Netanyahu's ruling coalition. The sensitive final status of Jerusalem, the refugees, and the Israeli borders, will demand a nationwide vote, and calls for new elections.

In the phased withdrawal of Jewish land, the atmosphere will change. Money for expansion of housing and facilities will be asked. Moshe Fogel, and Israeli spokesman said, "Much will depend on whether the Palestinian leader and his forces live up to the promise to rein in the militants. The CIA security for imprisoning the terrorists will be helpful. Israel will carry out the phased withdrawal over a three month period.

Leading up to the signing of the interim agreement, was an all-night peacekeeping slowdown. At a pivotal time, President Clinton lost his patience with posturing; got up from the table, and walked out, saying "Get serious about this, or we are not going to continue."

There was a noted gravity of what the president meant, and the situation changed, for real negotiation.

Netanyahu's final push was to President Clinton, who asked for the release of the Jewish spy, Jonathan Pollard. The president advised his friend his authority was limited, with no commitment, but he would review the status of the Pollard case. Pollard had been in prison for the last 12 years. He stole secret files from the CIA.

Several people have been instrumental in bringing the peace process closer; notably King Hussein, of Jordan, who is in the United States for treatment of cancer. The King said, "there has been enough destruction, enough death, enough waste; and it's time that together we occupy a place beyond ourselves, and our peoples. We should be worthy of them and of their sons, the descendants of the children of Abraham.

The tireless devotion of Envoy, Dennis Ross, the relentless energy of the Secretary of State, Madeleine Albright, and the former Cabinet minister, Hanan Ashrawi, of the Palestinians desire for Statehood; and others of the delegation, were keys that unlocked the deep distrust. The real test is the implementation of the Oslo Accords, and the final division of the land-for-peace.

After 19 months of stalemate, Prime Minister, Netanyahu of Israel; P.L.O. Chairman, Arafat, have reached an accord, with more of the West Bank under Palestinian supervision, and in return, there is safeguards for the Israelis and the Settlers living nearby.

What will happen in the future, only God knows, however there is exceptional courage for the Middle East leaders, in these negotiations.

Under terms of the Interim Accord, Israel will withdraw from 13% of the West Bank territory, in three phases over a 12 week period, in exchange for reciprocal Palestinian follow-up actions. For the moment, Israel will retain authority over security in most of the ceded land, however Palestinians will run their own civil affairs.

The Jewish State agrees to transfer an additional 15% of their land to the Palestinians from partial to full Palestinian control, if all the security conditions are met, this includes the jailing of terrorists, who would destroy the Jewish settlers located in the area, as well as towns and villages surrounding the disputed territory.

The agreement contains achievements and potential risks for both leaders, Netanyahu and Arafat. There is a commitment from the Israelis to open an airport in Gaza, with two safe passages; routes between the West Bank and the Gaza Strip. The Israelis will release 750 of the 3000 estimated political prisoners, if the P.L.O. revokes dozens of Anti-Israeli clauses in their National Charter.

President Clinton, of the United States, will attend the Palestinian convention if success is achieved, three months from the signing of the Interim Accord in

Washington, D.C. in October 1998. The land that the P.L.O. Chairman received from the Israelis will increase his stature among the Palestinian people, and in the world.

11-12-98
The Cabinet Israel Ratifies Wye Pact

Demands were placed on the Palestinians to follow-up with action they agreed on at the Wye retreat in Maryland of the United States. After nearly two weeks of postponements, the Israeli Cabinet, by a slim majority approved the land-for-peace security proposal, with conditions.

The Israeli Cabinet insisted that the Palestinians repeal clauses in their Charter that call for the destruction of Israel. After the current Accord is implemented, the Israelis will withdraw no more than 1% of West Bank land, and proceed with stage withdrawal over a period of time. An explicit threat to Yasser Arafat, Chairman of the P.L.O., was if he declares an independent state in May 1999, the peace process stalls, and Israel will annex areas it still controls on the West Bank.

As of now, the government of Israel approved the release of bids for construction of a disputed East Jerusalem housing project, for 1000 homes on a hilltop known as Har Homa. Prime Minister, Netanyahu said, "We reserve the right to apply Israeli law to the security areas, and settlements, accepted as vital to our national interests." The Cabinet declared, any additional troop withdrawal from the West Bank, beyond the 13% agreed to, will cover no more than 1% of the territory.

12-15-98
Palestinians Must Observe Wye Accord

The Palestinians have to follow through with the details of the Wye Accord, signed by President Netanyahu of Israel and Chairman Arafat of the P.L.O.
In Jerusalem on December 15, 1998, the Prime Minister of Israel said the Palestinians need to carry out further steps before he will approve a withdrawal from the West Bank. They have to keep all the provisions agreed to in the signing of the Wye Accord, in the United States. A day in which the President of the United States was honored by both parties for his strong support, the Palestinians said his visit endorsed the legitimate right of the land they had occupied.
The Israelis indicated there had to be an end to violence; a collection of illegal weapons, and a retraction of the Palestinian council, in writing of Hebrew, English, and Arabian language, denying the Jewish State the right to exist. In the Oslo Accord, there is nothing that states a declaration of a Palestinian statehood.
Prime Minister, Netanyahu, is facing a critical vote in the Knesset to determine the fate of his government, and any pullback is shaky to keep his coalition intact.
Pressing both sides to reconcile, President Clinton spoke to former guerilla fighters and top Palestinians, indicating the peace process has brought reward to them, with elections and self-government in Gaza and the West Bank, with a Palestinian Airport. You will be living with one another in peace or war; which do you prefer? The President of the United States congratulates the Palestinian leader, Arafat, after witnessing the National Council vote to support abolition of the resolutions of the Palestinian Charter that called for the destruction of the State of Israel, the Gaza City. President Bill Clinton, is the first American president to step on Palestinian-ruled soil. Thousands of people lined the freshly scrubbed streets to see the American president.

5-4-99
Timetable for Peace Passes
Jerusalem, Israel

A group of Jewish radicals will be out today, May 4, 1999, gathering in an Arab neighborhood to celebrate the end of an Oslo Accord peace process.
Some with relief, others with sadness, have decided to observe this day with only a passing nod.

May 4, 1999, was to have been the conclusion of a five-year transition period that would establish a permanent peace between Israel and the Palestinians. Also it was to have defined Palestinian self-rule, and settle hard disputes, such as the amount of territory the Arabs would govern, and who would control the Holy city of Jerusalem. In addition, the P.L.O. leader, Yasser Arafat, had promised his people that he would proclaim and independent state for the Palestinians on this day. Instead, Arafat and his directors will postpone the event until June 1999, at least, when the Jewish Nation elects the President.

Overshadowed by mistrust, and delays, and unfulfilled dreams, the leaders reasoned Israel has to be made to feel safe, and the Palestinians made to feel sovereign.

Timetable for Peace

Major events in the Middle East peace process:

Sept. 13, 1993: Landmark Oslo peace accords are signed by Israeli Prime Minister Yitzhak Rabin and Palestinian leader Yasser Arafat, establishing mutual recognition and formally ending decades of hostility.

May 4, 1994: "Gaza-Jericho" agreement is signed in Cairo, starting five-year countdown to Palestinian independence. Israel begins troop withdrawal from parts of the West Bank and Gaza Strip; Palestinians begin creating institutions for self-rule.

Sept. 28, 1995: Israel and the Palestinians sign accord on further Israeli withdrawals from West Bank villages; elections are planned for Palestinian Legislative Council to act as primary Palestinian governmental body.

Nov. 4, 1995: Rabin is assassinated; despite concerns for future of peace process, implementation of most recent agreement is accelerated.

Jan. 20, 1996: Palestinian Legislative Council is elected; Arafat elected Palestinian Authority president with 87.1% of vote.

May 5, 1996: "Final-status" talks on Palestinian autonomy begin.

May 29, 1996: Conservative Likud Party wins Israeli elections; Benjamin Netanyahu becomes prime minister. Progress on implementation of accords slows.

Jan. 17, 1997: Arafat and Netanyahu reach agreement on partial Israeli withdrawal from West Bank city of Hebron.

Oct. 23, 1998: Prolonged stalemate over further implementation of accords is ended with historic Wye Plantation pact reached in Maryland by Netanyahu and Arafat, which places more of the West Bank under Palestinian supervision in return for renewed efforts to protect the security of Israelis.

5-17-99
Israel Votes for a Change

A new Prime Minister, Ehud Barak, a highly decorated military officer, is elected to serve as the new Prime Minister of Israel. Presenting himself as a candidate of the center for the people, and the voters deeply suspicious of the Prime Minister, Benjamin Netanyahu, Barak wisely aimed his campaign at the soft right, in which the centralized government was also suspicious of the P.L.O. leader, Yasser Arafat, but prepared to make substantial concessions if their security fears are respected.
The only Arab leader feared in Barak's campaign was the highly honored Jordan Chieftan, King Hussein. The Israeli President who was assassinated by a Jew, Yitzhak Rabin, and Labor Leader of the Israelis, was shown in pictured blowups on street corners of the cities. This election was a deferred referendum on Rabin's approach to peace.
Barak promises to be the Prime Minister to all the people, and he reached out to constituencies long ignored by the Labor leaders, like moderate religious Jews and the working-class Sephardim, that is the Jews of Middle Eastern origin. The bruising campaign pitted religious against the secular, but a number of Barak's followers crave peace at home as well as with its Arab neighbors.
Barak's one exception of inclusiveness was his consistent attacks of the Ultra-Orthodox, who refused to share the burdens of Israeli society, especially military service, but who have enjoyed massive government financial support. The principle position will now be tested, as he tries to construct a coalition without the Ultra-Orthodox Sephardi party, which appears to have won 15 seats in the Parliament of 120. Barak will attempt to present a centrist position, to heal the nation's internal structure. If he remains faithful to this agenda, he can be the savior of Israel.
The former Army Chief of Staff is a pragmatist, who unlike the man he replaces is inclined to seek common ground among disparate groups.

Prime Minister Barak Will Form Government by June 7, 1999

Barak, the new Prime Minister of Israel has to balance the demands of a secular majority that supports him, with those of religious and ethnic opponents. Despite the secular mood of the voters, the Shapardic, Shas, party soared to a close third place finish, near Netanyahu's center-right Likud party. The Shas won 17 seats in the Parliament or Knesset, and the Likud, under the former Prime Minister lost 15 seats, receiving only 19 seats in the Knesset.
The Sahs trace their roots to Middle Eastern and North African countries, and they have suffered at the hands of Israel's European elite. They control the Yestivas and other schools, and also social programs for its faithful.
Barak and most of his allies have said they would refuse to deal with the charismatic Rabbi, Aryeh Deri, who was convicted of bribery and corruption, and sentenced to four years in prison. He has appealed.
Deri indicated he would continue to lead his party's social and spiritual movement, but would relinquish his political role and quit the Parliament or Knesset. This will clear the way for the new Prime Minister, Barak, to begin negotiations with the Shas.

Barak Is Elected Israeli Leader by a Landslide

■ Mideast: Netanyahu stuns the nation by quickly conceding and quitting as head of the Likud Party. The new prime minister is expected to improve U.S. relations, re-energize stagnant peace process.

By TRACY WILKINSON
TIMES STAFF WRITER

Benjamin Netanyahu, with wife Sarah, after conceding defeat.

JERUSALEM—In a stunning upheaval of Israeli politics, Ehud Barak—a decorated soldier who has vowed to seek peace with the same Arabs he once was assigned to kill—on Monday defeated Prime Minister Benjamin Netanyahu in a landslide.

Netanyahu, faced with a devastating indictment of his three-year tenure, abruptly quit the leadership of his center-right Likud Party after the overwhelming loss.

"This is, indeed, the dawn of a new day," Barak, head of the center-left Labor Party, declared early today to thousands of jubilant supporters who jammed into Tel Aviv's Rabin Square, where Prime Minister Yitzhak Rabin—Barak's mentor—was assassinated four years ago.

"It is time to end the division and to find harmony," Barak said, "whoever we are."

With 99.9% of the vote counted, Barak had 56% to Netanyahu's 44%, according to unofficial returns. Voters Monday also chose a parliament, which promises to be fragmented.

The election of Barak, who retired from a 35-year military career to be catapulted into leadership of the Labor Party two years ago, is expected to improve tense relations with Washington and breathe life into a peace process that has come undone under Netanyahu.

After calling the winner, President Clinton said in a statement: "I will continue to work energetically for a just, lasting and comprehensive peace that strengthens Israel's security. I look forward to working

Please see ISRAEL, A10

A More 'Sober' Peace Process for Mideast

By REBECCA TROUNSON
TIMES STAFF WRITER

JERUSALEM—With an overwhelming victory in Monday's elections, incoming Israeli Prime Minister Ehud Barak is expected to move quickly to revive the peace process with the Palestinians after three years of bitter stalemate.

But even in the first flush of victory over incumbent Benjamin Netanyahu and his right-of-center Likud Party, Barak's supporters cautioned that the prime minister-elect, a former army chief of staff, is likely to take a more "sober"—in other words, tougher—approach to the U.S.-led negotiations than his Labor Party colleague, former Prime Minister Shimon Peres.

"We want a sober peace process, not excessively romantic as we had in the last phase of Peres," said Shlomo Ben-Ami, a historian and Labor legislator who has helped

Please see ADVISER, A11

Natan Sharansky, a former Soviet refusnik, who heads a large immigrant party, will fight hard for the Interior Ministry post that the Shaphardic group held under Natanyahu's coalition government. The Interior Ministry controls passports, identity

cards, and other benefits for new immigrants. Sharansky's party won seven seats in the Knesset.

The broader the coalition, the better. Barak may want to invite his enemies first to join his government, then his friends. It is one way to prevent a sectarian crisis.
In the meantime, the P.L.O. leader, Yasser Arafat, was reported to be in good spirits about the election outcome.

7-6/7-99
Israel's Prime Minister, Ehud Barak
Names Cabinet
Tel Aviv, Israel

The new Prime Minister, Ehud Barak, will launch a new era of Middle East peacemaking when he is sworn in, today, July 6, 1999, as Prime Minister of Israel.
　　Meeting difficulty from his party members Labor Party, they overwhelmingly rejected his candidate for a crucial post of speaker of the Knesset. Demanding absolute loyalty and discipline from his coalition, he is finishing the assembly of his government. Today he holding 75 of the 120 assembly seats, however his central committee protested, vehemently his choice as Speaker of the Knesset or Parliament. Party members voted for a long-time labor activist, Avraham Burg. Recovering from a slap in the face, Barak praised the "Internal Democracy" of his party, and vowed to fulfill a campaign reform of peace and security.

　　The remaining slate of candidates were approved for cabinet appointments without rejection.

　　As a former head of Army of Israel, Barak places a high value on loyalty and discipline. The powers of the Prime Minister that is chosen directly by election since 1996, resemble those of a president in a presidential election. The important post of Foreign Minister went to David Levy, who only recently joined the Party of Barak.

　　The way Barak grants appointments spoke of his management style and personality. He clearly intends to retain power, with people he trusts.

7-15-99
Prime Minister, Ehud Barak, Seeks U.S. Aid

President Clinton and the new Prime Minister, Ehud Barak,

on Thursday, July 15, 1999, opened what both called an era of renewed U.S.-Israeli cooperation, carefully smoothing over some budding disputes and pledges in a drive for Middle East peace. The six-day visit to the United States for Barak bagan in the Whitehouse Rose-Garden, in which both men were determined to end the friction with the former Prime Minister, Benjamin Netanyahu.

　　The two men and their contingent continued on Thursday, their discussions at Camp David, Maryland, in the mountains. Barak calls for a lower profile in the Arab-Israeli peacemaking, that may make the United States more effective as a partner. Barak said he intends to turn over to the Palestinians an additional 13% of the West Bank land as required in the Wye agreement, which Netanyahu and the Palestinian leader, Yasser Arafat, signed last year.

There will be in the coming weeks a very serious attempt to restart negotiations with Syria's President, Assad. Barak intimated that the United States can contribute to the process more as a facilitator than a policeman, judge, and arbitrator at the same time. President Clinton, of the United States, agreed we are better at solving situations than being in the center of the conflict.

Israel's next prime minister, Ehud Barak, greets supporters in Tel Aviv after his decisive election victory.

9-3-99
Barak, Arafat Reaches Accord
Sharm El Sheik, Egypt

Converging on a neutral country, Prime Minister Ehud Barak of Israel and Yasser Arafat of the Palestinian Authority, signed a new agreement early today, September 3, 1999, in which both were anxious to reach a final settlement toward peace in the region of occupied Israel.
    With the Egyptian President Hosni Mubarak, U.S. Secretary of the United States, Jordan's King Abdullah the Second as a witness, Barak and Arafat basked in a process they both called, "The Peace of the Brave." Old adversities that may have delayed their path to peace were muffled as the old warriors leaped up to give a warm handshake, and both kissed Madeleine Albright of United States on the cheek.
    The chances for a permanent peace treaty look bright, as a framework for the next negotiations is the Israel will turn over 11% of the West Bank and Gaza to the Palestinians. Palestinian Statehood for Arafat and the status of Jerusalem remain in doubt.
    The Secretary of the U.S., Madeleine Albright said in her speech at the ceremony, "the two sides have begun their partnership that is vital to the region and their future."

Israeli Premier Ehud Barak and Palestinian leader Yasser Arafat sign pact in Egypt. Egyptian President Hosni Mubarak, center, is flanked by Jordan's King Abdullah II and Secretary of State Madeleine Albright.

9-3-99
Barak, Arafat Reaches Accord
Sharm El Sheik, Egypt

Converging on a neutral country, Prime Minister Ehud Barak of Israel and Yasser Arafat of the Palestinian Authority, signed a new agreement early today, September 3, 1999, in which both were anxious to reach a final settlement toward peace in the region of occupied Israel.

With the Egyptian President Hosni Mubarak, U.S. Secretary of the United States, Jordan's King Abdullah the Second as a witness, Barak and Arafat basked in a process they both called, "The Peace of the Brave." Old adversities that may have delayed their path to peace were muffled as the old warriors leaped up to give a warm handshake, and both kissed Madeleine Albright of United States on the cheek.

The chances for a permanent peace treaty look bright, as a framework for the next negotiations is the Israel will turn over 11% of the West Bank and Gaza to the Palestinians. Palestinian Statehood for Arafat and the status of Jerusalem remain in doubt.

The Secretary of the U.S., Madeleine Albright said in her speech at the ceremony, "the two sides have begun their partnership that is vital to the region and their future.

9-14-99
Final Settlement Issues Between Israelis and the Palestinians

Israel and the Palestinians open final status talks on Monday aimed at drafting a peace settlement within 12 months. These are the main issues confronting the negotiators:

Jerusalem - Israel captured the traditionally Arab East Jerusalem from Jordan, along with the West Bank in June 1967, during the Six-Day War. It regards all of Jerusalem as its united and eternal capital. It will not relinquish control. The Palestinians want East Jerusalem, including the walled Old City, with its major Muslim, Jewish, and Christian shrines, as the capital of a state. The internal community does not recognize Israel's claim to sovereignty. The United States and the interim peace deals say both parties must resolve the city status in their talks.

Jewish settlements - More than 180,000 Jews live in settlements on land that Israel continues to occupy in the West Bank and the Gaza Strip. Israel Prime Minister, Ehud Barak and the Parliament are in accord to keep the settlements under Israeli sovereignty. Under the Geneva Convention, it is illegal, and the U.S., call them obstacles to peace.

Borders and security arrangements - The Palestinians want to establish an independent Palestine, with sovereign powers in all the West Bank and Gaza Strip. Israel's Prime Minister, Ehud Barak states he intends to keep the settlement blocs under Israeli control with self-rule for the Palestinians in isolated areas.

Palestinian refugees - There are about 3.6 million U.N. registered refugees on the West Bank and on the Gaza Strip, with a few in Jordan, Lebanon, and Syria. Some are descendants of the 1948 War when Israel was created, and from the 1967 Six-Day War. Water is also an issue, with part or full control.

Peace with Syria Will Provide Peace with All Arabs
Tel Aviv, Israel

The aggression in the region of Palestine have caused economic stagnation, especially among the Arab nations.

President Clinton meets with Palestinian Authority President Yasser Arafat and aides at Camp David.

The importance of the peace agreement with Syria is not limited to Israel's relationship with Syria. If a peace accord can be attained, it will lead to peace with all the surrounding countries.

The Middle East comprises 24 nations, one which is Jewish. Deep resentments have led to numerous wars. The only way to settle the conflicts is at the negotiating tables. This is what the former Prime Minister of Israel, Shimon Peres, implies. The arms race has continued at the expense of the Arab standard continuing fear for any real hope and economic growth. Countries like Saudi Arabia and the Gulf states, as well as North Africa, indeed all the countries in the Middle East, other than the rogue states, Iraq, Iran, and Libya, have indicated on more than one occasion that when the peace treaty is signed with Syria, the state of war between them and Israel would become redundant.

The Middle East must, and can save itself by moving from a military orientation to a civil one. Painful problems will certainly be encountered on the way to an accord.

Security measures, border definitions, demilitarization, water resources, diplomatic relations, economic ties, are things to contend with, but they can be resolved.

In a tense situation, President Clinton of the United States, Prime Minister Ehud Barak, of Israel, and Yasser Arafat of the Palestinians will attempt to forge an agreement for land for peace in the Middle East.

Word is that the two leaders of the Middle East are tantalizing close to a deal. As of the 19th of July, 2000, there is no official action for a peace treaty. The Hebrew daily newspaper reported in today's edition that Barak offered Arafat a plan that would create a Palestinian State and give the Palestinians broad autonomy, but not sovereignty, in predominately East Jerusalem. Also some Palestinian refugees would be allowed to move to Israel for family unification, but most who fled during the 1948 war with Israel, the War of Independence, and their offspring, would be offered monetary compensation and be required to give up any claim to their ancestral homes.

Arafat's demand for political sovereignty over East Jerusalem will bring a total collapse of the Summit. Israel's credo is "Jerusalem is the 'Eternal and undivided Capital' of Israel."

After eight days of meetings, some of the minor mine fields have been agreed to, but the major issues still need to be resolved, with both parties surrendering some of their position.

No matter how the Camp David Summit ends, there may be violence with the disgruntled masses. Arafat has said he will unilaterally proclaim an independent State, which could lead to bloody clashes with Israel, if a settlement is not reached. The extremists of Israel will take their anger into the streets, with burning and looting. The Israeli Army is bracing itself against the worst scenario, and against large-scale demonstrations.

As of now, there is hope for a friendly exchange of views, but no signed treaty.

Mideast Talks Collapse
Camp David, Maryland - United States

Jerusalem proves to be a deal-breaker, but Israeli Prime Minister, Ehud Barak, and Chairman of the P.L.O., Yasser Arafat pledge to meet again. Arafat refuses to drop the threat of unilaterally declaring Statehood for the Palestinians that he plans before the end of the new year 2001.

After more than two weeks fo intense negotiations in July, the future of Jerusalem remains the same. It was a stinging defeat for the President of the United States who said, "The differences of the two leaders remains deep, but they have come a long way." Real headway is not possible at this time, because there is an intractable difference in the "Holy City, Jerusalem."

As the talks at Camp David, Maryland, broke off on Tuesday, July 25, 2000, the Jewish people in the settlement areas breathed a sigh of relief at the failure, and at the same time, the Settlers braced for what they fear may be a bloody conflict with the West Bank Palestinians. Some of the more militant Arabs cited a new "Intifada," or Holy War.

The Kirat Araba, a powerful Settlement of the Israelis, would fall under the Camp David peace plan, which means the settlement would close, and the people have to move from Israel's Northern Galilee region. They are deeply religious and portray themselves as standard bearers of Judaism and Zionism.

Barak offered Arafat full Palestinian sovereignty over some East Jerusalem neighborhoods in exchange for Israel's annexation of several West Bank settlements adjacent to the city. Since its capture by the Israelis the "Walled Old City" and the surrounding area of the Arabs. The Jewish State has proclaimed Jerusalem as its "Undivided and Eternal Capital."

Arafat, for him and the Palestinians, it has been all or nothing. His remarks to the President of the United States was, "If I make concessions on Jerusalem, I will be killed."

The Author - Clete Hinton

      The author, Clete Hinton was born in a small town outside of Chicago, Illinois, March 12, 1925. His formative years were spent in Topeka, Kansas, where his father worked on the Santa Fe Railroad. He grew up in an atmosphere of competition and survival in a township called Highland Park. His family moved to California previous to the bombing of Pearl Harbor by the Japanese in 1941. His high school and junior college years were in Southern California in Long Beach and Compton, California. He also attended R.O.T.C. Military in Long Beach.

      Mr. Hinton served in the Armed Forces in the Navy after graduation from high school from 1943 to 1946. The Author joined the Los Angeles County Fire Department in August of 1949, and worked for nearly 29 years, retiring as an engineer. He studied for his Associates of Arts degree, majoring in Fire Science, Hydraulics, and Business Administration.

      After retirement in 1978, Mr. Hinton wrote a few articles for "Firehouse Magazine," edited by a New York firefighter, Dennis Smith.

The Author has studied Foreign History and done extensive research in the Middle East Theater involving Israel and her neighbors. Most of his writing is factual and in chronological order. This writing, "The Return of the Sinai from 1979," is a sequel of his previous book, "The Camp David Accords."

www.ingramcontent.com/pod-product-compliance
Lightning Source LLC
Chambersburg PA
CBHW062037220426
43662CB00010B/1539